EU Annex 11 Guide to Computer Validation Compliance for the Worldwide Health Agency GMP

EU Annex 11 Guide to Computer Validation Compliance for the Worldwide Health Agency GMP

Orlando López

CRC Press
Taylor & Francis Group
Boca Raton   London   New York

CRC Press is an imprint of the
Taylor & Francis Group, an **informa** business

CRC Press
Taylor & Francis Group
6000 Broken Sound Parkway NW, Suite 300
Boca Raton, FL 33487-2742

© 2015 by Taylor & Francis Group, LLC
CRC Press is an imprint of Taylor & Francis Group, an Informa business

No claim to original U.S. Government works

Printed on acid-free paper
Version Date: 20150224

International Standard Book Number-13: 978-1-4822-4362-8 (Hardback)

Visit the Taylor & Francis Web site at
http://www.taylorandfrancis.com

and the CRC Press Web site at
http://www.crcpress.com

For Edelmira and Alfonso

Contents

Preface

Good Manufacturing Practice (GMP) describes a set of principles and procedures that when followed helps ensure that therapeutic goods are of high quality.

GMP is that part of quality assurance that ensures that medicinal products are consistently produced and controlled to the quality standards appropriate to their intended use and as required by the marketing authorization (MA) or product specification. GMP is concerned with both production and quality control.

The increased use of computer systems with both production and quality control of medicinal products requires the understanding and application of the expectations of the regulatory agencies or competent authority on these systems.

The European Union (EU) Annex 11[*] (Annex 11) details the European Medicines Agency (EMA) GMP requirements applicable to computer systems. The first edition of the EU Annex 11 dates back to 1992. As the first edition, the updated version of Annex 11[†] provides direction for the interpretation of the principles and guidelines of GMPs of computer systems performing functions established in Directive 2003/94/EC[‡] and Directive 91/412/EEC.[§]

---

[*] EC (1992) *Guide to Good Manufacturing Practice: Medicinal Products for Human and Veterinary Use—Annex 11: Computerised Systems*, The Rules Governing Medicinal Products in the European Union, Volume IV. Office for Publications of the European Communities, Luxembourg, January, pp. 139–142.

[†] EC (2011) *EU Guidelines to Good Manufacturing Practice: Medicinal Products for Human and Veterinary Use—Annex 11: Computerised Systems*, Volume 4, European Commission, Brussels, June, pp. 1–4.

[‡] European Union Directive 2003/94/EC, *European Commission Directive Laying Down the Principles and Guidelines of Good Manufacturing Practice for Medicinal Products for Human Use and Investigational Medicinal Products for Human Use*, 2003.

[§] European Union Directive 91/412/EEC, *European Commission Directive Laying Down the Principles and Guidelines of Good Manufacturing Practice for Veterinary Medicinal Products*, 1991.

Annex 11 is not a legal requirement; it is a guideline in the context of the EMA GMPs. However, Annex 11 is mandatory on each EU national level because the member states have to endorse the EMA GMP Guideline within the scope of the national healthcare legislation.

The purpose of Annex 11 is to provide to the EMA healthcare industry consistent criteria for effective implementation, control, and use of computer systems. In addition, computer systems resulting from the precise implementation of Annex 11 ensure that the systems can be used in the manufacture of medicinal products without any adverse impact on quality, efficacy, or patient safety.

The use of Annex 11 can be extended to other regulated applications. For example, the EU Good Clinical Practice (GCP) inspectors agreed to use as the reference for inspection of computer systems the published PIC/S Guidance on "Good Practices for Computerised Systems in Regulated 'GXP' Environments" (PI 011-3).* This guidance is an internal document helping inspectors with the interpretation of Annex 11. However, it also can be used by the industry for self-inspection or for preparing for a forthcoming official inspection.

Except for medical device software, Annex 11 may be applicable for software used in the production of a device (e.g., programmable logic controllers in manufacturing equipment) and software used in implementation of the device manufacturer's quality system (e.g., software that records and maintains the device history record).

Inspectorate countries outside the EU are adopting the content of Annex 11. It improves the standards for regulated users and systems. Refer to the table containing the list of countries following a guideline or following Annex 11.

As an example, the Canadian GMPs requirements for Medicinal Products for Humans† references the PIC/S Annex 11‡ as Canada's guideline applicable to computer systems performing GMP-regulated activities. In addition, since May 2013, Annex 11 is applicable to Active Pharmaceutical Ingredients (APIs) in Canada.

Another example of another inspectorate country outside the EU embracing the content of Annex 11 is the China Food & Drug Administration

---

* Annex 11 to *PIC/S Guide to Good Manufacturing Practice for Medicinal Products*, Document PE 009-10, PIC/S Secretariat, 14 rue du Roveray, CH-1207 Geneva, January 2013.
† Health Canada, Good Manufacturing Practices (GMP) Guidelines—2009 Edition, Version 2 GUI-0001, March 2011.
‡ Annex 11 to *PIC/S Guide to Good Manufacturing Practice for Medicinal Products*, Document PE 009-10, PIC/S Secretariat, 14 rue du Roveray, CH-1207 Geneva, January 2013.

(CFDA). The 2014 draft GMP Annex 2, covering computer systems, incorporates the majority of Annex 11 clauses.

As of the writing of this book, the following EU member countries in which Annex 11 is applicable are Austria, Belgium, Bulgaria, Croatia, Cyprus, Czech Republic, Denmark, Estonia, Finland, France, Germany, Greece, Hungary, Ireland, Italy, Latvia, Lithuania, Luxembourg, Malta, Netherlands, Poland, Portugal, Romania, Slovakia, Slovenia, Spain, Sweden, and United Kingdom.

The worldwide importance of Annex 11 is noticeable. In addition to being applicable to the EU and Canada, the following table comprises a list of countries conforming to a guideline or following Annex 11: the regulatory organization members of the PIC/S* (44 participating Authorities, including most EU Member States, Switzerland, Japan and the USA) and the Association of Southeast Asian Nations (ASEAN).

PIC/S	ASEAN
Members: Argentina, Australia, Austria, Belgium, Canada, China (Taiwan), Cyprus, Czech Republic, Denmark, Estonia, Finland, France, Germany, Greece, Hungary, Iceland, Indonesia, Ireland, Israel, Italy, Japan, Korea, Latvia, Liechtenstein, Lithuania, Malaysia, Malta, Netherlands, New Zealand, Norway, Poland, Portugal, Romania, Singapore, Slovak Republic, South Africa, Spain, Sweden, Switzerland, Ukraine, United Kingdom, United States	Brunei Darussalam, Cambodia, Indonesia, LAO PDR, Malaysia, Myanmar, Philippines, Singapore, Thailand, Vietnam
Partners: European Directorate for the Quality of Medicines & HealthCare, European Medicines Agency, UNICEF, World Health Organization	
Armenia, Belarus, Brazil, Chile, Philippines, Mexico, Hong Kong, Iran, Kazakhstan, Thailand, and Turkey applied recently for PIC/S membership.	

---

* PIC and PIC/S: Pharmaceutical Inspectors Convention (PIC)/Pharmaceutical Inspection Cooperation Scheme (PIC/S), http://www.picscheme.org. 39 Regulatory Agencies, within 37 countries, are members of the PIC/S. This organization develops and promotes guidance documents for regulatory inspectors. These guides are very valuable for the industry because they represent the inspector's perspective for regulatory inspection.

Medicines imported into EU need to take into account as an applicable requirement.

The primary three (3) principles of the updated version of Annex 11 states that

> This annex applies to all forms of computerised systems used as part of a GMP regulated activities. A computerised system is a set of software and hardware components which together fulfill certain functionalities.

> The application should be validated; IT infrastructure should be qualified.

> Where a computerised system replaces a manual operation, there should be no resultant decrease in product quality, process control or quality assurance. There should be no increase in the overall risk of the process.

The updated version of Annex 11 then continues with 17 specific items explicitly for computer systems.

Item 4.1 of this Annex specifically refers to the need of ensuring that the computer system has been developed under a quality management system that must incorporate a system life cycle (Chapter 2) and associated risk management (Chapter 4).

In addition, the revised Annex 11 adopts a risk-based approach, and is aligned with current industry computer systems good practices.

With the introduction of the updated revision of Annex 11, computer systems validation (CSV) practitioners are implementing comprehensive guidelines on a quality system for computer systems performing GMP-regulated activities.

Annex 11 is a superb framework as a quality system for computer systems performing GMP-regulated activities in any worldwide regulated environments.

Enjoy the reading. If you have any suggestions for improvement or questions, send them to olopez6102@msn.com.

Orlando López
SME - GAMP Data Integrity SIG

Author

Orlando López is a Data Integrity Subject Matter Expert. He has 25 years of experience in the worldwide pharmaceutical industry with relevant work in computer systems regulatory requirements including US, EU, Australian, Japanese, WHO, PIC/S, and ICH regulations and guidance. His special interest is the GMP compliance issues applicable to computer systems. He has experience with direct participation in FDA agency remedial action plans, regulatory inspections, response activities, and consent decree remediation-related verifications. He is the author of two earlier books: *21 CFR Part 11—A Complete Guide to International Compliance*, Taylor & Francis/CRC Press, 2004, and *Computer Infrastructure Qualification for FDA Regulated Industries*, Davis Healthcare International Publishing, 2006.

Contributors

Dr. R.D. McDowall is an analytical chemist with more than 40 years of experience including 6 years as a forensic toxicologist, 15 years working in the pharmaceutical industry, and 21 years as a consultant specializing in process improvement, informatics, and interpretation of regulations. His formal experience of computerized system validation started in 1986 and he has written on the topic and presented many short courses both in-house and publicly. Dr. McDowall edited the first book on LIMS in 1987 and has published extensively on the subject with over 60 published papers. In recognition of his input to the subject and teaching, the LIMS Institute presented him the 1997 LIMS Award. Dr. McDowall is also the writer of the Focus on Quality column in *Spectroscopy* magazine and the Questions of Quality column in *LC-GC Europe*. He has written widely on the subject of electronic working and the use of electronic signatures and is the author of a book on validation of chromatography data systems. He is currently principal of McDowall Consulting and was visiting research fellow at the University of Surrey, UK from 1991 to 2001. Dr. McDowall has contributed to the GAMP *Good Practice Guide on Risk Based Validation of Laboratory Computerised Systems,* 2nd ed. and is an industry expert of the GAMP Data Integrity Special Interest Group core group and a member of the GAMP DACh Special Interest Group on raw data.

Dr. Bernd Renger is director of the consulting firm Bernd Renger Consulting, Germany. He is a member of the European Compliance Academy (ECA) Advisory Board and co-founder and immediate past chair of the European Qualified Person (QP) Association. Since 2011, he has run his own consultancy business. Before that he worked for more than 34 years in several quality management positions in the pharmaceutical industry.

Markus Roemer is managing director at comes compliance services, Ravensburg, Germany. He is an auditor, and manages business management compliance projects and support, audit service center, GMP compliance projects, and is an IT validation expert.

Yves Samson is founder and director of the consulting firm Kereon AG located in Basel, Switzerland. He has been in computerized system validation since 1992. He is the editor of the French version of GAMP®4 and GAMP®5 and he translated the PIC/S Guide PI 011 into French.

Chapter 1

Introduction

The EMA sets requirements in the EU applicable to the computer systems performing functions established[*] in the GMP[†] for medicinal products for human use, investigational medicinal products for human use, and veterinary medicinal products.

These requirements are delimited in the Commission Directive 2003/94/EC.[‡]

> "When electronic, photographic or other data processing systems are used instead of written documents, the manufacturer shall first validate the systems by showing that the data will be appropriately stored during the anticipated period of storage. Data stored by those systems shall be made readily available in legible form and shall be provided to the competent authorities at their request. The electronically stored data shall be protected, by methods such as duplication or back-up and transfer on to another storage system, against loss or damage of data, and audit trails shall be maintained."

Similar requirements can be found in 91/412/EEC.[§]

---

[*] *Establish* means define, document (in writing or electronically), and implement.

[†] In the EU context, "GMP-regulated activities" is defined as the manufacturing-related activities established in the basic legislation compiled in Volume 1 and Volume 5 of the publication "The Rules Governing Medicinal Products in the European Union," http://ec.europa.eu/health/documents/eudralex/index_en.htm.

[‡] Commission Directive 2003/94/EC Laying down the principles and guidelines of good manufacturing practice with respect to medicinal products for human use and investigational medicinal products for human use, October 1994.

[§] Commission Directive 91/412/EEC Laying down the principles and guidelines of good manufacturing practice for veterinary medicinal products, July 1991.

The Eudralex Volume 4, Annex 11, which refers specifically to computer systems and information technology (IT) infrastructure, provides guidance for the interpretation of the above requirement for all EU Member States, the three European Economic Area (EEA) states, and Switzerland. Annex 11 is found in Volume 4 of "The rules governing medicinal products in the European Union." Volume 4 includes the EU Guidelines to Good Manufacturing Practice Medicinal Products for Human and Veterinary Use, Parts I, II, and III and the Annexes.

Originated as PIC/S GMP Annex 5 in 1991, it was adopted in 1992 by the EMA GMP as Annex 11. It has later become a part of the Good Laboratory Practices (GLP)[*] and GCP[†] guidelines in Europe.

The updated version of Annex 11 was issued by the European Commission (EC) in January 2011 and it is effective since June 2011 as revision 1. The related Chapter 4 – Documentation of the GMP Guide Part I also became effective at the same date. The reason given for revising both parts was the increasing use of electronic documents within the GMP environment.

A comparison between the 1992 version (Appendix A) and the 2011 version (Appendix B) of Annex 11 reveals that although many topics are the same in the 1992 and 2011 Annex 11 versions, the depth of discussion and emphasis in 2011 reflect the increased experience and technical advances in the use of computerized systems during the nearly two decades between versions.[‡]

Some differences between the versions of Annex 11 include:[§]

■ Significant rewrite of the entire Annex to align with current standards developed by the industry to increase clarity and to reduce prescriptive characteristics of the Annex where possible
■ Various clauses: Introduction of quality risk management principles according to International Conference for Harmonisation (ICH) Q9
■ Clause 11: Introduction of a requirement to periodically review computer systems for their validated state, which is a further specification of

[*] Annex 11 is a reference in the OMCL Validation of Computerised Systems Core Documents (http://www.edqm.eu/medias/fichiers/Validation_of_Computerised_Systems_Core_Document.pdf), May 2009.

[†] Via PI 011-3, the EU GCP inspectors agreed to use as the reference for inspection of computer systems the published PIC/S Guidance on Good Practices for Computerised Systems in Regulated "GXP" Environments (PI 011-3) http://ec.europa.eu/health/files/eudralex/vol-10/chap4/annex_iii_to_guidance_for_the_conduct_of_gcp_inspections_-_computer_systems_en.pdf.

[‡] Stokes, T., "Management's View to Controlling Computer Systems," *GMP Review*, 10(2), July 2011.

[§] Australia TGA, "Comparison between the 2009 and 2013 editions of the PIC/S Guide to GMP," May 2013.

an existing requirement following Chapter 5 Clause 5.24 and Annex 15, Clauses 23 and 45 (as released in 2001)

■ Embracing a risk-based approach that is aligned with current industry computer systems good practices
■ Dropped the requirement for parallel testing

In addition, the major changes in the updated version of Annex 11 include:

■ Requirements traceability throughout a life cycle moves from a regulatory *expectation* to a regulatory *requirement* for the first time
■ New requirements for the need to keep and manage all electronic records throughout their life cycle
■ Validation phase has been extensively expanded to include the complete life cycle

In total, there were 3 major changes and 12 minor ones.

The origins of the updated version of Annex 11 can be found in the expansion works for the PIC/S Guide PI 011.[*] Released in 2003, the purpose of the PIC/S Guide is to provide the GMP inspectors uniformity and recommendation to inspect computer systems.

At the time of publication, PIC/S has not yet rewritten PIC/S PI-011 to reflect the updated version of Annex 11.

During a PIC/S event in Kiev, Ukraine, September 30–October 5, 2012, members reviewed the revision of several PIC/S GMP Guides and Annexes based on the revisions of the EU GMP Guides and Annexes. As part of this review, the PIC/S members accepted the EU Annex 11. On December 11, 2012, the PIC/S posted the revised Guide to Good Manufacturing Practices for Medicinal Products (PIC/S PE 009-10). As part of the Annexes[†] of this PIC/S Guide, the EU Annex 11 was included as an Annex 11 as well.

This harmonization between the EU and PIC/S has a powerful impact on more than 40 countries, including PIC/S non-EU countries, such as the United States, all ASEAN member countries, and Canada. Annex 11 could be considered as a kind of "common denominator" applicable to computer systems supporting GXP-regulated operations.

---

[*] PI 011-3. "Good Practices for Computerised Systems in Regulated 'GXP' Environments," Pharmaceutical Inspection Cooperation Scheme (PIC/S), September 2007.

[†] PIC/S GMP, PIC/S GMP Document PE 009-10, January 2013. http://www.picscheme.org/publication. php?download&file=cGUtMDA5LTExLWdtcC1ndWlkZS14YW5uZXhlcy5wZGY_

Annex 11 is a good framework for validation and use of computer systems and handling electronic records in any worldwide-regulated environment.

The computer systems validation program for regulated operations can be established based on Annex 11, software quality assurance (SQA) practices, software quality engineer (SQE) practices, and type of software Good Automated Manufacturing Practices Rev 5 (GAMP®5).

This book, which is relevant to regulated operations, provides practical information to enable compliance with computer systems validation requirements, while highlighting and efficiently integrating the Annex 11 guidelines into the computer validation program. The ideas presented in this book are based on many years of experience in the US Department of Defense and regulated industries in various computer systems development, maintenance, and quality functions. A practical approach is presented to increase efficiency and to ensure that software development and maintenance is achieved correctly. The topics addressed in this book are equally relevant to other types of software development industries.

It is not the intention of this book to develop a paradigm or model for the regulated industry.

Chapter 2 discusses the integration of the system life cycle (SLC), computer validation, and Annex 11.

Chapter 3 discusses the three principles in Annex 11.

Since early 2003, a risk management system covering computer systems should be established and integrated into the Pharmaceutical Quality System (PQS). Chapter 4 introduces the risk management guidelines.

Chapter 5 discusses the guidelines on personnel in a regulated company.

Suppliers and service providers applicable to computer systems are discussed in Chapter 6.

Chapter 7 contains a practical approach for CSV based on Annex 11. This chapter provides the reader with the foundations of a CSV approach.

Chapters 8, 9, 10, 11, and 12 discuss particular issues on electronic records integrity and printouts associated with the stored information. A comprehensive discussion on electronic records integrity can be found in Chapter 26.

Change management is covered in Chapter 13.

Chapter 14 covers the periodic evaluation of computer systems.

The Annex 11 guidelines on security, one of the key elements to achieve the integrity of electronic records, are discussed in Chapter 15.

The management of incidents in computer systems is contained in Chapter 16.

Chapter 17 covers the subject of electronic signatures and their implementation.

The guidance given in Annex 11 concerning batch certification by a Qualified Person (QP) and release is covered in Chapter 18.

Business continuity and data archiving are discussed in Chapters 19 and 20, respectively.

Based on an SLC, Chapter 21 provides the documentation required for a computer system.

Procedural controls required for computer systems are covered in Chapter 22.

Maintenance, the most difficult phase in computer systems, is discussed in Chapter 23.

Chapter 24 covers the environments of Cloud Computing and how Annex 11 can be a model for compliance.

Chapter 25 intends to provide some advice regarding how to take advantage of the software categories as defined in GAMP® 5 for qualifying IT infrastructure systems.

Chapter 26 covers the integrity of electronic records based on Annex 11.

Chapter 27 contains a comparison of Annex 11 and US FDA 21 CFR Part 11. Appendix E is a reference used for this chapter.

This book examines the released final version of Annex 11 and provides recommendations to implement Annex 11. There are many other ways to implement the same requirements. For bringing the reader additional information, it references relevant regulations/guidelines. The purpose of this book is not to find gaps between Annex 11 and the referenced regulations. Some descriptions are based on listed guidelines with judicious editing where necessary to fit the context of this book.

The recommendations to implement Annex 11, as described in this book, are purely from the standpoint and opinion of the authors and should serve as a suggestion only. They are not intended to serve as the regulators' official implementation process.

References

Commission Directive 2003/94/EC, Laying down the principles and guidelines of good manufacturing practice in respect of medicinal products for human use and investigational medicinal products for human use, October 2003.

Commission Directive 91/412/EEC, Laying down the principles and guidelines of good manufacturing practice for veterinary medicinal products, July 1991.

EU Annex III to Guidance for the Conduct of Good Clinical Practice Inspections Computer Systems, May 2008. http://ec.europa.eu/health/files/eudralex/vol-10/chap4/annex_iii_to_guidance_for_the_conduct_of_gcp_inspections_-_computer_systems_en.pdf.

EudraLex Volume 4, "EU Guidelines to Good Manufacturing Practice, Medicinal Products for Human and Veterinary Use, Annex 11–Computerised Systems," June 2011. http://ec.europa.eu/health/files/eudralex/vol-4/annex11_01-2011_en.pdf.

European Directorate for the Quality of Medicine and Healthcare, OMCL Validation of Computerised Systems Core Documents, May 2009. http://www.edqm.eu/medias/fichiers/Validation_of_Computerised_Systems_Core_Document.pdf.

ISPE, "Regulatory Framework—EMEA," Dr. Kate McCormick, 2009.

ISPE, "Regulatory Framework—PIC/S and ICH," Dr. Kate McCormick, 2009.

Jacobs, D., European Medicines Agency (EMA), *Encyclopedia of Pharmaceutical Science and Technology*, Fourth Edition. New York: Taylor & Francis. Published online 23 Aug 2013; 1449–1460.

Stenbraten, A., *Cost-Effective Compliance: Practical Solutions for Computerised Systems, EU-GMP Annex 11*. Paper presented at the ISPE Brussels Conference, GAMP®—Cost Effective Compliance, 2011-09-19/20.

Chapter 2

SLC, Computer Validation, and Annex 11

Centered on a quality system approach, the development and subsequent modifications of computer systems must follow an appropriate development methodology.

Regulatory Guidance

"The validation documentation and reports should cover the relevant steps of the life cycle."

EU Annex 11-4.1

The above is satisfied through a phased approach that has come to be known as the system life cycle (SLC) (Annex 11-4.1). The SLC is the "phases in the life of the system from initial requirements until retirement including design, specification, programming, testing, installation, operation, and maintenance."[*]

The life cycle phases defined in Annex 11 should be scaled based on risk, criticality, complexity of each computer system, and which primary party initiates or performs the development, operation, or maintenance of software products (refer to Chapter 7).

---

[*] Definition in Annex 11 to Volume IV of the Rules Governing Medicinal Products in the European Community Computerised Systems, June 2011.

During the execution of the SLC process, the computer system is simultaneously validated. If the SLC process is approached accurately, no supplementary work is necessary to complete the computer systems documentation supporting the implementation and the associated validation process. The SLC is a vital element of the CSV process.

The prescribed SLC ensures the formal assessment and reporting of quality and performance measures for all the life-cycle stages of software and system development, its implementation, qualification and acceptance, operation, modification, requalification, maintenance, and retirement. The SLC enables both the regulated user and competent authority to have a high level of confidence in the integrity of both the processes executed within the controlling computer systems and in those processes controlled by or linked to the computer systems, within the prescribed operating environments.[*]

The most important question, as part of the nonfunctional requirements applicable to computer systems, is if a formal SLC is to be employed in the implementation of this system. If the evidence indicates that a formal SLC approach will not be used, there is high probability that the system under study will have significant problems with its quality and reliability.

Figure 2.1[†] depicts a typical SLC. It includes the following periods:

- Conceptualization
- Development
- Operational life
    - Early operational life
    - Maturity
    - Aging

The SLC model (Figure 2.1), can be successfully used when requirements are well understood in the beginning and are not expected to change or evolve over the life of the project. Project risks should be relatively low.

---

[*] PI 011-3. "Good Practices for Computerised Systems in Regulated 'GXP' Environments," Pharmaceutical Inspection Cooperation Scheme (PIC/S), September 2007.

[†] George J. Grigonis, Jr., Edward J. Subak, Jr., and Michael L. Wyrick, "Validation Key Practices for Computer Systems Used in Regulated Operations," *Pharmaceutical Technology*, 74–98, June 1997.

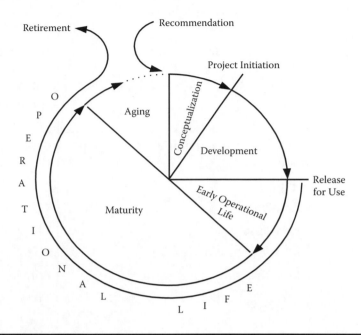

Figure 2.1   Typical system life cycle.

Table 2.1 lines up the life-cycle periods, high-level approach, and the associated Annex 11 item.

Table 2.1

SLC	*Approach*	*Annex 11*
Conceptualization	Defining project	11-4.5
	Generating quality plan	11-3; 11-4.5
Development	Establishing requirements specification	11-4.4
	Performing risk analysis	11-1
	Generating design specifications	11-5; 11-6; 11-9; 11-14
	Developing system components (software and infrastructure)	11-4.1; 11-4.6
	Developing the user and the system manual	11-8
	Installing the systems and qualifying	11-4.1; 11-4.8
	Planning and executing the acceptance test	11-4.7

(continued)

SLC	Approach	Annex 11
Operational Life	Releasing the system for operations	No specific Annex 11 item addressing criteria releasing the computer system to the operational life
	Operating and maintaining the computer systems Operating • Archiving • Backups • Business continuity • Infrastructure maintenance • Periodic review • Problem reporting • Problem management • Retirement • Security • System monitoring • Training Maintaining • Change and configuration management	Operational Phase 11-17; 11-7.1 11-7.2 11-16 Principle 11-11 11-13 11-4.2 11-12 11-6 (3rd sentence) 11-2 11-10

As depicted in the previous table, Annex 11 provides guidelines on how to implement each typical activity.

The only activity not explicitly covered in Annex 11 is the computer systems retirement. The retirement of computer systems is covered implicitly as part of 11-10. The retirement is considered a change of state of the computer, from active to inactive.

Last, as in any healthcare-regulated activity, procedural controls must be available for all life-cycle phases (Chapter 22). These should describe the activities in sufficient detail for the regulated user. The results of the procedural controls should be verified and, if necessary, corrected until the outputs of such activities comply. This ensures a formal quality system.

For a practical SLC process applicable to the healthcare industry, refer to Grigonis, Jr., Subak, Jr., and Wyrick (1997).

Life-Cycle Principles*

1. The SLC is independent from any specific development and maintenance methodologies. It includes the following periods: Conceptualization, Development, Early Operational Life, and Maturity and Aging; and the following events: Project Recommendations, Project Initiation, and Release for Use and Retirement.
2. "The validation documentation and reports should cover the relevant steps of the life cycle" (Annex 11-4.1).
3. Requirements specification should describe the required functions of the computer system and be based on documented risk assessment and GMP impact. The requirements should be traceable throughout the life cycle[†] (Annex 11-4.4).
4. Risk management should be applied throughout the life cycle of the computer system taking into account patient safety, data integrity, and product quality. As part of a risk management system, decisions on the extent of validation and data integrity controls should be based on a justified and documented risk assessment of the computer system (Annex 11-1).

References

PI 011-3. "Good Practices for Computerised Systems in Regulated 'GXP' Environments," Pharmaceutical Inspection Cooperation Scheme (PIC/S), September 2007.

George J. Grigonis, Jr., Edward J. Subak, Jr., and Michael L. Wyrick, "Validation Key Practices for Computer Systems Used in Regulated Operations," *Pharmaceutical Technology*, 74–98, June 1997.

---

[*] O. López, "Computer Systems Validation." In *Encyclopedia of Pharmaceutical Technology*, 4th ed. Taylor & Francis: New York, published online August 23, 2013; 615–619.

[†] O. López, "Requirements Management," *Journal of Validation Technology*, 17(2), Spring 2011.

Chapter 3

Annex 11 Principles

1. This annex applies to all forms of computerised systems used as part of GMP-regulated activities. A computerised system is a set of software and hardware components which together fulfill certain functionalities.
2. The application should be validated; IT infrastructure should be qualified.
3. Where a computerised system replaces a manual operation, there should be no resultant decrease in product quality, process control, or quality assurance. There should be no increase in the overall risk of the process.

Analysis

Principle 1

Confirming 2003/94/EC and 91/412/EEC, this first principle establishes that computer systems can be used to perform operations covered in the basic legislation compiled in Volume 1 and Volume 5 of the publication "The Rules Governing Medicinal Products in the European Union."[*]

> Regulatory requirements for data do not change whether data are captured on paper, electronically, or using a hybrid approach.

---

[*] http://ec.europa.eu/health/documents/eudralex/index_en.htm.

Table 3.1 Definition of Computer/Computerized Systems

	Computer Systems	*Computerized Systems*
EU Annex 11		A computerized system is a set of software and hardware components that together fulfill certain functionalities.
PIC/S PI 011-3	Computer hardware components assembled to perform in conjunction with a set of software programs that are collectively designed to perform a specific function or group of functions.	A computer system plus the controlled function that it operates.
EU GMP Glossary*		A system including the input of data, electronic processing, and the output of information to be used either for reporting or automatic control.

* http://ec.europa.eu/health/files/eudralex/vol-4/pdfs-en/glos4en200408_en.pdf

This first principle provides as well the definition of "computerized system." The difference about the subject of the definitions of a computer system between the PI 011-3* and the Annex 11 is curious. Refer to Table 3.1.

As depicted in Table 3.1, the term "computerized systems" has different connotations when this term is compared between Annex 11 and PI 011-3. PI 011-3 includes controlled functions and associated documentation in the definition of computerized systems. The definition in PI 011-3 is consistent with Figure 3.1.

Note that a fundamental concept recognized in the validation key practices[†] is that the term "computerized systems" applies not just to the computer system (i.e., software and hardware) but to the *combination* of:

- the computer system
- the process being controlled or monitored by the system
- the people

---

* PI 011-3. "Good Practices for Computerised Systems in Regulated 'GXP' Environments," Pharmaceutical Inspection Cooperation Scheme (PIC/S), September 2007.

† George J. Grigonis, Jr., Edward J. Subak, Jr., and Michael L. Wyrick, "Validation Key Practices for Computer Systems Used in Regulated Operations," *Pharmaceutical Technology*, 74–98, June 1997.

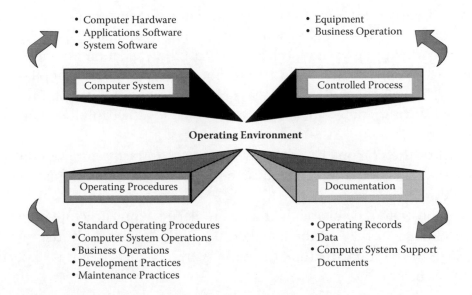

Figure 3.1   Computer systems operating environment.

- the documentation (including standard operating procedures) required to use, operate, and support the system
- any equipment or instruments being controlled or monitored by the system

In this book, a computer system is defined as in the validation key practices directly above.

Principle 2

In the case of computer systems implementing GMP-regulated activities,[*] certain functionality is required by the software application to implement master production records via operational checks (e.g., process specifications, conditions, sequencing, decision criteria, and formulas) and collect and manage critical data.[†] Some of these operational checks will provide data to determine the quality and the efficacy of drug products. In addition, managing the data collected must follow the data integrity principles contained in

---

[*] The term "GMP-regulated activities" in the EU context is defined as the manufacturing-related activities established in the basic legislation compiled in Volume 1 and Volume 5 of the publication "The Rules Governing Medicinal Products in the European Union," http://ec.europa.eu/health/documents/eudralex/index_en.htm.

[†] The term "critical data" in this context is interpreted as meaning data with high risk to product quality or patient safety. ISPE GAMP COP Annex 11 – Interpretation, July/August 2011.

Annex 11 (Chapter 26). Because the application is implementing a manufacturing process, the computer system needs to be validated (Chapter 7).

Consistent with the validation key practices, the validation principles pertinent to the application software are not limited only to the application software. They also include the usage, practice, and operations of a regulated activity within the regulated activity, which together fulfill certain GMP functionalities.

As part of the computer system, the computer infrastructure or computer hardware is considered equipment. As equipment, computer infrastructure is qualified.

To demonstrate the suitability of a given piece of infrastructure component, product, or service to the intended use and, consequently, the qualification state of the infrastructure, the main work products that it is expected to perform include:[*]

- a written design specification that describes what the software is intended to do and how it is intended to do it
- a written test plan and procedures[†] based on the Design Specification
- test results and an evaluation[‡] of how these results demonstrate that the predetermined design specification has been met

The information obtained from the executed test plan and procedure is used to establish written procedures covering equipment calibration, maintenance, monitoring, and control.

The qualification of the computer infrastructure consists of bringing it into conformance following the regulated company's standards and Annex 11 requirements. This is performed through a planned verification process. Once the computer infrastructure is in conformance, this state is maintained by following the operational and maintenance activities contained in Chapters 2 and 23 in this book.

The qualified state of the infrastructure must be periodically verified (Annex 11-11).

---

[*] O. López, *Computer Infrastructure Qualification for FDA Regulated Industries*, Davis Healthcare International Publishing, 2006.

[†] Written test plan and procedures are equivalent to Qualification Protocols.

[‡] Test results and an evaluation are equivalent to executed Qualification Protocols and the associated Summary Reports.

Principle 3

The use of a computer system does not reduce and should not add the requirements that would be expected for a manual system of data control and security. The computer system automates a manual repetitive operation and should meet the same quality systems requirements for those manual functions that it replaces.

This is why previous to converting a process from manual to automatic it is important to contemplate any quality assurance and safety issues as part of an impact assessment of risks. It is convenient that risks reduction measures should be implemented as part of the system's design. If the risks reduction measure cannot be incorporated as part of the computer system, then it is integrated in a procedural control.

This principle is verified during the validation and periodically, after the validation, during the operation of the systems. The statistical equivalence of the products between manually and automatically manufactured batches must be established.

References

Commission Directive 2003/94/EC, Laying down the principles and guidelines of good manufacturing practice in respect of medicinal products for human use and investigational medicinal products for human use, October 2003.

EudraLex Volume 4, "EU Guidelines to Good Manufacturing Practice, Medicinal Products for Human and Veterinary Use: Glossary," February 2013.

ICH Harmonised Tripartite Guideline, "Good Manufacturing Practice Guidance for Active Pharmaceutical Ingredients, Q7" November 2000.

ISO 13485:2003, "Medical Devices—Quality Management Systems—Requirements for Regulatory Purposes," Sections 7.2; 7.2.1; 7.2.2; 7.3.6; 7.5.2, February 2012.

PI 011-3. "Good Practices for Computerised Systems in Regulated 'GXP' Environments," Pharmaceutical Inspection Cooperation Scheme (PIC/S), September 2007.

WHO—Technical Report Series, No. 937, Annex 4, Appendix 5, "Validation of Computerized Systems," Section 7.1 (Hardware), 2006.

Chapter 4

Risk Management

EU Annex 11-1, General

Risk management should be applied throughout the life cycle of the computerized system taking into account patient safety, data integrity, and product quality. As part of a risk management system, decisions on the extent of validation and data integrity controls should be based on a justified and documented risk assessment of the computerized system.

Related References

3.2 The competence and reliability of a supplier are key factors when selecting a product or service provider. The need for an audit should be based on a risk assessment.

4.1 The validation documentation and reports should cover the relevant steps of the life cycle. Manufacturers should be able to justify their standards, protocols, acceptance criteria, procedures, and records based on their risk assessment.

4.4 User Requirements Specifications should describe the required functions of the computerized system and be based on documented risk assessment and GMP impact. User requirements should be traceable throughout the life cycle.

6.0 For critical data entered manually, there should be an additional check on the accuracy of the data. This check may be done by a second operator or by validated electronic means. The criticality and the potential consequences of erroneous or incorrectly entered data to a system should be covered by risk management.

16.0 For the availability of computerized systems supporting critical processes, provisions should be made to ensure continuity of support for those processes in the event of a system breakdown (e.g., a manual or alternative system). The time required to bring the alternative arrangements into use should be based on risk and be appropriate for a particular system and the business process it supports. These arrangements should be adequately documented and tested.

Analysis

This item, Annex 11-1, is a new one in Annex 11. It creates the expectations of managing computer systems risks through the system life cycle taking into account factors such as patient safety, product quality, and data integrity.

Software development is one of the most risk-prone management challenges. Risk factors are usually present that can negatively influence the development process and, if neglected, can lead to project failure. To counteract these factors, system risk must be actively identified, controlled, and reduced on a routine basis.[*]

Risk is defined as the probability of an undesirable event occurring and the impact of that event if it does occur. The result of this analysis will influence the degree to which the system development, implementation, and maintenance activities are performed and documented.

The purpose of risk management is to manage the risks of a computer system project by tracking them throughout the life cycle and performing risk mitigation as necessary.

Risk management includes risk assessment; cost-benefit analysis; and the selection, implementation, test, and evaluation of safeguards. Figure 4.1 depicts the risk management sequencing.

---

[*] Guidelines for Successful Acquisition and Management of Software Intensive Systems, Vol. 1, Software Technology Support Center, DAF, February 1995.

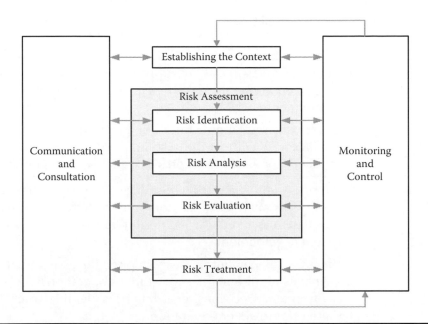

Figure 4.1   Risk management sequencing.

This overall system review considers both effectiveness and efficiency, including impact on the process controlled by the computer system and constraints due to policy, regulations, and laws.

Specifically for computer systems, factors to account are data integrity and the integrity of the processes executed surrounded by the controlling computer system within the prescribed operating environment (a.k.a. integrity of the intended use).

For a better benefit of the risk management, an integration of the SLC management and risk management activities should be achieved. Table 4.1* provides the integration of risk management and the SLC.

Based on the intended use and the safety risk associated with the computer system to be developed/configured, the developer should determine the specific approach, the combination of techniques to be used, and the level of effort to be applied.

The following is one of many techniques to implement a risk management process.

Risk management encompasses two processes: risk assessment and risk treatment. The risk assessment is composed of risk identification, risk analysis, and risk evaluation.

---

* NIST 800-30 r1, "Guide for Conducting Risk Assessments," September 2012.

Table 4.1   Risk Assessment and SLC

SLC Phase	Support from Risk Management
General	Identified risks are used to support the development of the system requirements document, including security requirements. A first risk assessment should be performed to determine the GMP criticality of the system. Does the system have an impact on patient safety, product quality, or data integrity?
Project Phase	The risks identified during this phase can be used to support the security analyses of the computer system. These analyses may lead to architecture and design trade-offs during the system development. The risk management process supports the assessment against its requirements and within its operational environment. Decisions regarding risks identified must be made prior to system operation. Requirements usually are developed with consideration of potential risks and form the basis for the first formal risk assessment.
Operational Phase	Risk management activities are performed for periodic reviews or whenever major changes are made to the computer system in its operational production environment (e.g., new system interfaces).
Retirement	Risk management activities are performed for system components that will be replaced to ensure that the hardware and the software are properly retired, that residual data is appropriately handled, and that system migration is conducted in a secure and systematic manner.

During the management of the risk, there must be a process to monitor and control the risks.

Risk Assessment

Risk assessment is the method to evaluate and characterize the critical parameters in the functionality of an equipment or process.[*]

---

[*] EudraLex, Volume 4, "EU Guidelines to Good Manufacturing Practice, Medicinal Products for Human and Veterinary Use, Annex 15 – Validation and Qualification," May 2014 (Draft).

During the risk evaluation, processes, systems, and functions should be assessed considering how possible hazards and potential harms arising from these hazards may be controlled or mitigated. For some processes, systems, or functions, a detailed assessment should also be performed.

This initial risk assessment, also called system risk assessment, is performed to evaluate the effect of the computer system on product safety, performance, and reliability. From this evaluation, the extent of validation required can be determined. Computer systems that control critical manufacturing areas will require more extensive validation activities and documentation than those that are of lesser risk. Likewise, computer systems whose output is subject to subsequent inspection or review will also require less rigor. The inspection or review will be a mitigation factor as part of the risk assessment.

A detailed risk assessment or Functional Risk Assessment (FRA) is performed based on the initial risk assessment executed at the concept phase. The FRA evaluates risks associated with processes and functions defined in the requirements specification. The evaluation consists of:

■ identifying processes/functions/transactions (as appropriate)
■ assessing risks by analyzing:
  – risk scenarios
  – effects for each event
  – likelihood of events
  – severity of impact
  – likelihood of detection
■ planning for reduction or elimination of those risks, based on the analysis

By evaluating the system risk analysis, the system owner may uncover potential problems that can be avoided during the development process. The chances of a successful, if not perfect, system implementation are improved.

To adequately analyze the risks, a comprehensive requirements specification deliverable is essential. The best time to perform an initial risk analysis is just after the project team has completed the review of the requirements specification deliverable. The risks found during the assessment may add requirements that need to be part of the requirements specification.

Some of the items to consider when conducting the risk analysis include:

■ regulatory areas of the system
■ size of the computer system and number of users
■ complexity of the system in terms of the design

- type of data the system handles
- functionality of the system
- interaction with and impact on existing systems
- vendor reliability
- effect/impact of system noncompliance
- safety to the customer, employee, and community
- cost versus benefit of the system

In addition, after performing the system risk assessment, it should determine the extent of validation necessary based on the identified risks, and then develop your test plan and test cases accordingly.

According to the ICH Q9,[*] the extent of validation may include:

- selection of the design
- code reviews
- extent of testing and test method

The Canadian Health Products and Food Branch Inspectorate[†] (Canadian Inspectorate) provides a look at how inspectors may associate risk as part of GMP inspections. The Canadian Inspectorate considers three types of risk associated with manufacturing computer systems: critical, major, and other.

A critical observation[‡] consists of computer systems used for complex manufacturing operations of critical products that are not qualified and with evidence of malfunctioning or lack of appropriate monitoring.

The Inspectorate considers major observations as[§]:

- computer system does not operate within its specifications in the course of the critical steps of fabrication, packaging/labeling, and testing
- lack of preventative maintenance program for major equipment/no records maintained

---

[*] ICH Harmonised Tripartite Guideline, "Quality Risk Management," Q9. November 2005.

[†] Canadian Health Products and Food Branch Inspectorate, "Risk Classification of Good Manufacturing Practices (GMP) Observations (GUI-0023)," September 2012, http://www.hc-sc.gc.ca/dhp-mps/compli-conform/gmp-bpf/docs/gui-0023-eng.php.

[‡] Critical observation—Observation describing a situation that is likely to result in a noncompliant product or a situation that may result in an immediate or latent health risk and any observation that involves fraud, misrepresentation, or falsification of products or data.

[§] Major observation—Observation that may result in the production of a drug not consistently meeting its marketing authorization.

- no calibration program for automatic, mechanical, electronic, or measuring equipment/no records maintained
- unapproved/undocumented major changes compared to Master Production Documents (e.g., embedded Master Production in PLC code)
- lack of or insufficient change control system

The Inspectorate considers other observations as[*]:

- inadequate training records
- access to production areas restricted to unauthorized personnel

The above list can provide areas in which risks can be assessed when computer systems are performing functions applicable to Annex 11.

Risk Mitigation

As part of the risk analysis, strategies for mitigation of the identified risks may[†] include modifying the process or system design, modification of project approach or structure, or modifying the validation and testing approach.

Reduction or elimination of those risks is performed during the system development life cycle (SDLC). Based on the risks identified, planning of the design validation, design verification, and qualification testing should begin. The test plan and test cases should be developed accordingly.

Risk Evaluation

Inputs to the evaluation of the risk include implementation strategies for selected courses of action for risk responses and the actual implementation of selected courses of action.

The risk evaluation consists of:

- Assess processes, systems, or function, considering:
  - Possible hazards.
  - How potential harm arising from these hazards may be controlled or mitigated.

---

[*] Other observation—Observation that is neither critical nor major but is a departure from GMP principles.
[†] May—This word, or the adjective "optional," means that an item is truly optional.

■ For some processes, systems, or functions, a detailed risk assessment should be performed. Example of a detailed risk assessment is FRA.

Risk Monitoring and Control

The purpose of risk monitoring and control is to manage the risks of a computer system project by tracking them throughout the life cycle and performing risk mitigation as necessary.

This process is entered from the project management–related activities, project monitoring, and control process whenever a risk needs to be addressed, monitored, or tracked. There are two entry scenarios:

■ A periodic scheduled risk assessment is due.
■ Project information is discovered or received that affects risk.

It should also be performed whenever there is a significant change in the conditions affecting the risks. Criteria that often trigger risk reassessment include:

■ significant changes in scope, schedule, or budget
■ identification or discovery of a new risk
■ completion of a major phase of the software project (e.g., design)

Risk Monitoring and Control

Project Planning Process	Project Start-Up Process	Project Monitoring and Control Process
Risk Assessment		Risk Monitoring

Approach

Annex 20* summarizes an approach to a Quality Risk Management pertinent to computer systems and computer-controlled equipment.

- Determine the GMP criticality of the system, impact on patient safety, product quality, or data integrity; identify critical performance parameters; determine the extent of validation.
- Develop requirement specification with consideration from the basis of the criticality; perform a detailed risk assessment to determine critical functions.
- Select the design of computer hardware and software (e.g., modular, structured, fault tolerance); implement appropriate controls via design as much as possible.
- Perform code review.
- Determine the extent of testing and test methods of the controls implemented during the design.
- Evaluate reliability of electronic records and signatures, as applicable.
- Trace risks throughout the life cycle.

It is left to the competent persons to choose the risk analysis approach for the individual validation projects. The method should be implemented structurally.

During the project, risks may be reassessed. The reassessment should occur at regularly scheduled intervals. It should also be performed whenever there is a significant change in the conditions affecting the risks. Criteria that often trigger risk reassessment include:

- significant changes in scope, schedule, or budget
- identification or discovery of a new risk
- completion of a major phase of the software project (e.g., design)

---

* EudraLex, The Rule Governing Medicinal Products in the European Union, Volume 4, EU Guidelines for Good Manufacturing Practices for Medicinal Products for Human and Veterinary Use, Annex 20, Quality Risk Management, February 2008.

Summary

Computer systems performing GMP-regulated activities must be validated proportionally to the level of risk present to patient safety, product quality, and integrity of critical records.

References

EudraLex, Volume 4, "EU Guidelines for Good Manufacturing Practices for Medicinal Products for Human and Veterinary Use, Annex 20–Quality Risk Management," February 2008.

GAMP®/ISPE, Risk Assessment for Use of Automated Systems Supporting Manufacturing Process—Risk to Record, Pharmaceutical Engineering, Nov/Dec 2002.

GAMP®/ISPE, Risk Assessment for Use of Automated Systems Supporting Manufacturing Process—Functional Risk, Pharmaceutical Engineering, May/Jun 2003.

GHTF, "Implementation of Risk Management Principles and Activities within a Quality Management System," May 2005.

ICH Harmonised Tripartite Guideline, "Quality Risk Management, Q9," November 2005.

NIST, "Guide for Conducting Risk Assessments," 800-30 Rev 1, September 2012.

PIC/S, "Quality Risk Management: Implementation of ICH Q9 in the pharmaceutical field an example of methodology from PIC/S," PS/INF January 2010.

Pressman, Roger S., and Maxim, Bruce R., *Software Engineering—A Practitioner's Approach*, McGraw Hill, 2014.

Chapter 5

Personnel

EU Annex 11-2, General

There should be close cooperation between all relevant personnel such as Process Owner, System Owner, Qualified Persons, and IT. All personnel should have appropriate qualifications, level of access, and defined responsibilities to carry out their assigned duties.

Analysis

Annex 11-2 can be traced to the following Principle[*]:

"The correct manufacture of medicinal products relies upon people. For this reason, there must be sufficient qualified personnel to carry out all the tasks which are the responsibility of the manufacturer. Individual responsibilities should be clearly understood by the individuals and recorded. All personnel should be aware of the principles of Good Manufacturing Practice that affect them and receive initial and continuing training, including hygiene instructions, relevant to their needs."

---

[*] EudraLex, The Rule Governing Medicinal Products in the European Union, Volume 4, EU Guidelines for Good Manufacturing Practices for Medicinal Products for Human and Veterinary Use, Part 1, Chapter 2–Personnel, February 2014.

It is the responsibility of the senior management to determine and provide acceptable and appropriate resources to implement and maintain the computer systems' quality management system and continually improve its effectiveness.

The manufacturer should have an adequate number of personnel with the necessary qualifications and practical experience. It must ensure that a consistent division of roles and tasks between the relevant personnel is clearly defined and implemented.

Specifically for personnel planning, managing, or performing computer systems validation, it will help if the qualifications and practical experience include computer programming, analysis, and design.

In addition, continual training should also be ensured according to standard training programs in the tasks assigned to them personally.

Training should not only include system operation but also cover the significance of system faults (bugs), regulatory requirements, risk management, system changes, security procedures, manual operation of the system, and documentation of system errors. The organization must record the training of computer system–related personnel.

The success of the risk management depends on the education and training of management and employees to understand the importance of risk management in producing and supplying safe pharmaceuticals.[*]

A link should be provided between training programs and the change management process so that training requirements can be continually evaluated, adjusted, and maintained in alignment with the current state of the operational computerized system.

For additional GMP requirements about training, refer to Sections 2.10 to 2.14 in EudraLex (2014).

References

EudraLex, The Rules Governing Medicinal Products in the European Union, Volume 4, "EU Guidelines for Good Manufacturing Practices for Medicinal Products for Human and Veterinary Use, Part 1, Chapter 2–Personnel," February 2014, (http://ec.europa.eu/health/files/eudralex/vol-4/2013-01-18_chapter2_.pdf).

ICH Harmonised Tripartite Guideline, "Good Clinical Practice, E6," Sections 4.1, 4.2.3, 4.2.4, 5.4.1, 5.5.1, 5.6.1; June 1996.

---

[*] WHO—Technical Report Series No. 981, "WHO Guidelines on Quality Risk Management," 2013.

ISO 13485:2012, "Medical Devices—Quality Management Systems—Requirements for Regulatory Purposes," Sections 5.5, 5.5.1, 5.5.3, 6.2, 6.2.1, 6.2.2; February 2012.

ISPE GAMP®: *"A Risk-Based Approach to Compliant GXP Computerised Systems,"* Operational Appendix O12, International Society for Pharmaceutical Engineering (ISPE), 5th ed., February 2008.

US FDA 21 CFR Part 58.29, Good Laboratory Practice for Non-Clinical Laboratory Studies.

US FDA 21 CFR Part 110(c), Current Good Manufacturing Practice in Manufacturing, Packing, or Holding Human Food.

US FDA 21 CFR Part 312.53(a) and 53(d), Investigational New Drug Application.

US FDA 21 CFR Part 606. 160(b)(5)(v), Current Good Manufacturing Practice for Blood and Blood Components.

WHO—Technical Report Series No. 937, Annex 4. Appendix 5, "Validation of Computerized Systems," 2006.

WHO—Technical Report Series No. 981, "WHO Guidelines on Quality Risk Management," 2013.

Chapter 6

Suppliers and Service Providers

EU Annex 11-3, General

3.1 When third parties (e.g., suppliers, service providers) are used to provide, install, configure, integrate, validate, maintain (e.g., via remote access), modify, or retain a computerized system or related service or for data processing, formal agreements must exist between the manufacturer and any third parties, and these agreements should include clear statements of the responsibilities of the third party. IT departments should be considered analogous.

3.2 The competence and reliability of a supplier are key factors when selecting a product or service provider. The need for an audit should be based on a risk assessment.

3.3 Documentation supplied with commercial off-the-shelf products should be reviewed by regulated users to check that user requirements are fulfilled.

3.4 Quality system and audit information relating to suppliers or developers of software and implemented systems should be made available to inspectors on request.

4.5 The supplier should be assessed appropriately.

Analysis

Service providers are all parties who provide any services irrespective if they belong to an independent (external) enterprise, the same company group/structure, or an internal service unit.

The role of the service providers and supplier has been put in the spotlight due to the trend by the regulated users[*] of purchasing computer systems, software products, or software services.

The choice of a contractor/supplier management by a regulated user must be documented. The contractor/supplier's suitability is demonstrated by means of compliance with the prerequisites in the vendor requirements document or performance measurement contained in the system level agreement (SLA).

Even where tasks are partly contracted out to external companies, the regulated user is ultimately responsible for ensuring the suitability and operability of the computer systems. The regulated user must have processes in place to ensure the supplier's suitability for the service or task to which the supplier is to be entrusted and the quality of contracted tasks. The regulated user must have the control of outsourced activities (contractor/supplier management) and have the ability to measure the quality of contracted tasks.

The responsibilities and specific requirements should be clearly defined in the agreement between the contract giver and contract acceptor, service agreements, or quality agreements.

These processes and controls must incorporate quality risk management to determine whether a supplier should be audited[†] and include the following[‡]:

- The quality controls and quality assurance procedures, documentation, and records related to the development and production of the system, software product, or software service from a supplier are of critical importance. Compliance with a recognized Quality Management System (QMS) provides the regulated user and regulatory agencies or compe-

---

[*] In this chapter, the regulated user is also the "acquirer" or the organization that acquires or procures a system, software product, or software service from a supplier.

[†] Audit—conducted by an authorized person for the purpose of providing an independent assessment of software products and processes in order to assess compliance with requirements (ISO 12207:1995). (Note: The 1995 revision is not the most recent version.)

[‡] ICH Q10, *Pharmaceutical Quality Systems*, June 2008, Section 2.7, Management of Outsourced Activities and Purchased Materials.

tent authority with the desired confidence in the structural integrity, operational reliability, and ongoing support for system, software product, or software service utilized in the system.[*]

■ Evaluate[†] the suitability and competence of the provider to carry out the critical systems/activity using a defined supply chain prior to outsourcing operations. For application software used specifically for GMP-regulated activities, at least for GAMP type of software configured products (GAMP5 software category 4) and custom applications (GAMP5 software category 5), the validity of potential suppliers should be evaluated appropriately (11-4.5) and the evaluation documented. This evaluation should consider:
  – The potential impact of the system being supplied based on patient safety and data integrity
  – Vendor's QMS
  – Operational reliability
  – The novelty or complexity of the system
  – Software engineering practices
  – The history and experience in supplying these systems
  – Ongoing support for software and hardware products

■ The regulated user may wish to consider additional means of evaluation fitness for purposes against predetermined requirements, specifications, and anticipated risks. Techniques such as supplier questionnaires, (shared) supplier audits (11-3.2), and interaction with user and sector focus groups can be helpful.[‡]

■ Documented justification should be provided for not evaluating suppliers of GMP-regulated systems, software products, or software services.

■ A report of the documented supplier selection should exist for review by inspectors (11-3.4). Any deviation from the requirements observed during this evaluation or audit should be addressed. This report is an element of the validation life cycle and provides an insight into the evaluation processes. Confidentiality agreements should be adjusted accordingly.

---

[*] PI 011-3. "Good Practices for Computerised Systems in Regulated 'GXP' Environments," Pharmaceutical Inspection Cooperation Scheme (PIC/S), September 2007.

[†] Evaluation—a systematic determination of the extent to which an entity meets its specified criteria (ISO 12207:1995). (Note: The 1995 revision is not the most recent version.)

[‡] PI 011-3. "Good Practices for Computerised Systems in Regulated 'GXP' Environments," Pharmaceutical Inspection Cooperation Scheme (PIC/S), September 2007.

- The output from the evaluation or audit may:
  - Determine the level of governance by the regulated company.
  - Identify potential risks to the project due to gaps in the vendor QMS.
  - Use vendor's documentation results in support of the verification of the manufacturing critical aspects.
  - Build a common quality understanding/partnership between the supplier and the vendor.
- If the supplier proves the correct implementation of the established quality system for the application's intended use, except for the review of the performance of the supplier, no additional controls are required for the suppliers by the regulated user.

  The decision and justification to use vendor's documentation results in support of the verification of the manufacturing critical aspects should be based on the correct implementation of the established quality system, intended use of the computer system, and should be documented and approved by subject matter experts including the quality unit (ASTM, E 2500-13). These should not be repeated by the customer.
- Monitor and review the performance of the supplier or the quality of the services from the provider, and the identification and implementation of any needed improvements. The regulated user should check regularly that the external company is developing, maintaining, or operating the computer system properly and in accordance with the approved SLA.
- Monitor outsourced activities to ensure they are from approved sources using the agreed supply chain.

  It is the belief of particular regulated users that a mere certification of suitability from the vendor, for example, the off-the-shelf application is Annex 11 compliant, will be adequate. When validation information is produced by an outside firm, for example, computer vendor, the records maintained by the company need not include all the voluminous test data. However, such records should be sufficiently complete (including general results and protocols) to allow the company to evaluate the adequacy of the validation.

Following the ISO/IEC International Standard,* the primary SLC processes can be used to guide the reader as to how to put together the elements discussed in this chapter.

---

* ISO 12207:1995, "Information Technology—Software Life Cycle Processes." (Note: The 1995 revision is not the most recent version. The Primary SLC processes are discussed only in the 1995 revision.)

In the context of the regulated user, the Acquisition Process is the main process to acquire a system, software product, or service.

In the context of the service provider, the Supply Process is the main process to provide the system, software product, or software service to the regulated user. The referenced Annex 11 item, as applicable, can be found on each equivalent sub-process.

Acquisition Process

The activities of the Acquisition Process include:

- Acquisition Planning (11-1)
- Requirements gathering, including technical constraints (11-4.4)
- Requirements gathering and specification (11-4.4)
- Contract preparation and update (11-3.1)
- Supplier monitoring
  - In-process audits (11-4.5)
  - Code reviews, inspections, and audits (11-3-2)
- Acceptance and completion (11-4.7)
  - FAT
  - SAT

Supply Process

The activities of the Supply Process include:

- Initiation, preparation of response, contract (11-3.1)
- Planning (11-1)
- Execution and control
  - Develop product based on development process (project phase, relevant 11-4.1 and 4.5)
  - Maintain product based on maintenance process (operational phase)
- Review and evaluation
  - In-process audits (11-4.5)
  - Code reviews, inspections, and audits (11-3-2)
  - FAT (11-4.7)
  - SAT (11-4.7)
- Delivery and completion
  - Formal release for use

References

ASTM, E 2500–13 "Standard Guide for Specification, Design, and Verification of Pharmaceutical and Biopharmaceutical Manufacturing Systems and Equipment," 2013.

ICH Harmonised Tripartite Guideline, "Good Manufacturing Practice Guidance for Active Pharmaceutical Ingredients, Q7," November 2000.

ICH Harmonised Tripartite Guideline, "Pharmaceutical Quality Systems, Q10," Section 2.7, Management of Outsourced Activities and Purchased Materials, June 2008.

ISO 12207, "Information Technology—Software Life Cycle Processes," 1995.*

ISO 13485, "Medical Devices—Quality Management Systems," Sections 5.5, 5.5.1, 5.5.3, 6.2, 6.2.1, 6.2.2, 7.4, 7.4.1; July 2012.

ISPE GAMP 5: *A Risk-Based Approach to Compliant GXP Computerised Systems*, 5th ed., International Society for Pharmaceutical Engineering (ISPE), Management Appendices M2 and M6, February 2008.

O. López, "Hardware/Software Suppliers Qualification," in *21 CFR Part 11: Complete Guide to International Computer Validation Compliance for the Pharmaceutical Industry*, Interpharm/CRC, Boca Raton, FL, 2004, 107–109.

PDA, Technical Report No. 32, "Auditing of Supplier Providing Computer Products and Services for Regulated Pharmaceutical Operations," *PDA Journal of Pharmaceutical Science and Technology*, Sep/Oct 2004, Release 2.0, Vol. 58 No. 5.

WHO—Technical Report Series, No. 937, Annex 4, Appendix 5, "Validation of Computerized Systems," Section 6.2, 2006.

---

* *Note*: The 1995 revision is not the most recent version.

Chapter 7

Validation

EU Annex 11-4, Project Phase

4.1 The validation documentation and reports should cover the relevant steps of the life cycle. Manufacturers should be able to justify their standards, protocols, acceptance criteria, procedures, and records based on their risk assessment.

4.2 Validation documentation should include change control records (if applicable) and reports on any deviations observed during the validation process.

4.3 An up-to-date listing of all relevant systems and their GMP functionality (inventory) should be available. For critical systems, an up-to-date system description detailing the physical and logical arrangements, data flows, and interfaces with other systems or processes, any hardware and software prerequisites, and security measures should be available.

4.4 User requirements specifications should describe the required functions of the computerized system and be based on documented risk assessment and GMP impact. User requirements should be traceable throughout the life cycle.[*]

4.5 The regulated user should take all reasonable steps to ensure that the system has been developed in accordance with an appropriate quality management system. The supplier should be assessed appropriately.

---

[*] O. López, "Requirements Management," *Journal of Validation Technology*, 17(2), Spring 2011.

4.6 For the validation of bespoke or customized computerized systems, there should be a process in place that ensures the formal assessment and reporting of quality and performance measures for all life-cycle stages of the system.

4.7 Evidence of appropriate test methods[*] and test scenarios should be demonstrated. Particularly, system (process) parameter limits, data limits, and error handling should be considered. Automated testing tools and test environments should have documented assessments for their adequacy.

4.8 If data are transferred to another data format or system, validation should include checks that data are not altered in value or meaning during this migration process.

Analysis

Validation

Action of proving, in accordance with the principles of Good Manufacturing Practice, that any procedure, process, equipment, material, activity or system actually leads to the expected results.

EudraLex—Volume 4 GMP Guidelines, Glossary

"Validation" of computer systems is the process that ensures the formal assessment and reporting of quality and performance measures for all the life-cycle stages of software and system development, its implementation, qualification, and acceptance, operation, modification, requalification, maintenance, and retirement.[†]

---

[*] Test methods—With the Black-Box Test, the test cases are derived solely from the description of the test object; the inner structure of the object is thus not considered when creating the test plan. With the White-Box Test, the test cases are derived solely from the structure of the test object. With the Source-Code Review, the source code is checked against the documentation describing the system by one or several professionals. The APV Guideline Computerised Systems based on Annex 11 of the EU-GMP Guideline, April 1996.

[†] PI 011-3. "Good Practices for Computerised Systems in Regulated 'GXP' Environments," Pharmaceutical Inspection Cooperation Scheme (PIC/S), September 2007.

The key elements of the above definition are formal assessments, quality, and performance measures.*

The *formal assessment* activities and associated acceptance criteria are established. The products of those assessments provide the data supporting the state of the validation of the computer system.

In the CSV context, *quality* can be defined as the precise capability of the computer system to perform the intended use or the fitness for purpose and complying with all applicable requirements.

Performance measurement techniques can support the project-related activities and the management of such activities in the following ways:

- Defining effective metrics for sizing the project and measuring progress
- Using Earned Value Management (EVM) as the key integrating tool for control
- Defining quality goals in terms of project milestones and metrics
- Planning for incremental releases and rework
- Revising the plan for deferred functionality and requirements volatility
- Focusing on requirements, not defects, during rework
- Using testable requirements as an overarching progress indicator

The accurate implementation of a CSV process in compliance with the GMPs enables both the regulated user and competent authority to have a high level of confidence in the integrity of both the processes executed within the controlling computer system and the processes controlled by or linked to the computer system within the prescribed operating environment.†

Another key element of the CSV definition is "life cycle" and it is a key component in Item 4 of Annex 11.

Chapter 2 in this book describes how Annex 11 is contained in a typical SLC and depicts a suggested validation approach based on Annex 11 items.

Computer Systems Validation Regulatory Guidance

The computer systems validation process incorporates "planning, verification, testing, traceability, configuration management, and

---

* http://www.testablerequirements.com/Articles/solomon.htm
† PI 011-3. "Good Practices for Computerised Systems in Regulated 'GXP' Environments," Pharmaceutical Inspection Cooperation Scheme (PIC/S), September 2007.

many other aspects of good software engineering that together help to support a final conclusion that software is validated."

US FDA CDRH, General Principles of Software Validation; Guidance for Industry and FDA Staff, January 2002

The purpose of validation of a computer system (Principle 2) performing GMP-regulated activities is to ensure an acceptable degree of evidence (documented, raw data) (Annex 11-1 and 11-4.1), confidence (dependability and thorough, rigorous achievement of predetermined system specification[*]), intended use, accuracy, consistency, and reliability.[†]

Establishing intended use, proper performance, and operating environment of the computer system are essential elements to a successful CSV.[‡]

Key activities to establish the scope of the system (intended use, proper performance, and operating environment of a computer system) (Annex 11-4.4) are

- Identification of operational functions associated with the process to be automated and the users. These operational functions consist of authority checks and the associated controls of electronic data integrity.
- Delineation of the operational system checks.
- Identification of the applicable regulatory requirements, regulated user standards, and safety requirements.

After defining the operating environment and type of software and evaluating the organization of a system to accomplish the intended use and required performance, the key activities to successfully execute CSV projects are as follows[§]:

- Establish a requirements specification. This specification must include both structural and functional analysis (Annex 11-4.1 and Annex 11-4.7). This analysis describes what functionality is required and the data integrity controls (11-1) to be implemented, consequently, the intended use of the computer system.

---

[*] In this book, system specification corresponds to requirements, functional, or design specifications.
[†] WHO. Technical Report Series, No. 937, 2006. Annex 4, Appendix 5, Section 1.3.
[‡] O. López, "Computer Systems Validation." In *Encyclopedia of Pharmaceutical Technology*, 4th ed., Taylor and Francis, New York. Published online: August 23, 2013, 615–619.
[§] O. López, "Computer Systems Validation." In *Encyclopedia of Pharmaceutical Technology*, 3rd ed., Marcer and Dekker, Inc., New York, 2006.

▪ Write a validation plan based on a risks approach to determine the scope and extent of the validation (Annex 11-1) and, after executing the plan, to prove control of the critical aspects of the particular computer operation. In the absence of an applicable procedural control, the validation plan must cover the software development life cycle (SDLC) methodology and the associated maintenance methodology that best match the nature of the system under development (Annex 11-4.5 and Annex 11–Operational Phase). The validation plan must provide the document evidence of the validation process as well (Annex 11-4.1).

▪ Establish a system specification that describes how the computer system will comply with the requirements specification (Annex 11-4.1).

▪ Changes during the development phase must be recorded and assessed for potential impact to the system specification.

▪ Demonstrate that the predetermined system specification has been met (Annex 11-4.7).
  - Select the infrastructure supporting the application based on the capacity requirements and functionality (Annex 11-4.4 and Annex 11 – 2nd Principle).
  - Review, verify, and test the operational functions (Annex 11-4.1).
  - Identify and test the "worst case" operational/production conditions (Annex 11-4.7).
  - Replicate the test results based on statistics (Annex 11-4.1).

The above formal activities produce the objective confirmation that the system is "validated." Many of these activities must be completed in a predefined order and delimited as part of an SLC. The working products (refer to Chapter 2) in the SLC provide the objective evidence that is required to demonstrate that the computer system conforms to the needs of the user and the intended use and that all requirements can be consistently achieved.

Immediately after the computer system has been released into the production environment, the maintenance of the computer systems initiates. To successfully maintain the validated state of the computer systems, the key activities to consider are

▪ Availability of written procedural controls to maintain the validation state of the computer system and its operating environment (Annex 11–Operational Phase). Consider the following: performance monitoring, configuration management, backups and restoration of backups (Annex 11-7.2), data archiving and restoration of archived data (Annex 11-17), system and data security (Annex 11-7.1), calibration and maintenance, personnel training, emergency recovery, and periodic re-evaluation (WHO Technical Report Series, No. 937, 2006. Annex 4, Appendix 5, Section 1.6).

■ Assessment of any modification to a component of the system, its operating environment, or documentation to determine the impact of the modification to the computer system. If required, qualification/validation is to be re-executed totally or partially (Annex 11-10).

■ After a suitable period of running the new system, independently review and compare the system with the system specification and intended use (WHO Technical Report Series, No. 937, 2006. Annex 4, Appendix 5, Section 3.3).

■ Evaluate the system periodically (Annex 11-11) to confirm that it remains in a valid state and is compliant with GMP. Such evaluation should include, where appropriate, the current range of functionality, the intended use, deviation records, incidents (Annex 11-13), problems, upgrade history, performance, I/Os verification, reliability, security, and validation status reports (Annex 11-11).

Overall, the changes to the computer system, which may affect the validated state, must be evaluated to determine if revalidation is required. Refer to Chapter 13.

Completing the SLC, the retirement of the computer systems process must be comprehensive to remove the application, automated or manual interfaces, and associated infrastructure. Retirement without replacement may require the archiving of certain application records to satisfy the retention requirements of company policies and governing regulations relating to system documentation, operating records, application software, and data (Annex 11-17, Annex 11, 2nd Principle).

In addition, retirement with replacement may require critical data[*] be reformatted to adjust the new application record formats/database organization (Annex 11, 2nd Principle, and Annex 11-4.8). The considerations for data transfer and validation are discussed in Chapter 8.

As part of the computer systems portfolio management, a list of systems is required. This list depicts the representation of the systems supporting automated processes. It provides the status of the computer system during

---

[*] Critical data—in this context, critical data is interpreted as meaning data with high risk to product quality or patient safety. ISPE GAMP COP Annex 11 – Interpretation, July/August 2011.

its life cycles. Some of these statuses include implementation, operational changes, periodic reviews, revalidation, and retirements. In addition, for systems with an operational status, system description detailing the physical and logical arrangements, data flows and interfaces with other systems or processes, and any hardware and software prerequisites should be available (Annex 11-4.3).

Finally, the users of regulated computer systems have the ultimate responsibility for ensuring that documented validation evidence is available to the competent authority inspector for review (PIC/S PI 011-3).

Primary Life-Cycle Processes

Following the ISO/IEC International Standard,* primary SLC processes can be used to guide the reader in putting together all the elements in Annex 11. These processes summarize all aspects of a typical SLC. It is not the intention of this discussion to develop a paradigm or model for the regulated industry.

Primary SLC processes are contingent upon who initiates or performs the development, operation, or maintenance of software products. These primary parties are the acquirer, the supplier, the developer, the operator, and the maintainer of software products. The primary SLC processes consist of acquisition, supply, development, operation, and maintenance.

The following defines each ISO/IEC 12207 (1995 first edition) primary life-cycle process:

- Acquisition Process—Defines the activities of the regulated user acquirer, the organization that acquires a system, software product, or service.
- Supply Process—Defines the activities of the supplier, the organization that provides the system, software product, or software service to the regulated user acquirer.
- Development Process—This is the primary life-cycle process discussed in Chapter 2. It defines the activities of the developer, the organization that defines and develops the software product.

---

* ISO12207:1995, "Information Technology—Software Life Cycle Processes." (Note: The 2008 revision of ISO 12207 does not cover the primary life-cycle processes.)

■ Operation Process—Defines the activities of the operator, the organization that provides the service of operating a computer system in its live environment for its users.

■ Maintenance Process—Defines the activities of the maintainer, the organization that provides the service of managing modifications to the software product to keep it current and in operational fitness. This process includes the migration and retirement of the software product.

In addition to the above SLC processes, the retirement process is added as a primary life-cycle process. In the ISO/IEC 12207, this process is contained as part of the maintenance process. The retirement process completes the SLC as described in Chapter 2.

Acquisition Process

The acquisition process begins with the definition of the need to regulate users who acquire a system, software product, or software service. It continues with the preparation and issue of a request for proposal, selection of a supplier, and management of the acquisition process through to the acceptance of the system, software product, or software service.

The acquisition process activities include:

■ Initiation activities
■ Request for proposal
■ Contract preparation and update
■ Supplier monitoring
■ Acceptance and completion

From the context of the regulated user, the acquisition process activities are related with Annex 11-3 and Annex 11-4.5.

Supply Process

The supply process is initiated either by a decision to prepare a proposal to replay a regulated user acquirer's request for proposal or by signing and entering into a contract with the regulated user acquirer to provide the system, software product, or software service.

The supply process continues with the determination of procedures and resources needed to manage and ensure the project, including development of project plans and execution of the plans through delivery of the system, software product, or software service to the regulated user acquirer.

The list of activities include:

- Response to the request of proposal
- Contract
- Planning
- Execution and control
- Review and evaluation
- Delivery and completion

From the context of the supplier, Annex 11-4.5 is the applicable item to the supply process activities: purchasing computer systems, software product, or software services. The service supplier must ensure that the service to be provided has been developed with an appropriate quality management system.

Development Process

Development of software in a quality-assured manner involves the appropriate selection and implementation of software design and development methods that[*]:

- include a formal development process using models, methods, architecture, and design-modeling techniques appropriate for the development language and the safety criticality of the intended purpose and foreseeable use.
- cover different software life-cycle stages, for example, via compliance with ISO/IEC 12207, Software Engineering Body of Knowledge (SWEBOK) guide implemented with suitable tools that are linked in a systematic way and that systematically produce, derive, or generate detailed design source code, 486 traceability records, and 487 test specifications.

See Chapter 2 in this book.

---

[*] International Medical Device Regulators Forum (IMDRF) SaMD Working Group, "Software as a Medical Device: Possible Framework for Risk Categorisation and Corresponding Controls," March 2014 (Draft).

Operation and Maintenance Processes

See Chapter 13 in this book. Irrespective of the source of the software model (acquirer,[*] supplier,[†] or developer[‡]), the development of the computer system should follow accepted standards for system life cycle (SLC) including, but not limited to, proper design, system qualification procedures, change control, and detailed documentation.

Proposed documentation requirements are covered in Chapter 21.

References

Commission Directive 2003/94/EC, "Laying Down the Principles and Guidelines of Good Manufacturing Practice in Respect of Medicinal Products for Human Use and Investigational Medicinal Products for Human Use," Article 9 Section 2, October 2003

EudraLex, Volume 4, "EU Guidelines to Good Manufacturing Practice, Medicinal Products for Human and Veterinary Use, Annex 11 – Computerised Systems," June 2011.

EudraLex, Volume 4, "EU Guidelines to Good Manufacturing Practice, Medicinal Products for Human and Veterinary Use, Annex 15 – Validation and Qualification," May 2014 (Draft).

ICH Harmonised Tripartite Guideline, "Good Clinical Practice, E6," Sections 5.5.3 (a) and (b), June 1996.

ICH Harmonised Tripartite Guideline, "Good Manufacturing Practice Guidance for Active Pharmaceutical Ingredients, Q7," November 2000.

ICH Harmonised Tripartite Guideline, "Quality Risk Management, Q9," November 2005.

ISO 13485:2012, "Medical Devices—Quality Management Systems—Requirements for Regulatory Purposes," Sections 2.3, 7.2, 7.2.1, 7.2.2, 7.3.6.6.3, 7.5.1.2.2, 7.5.2; February 2012.

ISPE GAMP 5: *A Risk-Based Approach to Compliant GXP Computerised Systems*, International Society for Pharmaceutical Engineering (ISPE), 5th ed., Development Appendices: D1–D7; Management Appendices M1–M10; Operational Appendix O1, February 2008.

López, O., "Requirements Management," *Journal of Validation Technology*, Spring 2011.

---

[*] Acquirer—An organization that acquires or procures a system, software product, or software service from a supplier (ISO 12207:1995).

[†] Supplier—An organization that enters into a contract with the acquirer for the supply of a system, software product, or software service under the terms of the contract (ISO 12207:1995).

[‡] Developer—An organization that performs development activities (including requirements analysis, design, and testing through acceptance) during the software life-cycle process (ISO 12207:1995).

PI 011-3. "Good Practices for Computerised Systems in Regulated 'GXP' Environments," Pharmaceutical Inspection Cooperation Scheme (PIC/S), September 2007.

US FDA 21 CFR Part 58.61; 63(a) and (c); 58.81(c) and (d); 58.33, "Good Laboratory Practice for Non-Clinical Laboratory Studies."

US FDA 21 CFR Part 606.160(b)(5)(ii) and 606.100(b)(15), "Current Good Manufacturing Practice for Blood and Blood Components."

US FDA 21 CFR Part 803.17 and 18, "Medical Device Reporting."

US FDA 21 CFR 1271.160(d), "Human Cells, Tissues, and Cellular and Tissue-Based Products."

US FDA, "Blood Establishment Computer System Validation in the User's Facility," April 2013.

US FDA, "General Principles of Software Validation; Final Guidance for Industry and FDA Staff," CDRH and CBER, January 2002.

WHO, Technical Report Series No. 937, Annex 4. Appendix 5, "Validation of Computerized Systems," 2006.

Chapter 8

Data

R.D. McDowall
Principal, McDowall Consulting

EU GMP Annex 11-5, Operational Phase

Computerized systems exchanging data electronically with other systems should include appropriate built-in checks for the correct and secure entry and processing of data in order to minimize the risks.

Introduction

Annex 11 contains the requirement in Clause 5 that focuses on ensuring the integrity of data that are transferred electronically between computerized systems.

Before we discuss the clause in detail, we need to consider the impact of other sections of Annex 11 on how Clause 5 can be interpreted.

Impact of Other Sections of Annex 11

Clause 5 does not exist in isolation. Some other clauses of the Annex 11 regulation need to be considered to help interpret Clause 5. This is shown in Figure 8.1 and will be discussed in the following sections.

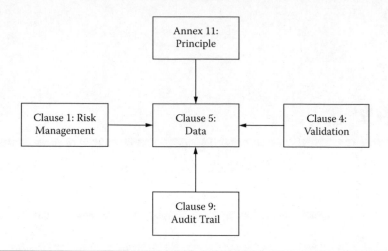

Figure 8.1   Impact of other Annex 11 clauses on interpretation of Clause 5 on data.

There are four clauses that impact the interpretation of Clause 5 on data transfer between systems.

The Principle of Annex 11 states:

> Where a computerised system replaces a manual operation, there should be no resultant decrease in product quality, process control or quality assurance. There should be no increase in the overall risk of the process.

Typically, electronic data transfers will replace a manual operation that is inherently error prone, as the existing manual process is operated by humans. However, simply replacing a manual process with an electronic one does not necessarily mean that the new process will work reliably or correctly and will be error free. The transfer process and associated software need to be carefully designed to ensure that the transfer has appropriate error-trapping mechanisms and sufficient capacity for anticipated data volumes to perform consistently and reliably. However, the primary aim of an electronic transfer should be to eliminate an existing manual process by making it error free, faster, and more effective as well as reducing human involvement in the process.

As with all requirements of Annex 11, Clause 5 should be interpreted with Clause 1 for risk management, which has two explicit mentions of data integrity:

■ Data integrity controls need to be risk based.
■ Appropriate controls should be based on the functions automated by the systems involved and criticality of data transferred between them.

Therefore, the controls required for ensuring the effectiveness and efficiency of electronic transfer will depend on the criticality of the data being transferred and the impact on the patient, process, and integrity if the data are corrupted or changed during the transfer between the systems.

An electronic transfer will usually be involved with the implementation and validation of a new system or new functionality. Alternatively, two existing systems will be integrated under a change control request. Regardless of the approach, the requirements of Annex 11 Clause 4 on validation will be applicable, for example, plan of the work, specification of requirements, traceability, testing, and release. This portion of the work will not be discussed here; the reader is referred to Chapter 7 for further information on this topic. This chapter will look at the options for electronic transfer and mechanisms for ensuring the integrity of the data.

As data will be entered into a system via electronic transfer, the audit trail of the receiving system needs to document the act, and therefore Clause 9 requirements could come into play. Although there may not be any operator interaction with the process, in the author's view, the transfer should be documented such as source or originating system, time and date of transfer, and the number of records received by the receiving system.

Preserving the Content and Meaning of Data

The prime consideration in any electronic transfer of data between systems is that the content and meaning of the transferred data are preserved. This implicitly requires that sufficient metadata are transferred with the main data element to ensure that contextual information is maintained. As an example, if a pH measurement, generated in either a laboratory or in-process manufacturing system, is transferred to another system, there needs to be additional metadata transferred as well:

- Assume that the actual pH measurement is 7.0. If only this number were transferred, what information does it provide? None. What are we measuring and why are we measuring it?
- Therefore, additional metadata is required to put context around the measurement to make it understandable and meaningful, such as:
  - What is being measured?
  - Where is it being measured?
  - When was the measurement made?

- Who made the measurement?
- What is the relevance of the result (e.g., inside a specification or process limit)?
- Is this part of a series of measurements or only a single one?

■ As an absolute minimum, the value plus a reference to the associated metadata in the source system are needed for transfer so that the content and meaning of the value are ensured. Otherwise, the data and sufficient metadata must be transferred to ensure that content and meaning are preserved.

■ Data migration is a special type of electronic transfer that will be discussed later in this chapter, but the aim of any automated migration is to preserve the content and meaning of data generated in the source system in the receiving system. If required, any differences between the data in the source and receiving systems are explained and justified via a risk assessment.

Some Data Transfer Options

The two main ways that data can be transferred from the source system to the receiving system are shown in Figure 8.2. These are direct data transfers from system to system or via a data file that is placed in an operating system directory by the source system and then the receiving system accesses the file and imports it. In either case, the source system can be in the same organization as the receiving system or external to it. Regardless of the situation, the same principles of data transfer are applicable to both.

The principle of electronic transfers is that they are best without human involvement, provided that the involved tools have been validated adequately. Involving users in the transfer process should be minimized if possible to reduce any errors.

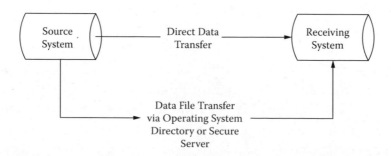

Figure 8.2   Schematic of electronic data transfer options.

Manually Driven Electronic File Transfers

In this section, we will discuss some of the ways to transfer electronic files between two systems. In many cases, the data file to be transferred may be in an Excel (xls or xlsx) or a comma separated value (CSV) file format, either of which can be subject to manipulation or corruption in transit or while in a directory, which will be discussed later.

Copy and Paste/Drag and Drop Electronic Transfers

There may be situations where a manual electronic transfer is the only mechanism possible. In such cases, procedural controls need to be in place. For example, many stand-alone laboratory systems generate electronic records that need to be protected. One of the simplest means of ensuring that the data are secured is to copy and paste or drag and drop the records from the workstation in the laboratory to a secure network location. In this case, there needs to be a procedure written with roles and responsibilities defined and a mechanism for ensuring that the records on the source system are the same as those transferred to the receiving system. In addition, there needs to be a second person review to check that the source and receiving files are the same, for example, number of files, data volume in the two locations are the same, the correct names of the files are present in the two locations and, in addition, the time and date stamps on both sets of files are identical. There also needs to be the provision of evidence to demonstrate that this is correct.

Security should be available to prevent access by unauthorized people; as a minimum, using groups defined in the operating system may be a way of achieving this. To avoid manipulation of the data, the disk on which the files are transferred could be made write protected. These requirements may also be applicable to other data transfer approaches.

As can be seen, this way of transferring data is laborious and potentially error prone, but it is better than storing data on a stand-alone workstation where it could be subject to loss or unauthorized manipulation.

A second type of file transfer is where a file, for example, a CSV formatted file containing data, is transmitted from the source system to a secure location on the network format. Here the file is imported into the receiving system under the command of a user. As such, it is similar to the first file transfer process in that it needs to be under control of a procedure, but the rigor of control will be less. Typically in this situation, there will be audit trail entries in the receiving system that a file was imported, by whom, and when.

A third type of manually driven electronic transfer uses a File Transfer Protocol (FTP) or secure FTP software. Files sent via FTP are sent in plain text that can be read if a more secure transmission mode is required. Then a secure FTP mode is required where data are protected or encrypted to ensure a more secure transfer. In essence, FTP software allows a user to browse directories and select the files to be transferred from the source system and then copies them in a secure location for import into the receiving system.

The problem with the manually driven electronic file transfer methods outlined thus far is that there is no built-in mechanism of ensuring the integrity of the transfer and answering the question, "Have there been any data changes or corruption?"

Ensuring Data Integrity

There are a number of mechanisms for ensuring the integrity of data transfer either by file transfer or by direct data transfer routes. Two of these are as follows:

■ Cyclic Redundancy Checks. CRCs, sometimes called check sums, are a means of detecting errors in transmitted data. Based on a mathematical interpretation of the data being transmitted, a check sum is added to the data; this increases the file size but does not alter the data being transferred. When the data are received, the system performs the same calculation on the data and compares the newly calculated value with that transmitted in the data set. If the two match, then the transmitted data have not been corrupted during transmission from the source system. If there is an error, the receiving system can request that the data be resent.

■ Encryption. Although CRCs are intended for ensuring the integrity of transmitted data, they are not intended for protecting against intentional manipulation of data. For this, data encryption is required. This takes the data to be transmitted and, using an encryption algorithm, coverts the data into a cyphertext that requires the key to convert the data into a readable format again. Encryption of data can also include the use of digital signatures to ensure the authenticity of the data.

Automatic Methods of Electronic Data Transfer

Rather than use manually driven electronic transfers, a better approach is to use automatic transfer of data between systems. This can work in a number of ways but requires software that can automatically identify the data to be transferred, there is a file to be imported, and the actual importing to the receiving system. With the introduction of software, we have to consider the impact of the other clauses of Annex 11 shown in Figure 8.1: risk management, validation, and audit trail.

When software is used, it is ideal that data transfer is achieved using a commercial package that either works as standard (GAMP category 3 software) or can be configured (GAMP category 4). Where there is a strong business case and there is no commercial alternative, then custom software (GAMP category 5 software) can be considered. However, this is the highest risk software category.

Two methods for transferring data automatically are as follows:

■ Some systems can use software agents that parse specific directories on a timed interval to then copy or transfer any data located in the directories. When data reach the receiving system, the data are checked against the original files in the source system to verify that there are no errors. The original data can be either left in the originating system or deleted automatically, if configured by the system administrator, so that there is only the copy in the receiving system.
■ Database views can be used to transfer data from one database to another application. A view is based on a query of the source system database and the output can be transferred to the receiving application.

Data Migration Issues

One specific type of data transfer that requires a separate discussion is data migration either from one version to another of the same application or between two different applications.

The first situation is easier to deal with, as typically there will be migration tools provided by the application provider that will perform the transfer, and validation will be undertaken in parallel. The second situation is more difficult, as data fields need to be mapped between the two systems. In some cases:

■ There will be an exact match between data in the two systems.
■ Data will be truncated when moving to the receiving system data, elements of strings cannot fit in the new system, and some data are lost. A risk assessment needs to be performed to assess if the content and meaning have changed and what, if anything, needs to be done to mitigate the risk.
■ Data cannot be migrated. This may apply to the audit trail entries in the source system that are protected and cannot be removed or there is no mechanism to import audit trail entries from one system to another. Alternatively, there is no field in the receiving system to store some data from the source system. Again, a risk assessment needs to be undertaken and options discussed. It may be that a read-only database for the source data is maintained after migration to the receiving system.

Once the mapping is complete, validation of the data migration will be undertaken before the actual migration. The migration should be accompanied with checks that the work has been successful at the database level and at the application level to demonstrate correct data migration.

Validation Considerations for Data Transfer

Validation of the transfer needs to consider two major elements for specification and acceptance testing. First, specify the requirements of the transfer including frequency of transfer and define the maximum data volume or size of each transfer. This is to ensure that the transfer mechanism is specified and tested on a worst-case basis rather than finding out issues when the interface is operational.

Second, test the transfer to pass as well as to fail (e.g., wrong data formats, corrupted file). In addition, one of the tests needs to include the maximum data size to be transferred or even exceeded as well as the frequency of transfers required. Acceptance criteria should be based on the preservation of the content and meaning of the data. If data elements are truncated during the transfer, this is because it is designed or the receiving system is known to truncate the data field, which should be part of the specification for the transfer.

For further information about the interpretation of the validation section of Clause 4 on validation, the reader is referred to Chapter 7 of this book.

Reference

EudraLex, Volume 4, EU Guidelines to Good Manufacturing Practice, Medicinal Products for Human and Veterinary Use, Annex 11 – Computerised Systems, June 2011.

Chapter 9

Accuracy Checks

EU Annex 11-6, Operational Phase

For critical data entered manually, there should be an additional check on the accuracy of the data. This check may be done by a second operator or by validated electronic means. The criticality and the potential consequences of erroneous or incorrectly entered data to a system should be covered by risk management.

Analysis

Regulatory Expectation

"There should be records of checks that the data/control/monitoring interface(s) between the system and equipment ensure correct input and output transmission."

PIC/S PI 011-3, Section 20.5, September 2007

Annex 11-6 is applicable to critical data* entered manually to the computer system. For example, values that are used for the rejection or approval of a semi-finished or final product batch, batch number, expiry date for packaging processes, keying in of laboratory data, and results from paper records or boundary values should be seen as critical data.

Critical input data need to be identified in the course of the development of the requirements document, assessed as part of the risk analysis (Annex 11-1). Critical input data are comprised of all data relevant to product quality.

Of those critical values, the ones to be entered manually need to be identified as well as the associated data type. In addition to the incorrect value entered, an inappropriate data type should be prevented.

The consequence of a faulty manual data input should be assessed as part of the risk analysis. Based on the impact level, there should be appropriate control measurements implemented. These controls may include verification by a second person.

The requirements document should describe the electronic prompts, flags, and data quality checks to be designed and implemented to address, for example, data inconsistencies, missing data, and entries out of range.

The intent of Annex 11-6 is to confirm that critical data entered manually by an authorized person was, in fact, entered accurately and that there is an independent verification record to show this. The persons carrying out the data entry and verification should be identifiable. The independent verification of the manually entered critical data can be performed by a second authorized person or a computer system.

A second authorized person with logged name and identification, with time and date, may verify data entry via the keyboard. The process applicable to the critical data entry requiring a second check must be established in a procedure.[†]

Accuracy Checks Performed by Computer Systems

The accuracy check can be performed by a computer system if and only if the automation of this verification can achieve the same or higher degree of guarantee as the verification by a second person (Annex 11, Principle C).

---

[*] Critical data—data with high risk to product quality or patient safety. (ISPE GAMP COP Annex 11 – Interpretation, July/August 2011.)

[†] PI 011-3. "Good Practices for Computerised Systems in Regulated 'GXP' Environments," Pharmaceutical Inspection Cooperation Scheme (PIC/S), September 2007.

In the context of this check, a verification is one that is programmed into the background of the data entry. This could be specific checks on data format, ranges, or values.

To minimize errors and omissions during manual data entry, it is encouraged to use electronic prompts, flags, and data quality checks. Reminders can be designed to alert the data entry person of missing data, inconsistencies, inadmissible values (e.g., date out of range), and to request additional data where appropriate to effectively complete the record. The data entry person should have the ability to enter comments about issues associated with the data.[*]

Accuracy checks can also be performed by computer systems featuring direct data capture linked to other databases and intelligent peripherals.

Special access, system control features, or special devices such as identification code bars and the inclusion and use of an audit trail to capture the diversity of changes possibly impacting the data may facilitate this check.[†]

The overall validation of the computer system, specifically the qualification of the verification step, and implementation of the normal operational controls (Chapter 23) ensure accuracy and repeatability of the implemented accuracy checks.

As part of the test plan and procedure it is critical to establish that the correct method confirms that the verification of critical data entered manually conforms to the applicable requirements implemented in Annex 11-6.

The requirements for critical data must include correct values and data types. Incorrect values and incorrect data types must be prevented or it will result in an error message (e.g., text in a numeric field or a decimal format in an integer field).

For numerical critical data entered manually, one of the testing methods used to verify the correctness of the accuracy checks is domain testing. This testing method is also known as boundary testing.

Domain testing is used to verify numerical processing software. Domain test values are set at the edges (i.e., slightly above and slightly below) of the valid input ranges and include the biggest, smallest, soonest, shortest, fastest members of a class of test cases. It should be noted that the presence of incorrect inequalities usually causes failures only at the code of algorithm boundaries. The objective of domain testing is to avoid making the

---

[*] US FDA, *"Guidance for Industry: Electronic Source Data in Clinical Investigations,"* September 2013.
[†] PI 011-3. "Good Practices for Computerised Systems in Regulated 'GXP' Environments," Pharmaceutical Inspection Cooperation Scheme (PIC/S), September 2007.

computer system involuntarily stop and demonstrate the correctness of error messages.

In assessing how well a computer system performs the accuracy check, it is necessary to demonstrate that the computer system examines the same conditions that a human being would look for, and that the degree of accuracy in the examination is at least equivalent.

References

PI 011-3. "Good Practices for Computerised Systems in Regulated 'GXP' Environments," Pharmaceutical Inspection Cooperation Scheme (PIC/S), September 2007.

US FDA, *"Guidance for Industry: Electronic Source Data in Clinical Investigations,"* September 2013.

Chapter 10

Data Storage

EU Annex 11-7—Operational Phase

7.1 Data should be secured by both physical and electronic means against damage. Stored data should be checked for accessibility, readability, and accuracy. Access to data should be ensured throughout the retention period.

7.2 Regular back-ups of all relevant data should be done. Integrity and accuracy of back-up data and the ability to restore the data should be checked during validation and monitored periodically.

Analysis

"The electronically stored data shall be protected, by methods such as duplication or back-up and transfer on to another storage system, against loss or damage of data, and audit trails shall be maintained."

Chapter II, Article 9, Section 2, Commission Directive 2003/94/EC

Data storage is a device that records (stores) or retrieves (reads) information (data) from any medium, including the medium itself.

In a typical process-manufacturing environment, typical data storages containing critical data are the SCADA (refer to Appendix F) and the data server containing MES-related data.

There are various key processes associated with the integrity to the data saved in a data storage device: inputs, outputs, storage, and retention of the electronic records.

Inputs and Outputs

The inputs and outputs (I/Os) to the data storage devices are managed by Annex 11-5, Data. They must include "appropriate built-in checks for the correct and secure entry and processing of data, in order to minimize the risks." The built-in checks are defined during the requirements phase (Annex 11-4.5). As an example, the hard points representing I/Os within the SCADA systems coming from a PLC must be subject to an interface verification. It must ensure that the data sent by the PLC to the SCADA was properly received by the SCADA and vice versa.

The controls to input data must include controls to prevent omissions in data (e.g., system turned off and data not captured).*

The accuracy of the I/Os to the data storage is tested during the qualification activities and after the qualification, as part of the computer system's ongoing performance evaluation program. I/Os verification after the qualification activities is based on the realistic expectation that the computer system's I/O errors can occur on validated systems. Computer components (logic circuits, memory, microprocessor), hardware interfaces, or devices (modems, displays), like mechanical parts, can fail after they have been installed and tested.

Storage

Design specification or similar document must describe the file structure in which the data are stored, the data capacity requirements, and how the security scheme is implemented. The file structure and security are tested during the qualification.

---

* Health Canada, "Good Manufacturing Practices (GMP) Guidelines for Active Pharmaceutical Ingredients (APIs)," GUI-0104, C.02.05, Interpretation #15, December 2013.

After the data are in the storage device, the data integrity must be ensured. Logical and physical protections must be adequate to the risk (Annex 11-12.2). Logical and physical protections comprise the protection of data storage devices from unauthorized parties (Annex 11-7.1 and 12.1) as well as the environmental impacts influencing the respective data storage devices (Annex 11-7.1).

As an element of the data integrity, there must be a record of any data change made that includes the previous entry, who made the change, and when the change was made* (Annex 11-9).

To reduce the risk of losing the data in the storage and guarantee data readiness to the users, periodic backups must be performed (Annex 11-7.2). The backup must be stored separate from the primary storage location and at a frequency based on an analysis of risk to GMP data and the capacity of the storage device.

The effectiveness of the backup and restore processes must be verified (Annex 11-7.2) as part of the qualification process. In addition, the capacity level of the storage must be monitored.

All the above must be written in a procedural control. Items to be considered as part of the backup procedure are as follows†:

- backup and restore procedures
- frequency of backup
- verification of the ability to retrieve backup data and files
- at least two generations or two copies of backups should be kept, unless other measures are taken to prevent backup versions from being damaged
- backup copies should be stored separate from the system in a way that it is highly unlikely that both the original and the backup copies can be damaged
- availability of the backup within an appropriate period

Accessibility, readability, and accuracy to the storage device and backups should be checked immediately after copying and periodically thereafter (Annex 11-11). If changes are proposed to the storage-related computer infrastructure (hardware and software) and the application accessing the records in storage, the above-mentioned checks must be performed as part of the qualification of the new component.

---

* Health Canada, "Good Manufacturing Practices (GMP) Guidelines for Active Pharmaceutical Ingredients (APIs)," GUI-0104, C.02.05, Interpretation #15, December 2013.
† Conseil Européen des Fédérations de l'Industrie Chimique (CEFIC), "Computer Validation Guide," Rev 2, December 2002.

The person who owns the stored records will be responsible for adequacy of storage and associated controls to these records.

Finally, when outside agencies are used to provide data storage services, there should be a formal agreement including a clear statement of the responsibilities of that outside agency (Annex 11-3).

Retention

Retention of records or exact copies of records in data storage devices does not differ from paper.

Records retention requirements are described in the Commission Directive 2003/94/EC, Chapter II, Article 9, Section 1. As an example, electronic manufacturing batch records must be kept for one year after expiry of the batch to which it relates or at least five years after certification of the batch by the Qualified Person, whichever is the longer. For investigational medicinal products, the electronic batch documentation must be kept for at least five years after the completion or formal discontinuation of the last clinical trial in which the batch was used. After completing the specified record requirements, the records can be archived (Annex 11-17).

Relevant Controls*

The following procedures and technical controls should be adopted for records retained by computer storage:

- Records should be regularly and progressively backed up, and the backup retained at a location remote from the active file (11-7.2)
- Data collected directly from equipment and control signals between computers and equipment should be checked by verification circuits/software to confirm accuracy and reliability (11-5)
- Interfaces between computers and equipment should be checked to ensure accuracy and reliability (11-5)
- Contingency plans and recovery procedures should be documented in the event of a breakdown. The recovery procedures should be

---

* TGA, "Australian Code of Good Manufacturing Practice for human blood and blood components, human tissues and human cellular therapy products," Rev 1, April 2013.

periodically checked for the return of the system to its previous state (11-16)

■ The system should be able to provide accurate printed copies of relevant data and information stored within it. Printed matter produced by computer peripherals should be clearly legible and, in the case of printing onto forms, should be properly aligned onto the forms (11-8).

References

APV, "The APV Guideline 'Computerized Systems' based on Annex 11 of the EU-GMP Guideline," Chapter 5, Version 1.0, April 1996.

Commission Directive 2003/94/EC, "Laying Down the Principles and Guidelines of Good Manufacturing Practice in Respect of Medicinal Products for Human Use and Investigational Medicinal Products for Human Use," Chapter II, Article 9, Sections 1 and 2, October 2003.

TGA, *"Australian Code of Good Manufacturing Practice for human blood and blood components, human tissues and human cellular therapy products,"* Rev 1, April 2013.

Chapter 11

Printouts

EU Annex 11-8, Operational Phase

8.1 It should be possible to obtain clear printed copies of electronically stored data.

8.2 For records supporting batch release, it should be possible to generate printouts indicating if any of the data has been changed since the original entry.

Analysis

Regulatory Expectation

"All data defined as critical data and associated metadata should be printable."

**Aide Memoire (Ref. #: 07121202) of the German ZLG
(Central Authority of the Laender for Health Protection)**

Even with the increased use in the GMP-regulated activities of computer systems and, subsequently, electronic records, it is very common to see regulated users rely on printouts as a hardcopy to be attached to the batch record or rely on printouts to perform regulated activities.

Due to incorrect inputs, programming, configuration, computer malfunctions, or other reasons, computer printouts, on occasion, do contain errors. If the errors are unnoticed, these printouts can result in a serious production error and the distribution of an adulterated product.

If, based on the regulated user's business practices, these printouts are used as quality records, then the design, qualification, and controls of these printouts are critical.

Based on the need of the regulated user, the reports are validated as per regulated procedural control. The format in which the data were stored should also be filed along with the reports.

In cases of internal audits (e.g., self-inspections [EudraLex Volume 4, Chapter 9]) or external audits (e.g., inspections by regulatory agencies or competent authority), it must be possible to obtain printed reports of electronically stored data that were neither specified nor validated during the implementation of the normal required reports.

In this particular case, in order to generate reliable printouts, a report generator can be utilized to take data from a source such as a database or a spreadsheet and use it to produce a document in a format that satisfies a particular human readership.

If satisfied with the computer system validation evidence, auditors can then study the computer system when it is being used and call for printouts of reports from the system and archives as relevant.

If a report generator creates the printout, then a verification of the printout must be performed before providing the printout to the auditor.

In any case, the printout functionality must provide the capability to print audit trails (Annex 11-8.2 and Annex 11-9). In addition, Annex 11-8.1 recommends that the printout be clear. "Clear printed" means printouts that apart from the values themselves, the units and the respective context can also be seen in the printout.* Units and the respective context are also known as metadata.

In case the supplier of the computer system is not capable to support Annex 11-8.2, it may be acceptable to describe in a procedure that additionally a printout of the related audit trail report must be generated and linked manually (e.g., paper-based revision history audit trail log) to the record.†

Printouts must be verified before hardware or software is exchanged. As part of the validation/qualification of the software/hardware, regression

---

* "Q&As on Annex 11," *Journal for GMP and Regulatory Affairs*, 8, April/May 2012.
† European Medicines Agency (EMA), "Q&A: Good Manufacturing Practices (GMP)," February 2011.

testing can be used to check that the data concerned can also be printed in the new configuration.

Should a change in the hardware or software not allow stored data to be printed in the new configuration, then one of the following procedures should be applied*:

■ The data in the format concerned should be converted into a format that can be printed in the new configuration.
■ The components of the old hardware or software configuration required for printing should be retained. In this case, it should be guaranteed that a suitable alternative system is available in case the retained system fails.
■ The data are transferred to another medium.

---

* APV, "The APV Guideline 'Computerised Systems' based on Annex 11 of the EU-GMP Guideline," Version 1.0, April 1996.

Chapter 12

Audit Trails—Ensuring Data Integrity

R.D. McDowall
Principal, McDowall Consulting

EU GMP Annex 11-9, Operational Phase

Consideration should be given, based on a risk assessment, to building into the system the creation of a record of all GMP-relevant changes and deletions (a system-generated "audit trail"). For change or deletion of GMP-relevant data, the reason should be documented. Audit trails need to be available and convertible to a generally intelligible form and regularly reviewed.

Introduction

Data integrity is an important regulatory topic, and one of the main ways to ensure and monitor this in a computerized system is via an audit trail. In the paper world, say, a laboratory notebook or a controlled worksheet, the audit trail is part of the document itself and any entries and changes are self-evident by signing or initialing entries and any subsequent changes on the paper. However, when a computerized system is involved, who entered data and the users who changed data are not always evident on the record itself, and this is why an audit trail is required to record this information.

Relationship of Clause 9 to Other Sections in EU GMP

It is important to realize that Clause 9 of Annex 11 does not sit in isolation; there are relationships between another clause in Annex 11* and Chapter 4 on documentation† as shown in Figure 12.1.

Clause 9 for audit trails is linked to Clause 12 in the security section of Annex 11. The requirements for audit trails are also linked to Chapter 4 on documentation. Here the regulations for good documentation practices, records retention, and the types of GMP-relevant documents are outlined, as shown in Figure 12.1. This chapter will focus on the requirements for audit trails in Annex 11 but will refer to Chapter 4 requirements where necessary.

Chapter 4: Documentation Essentials

From Chapter 4, Clauses 4.7 to 4.9 contain the requirements for good documentation practices that need to be followed both on paper and in

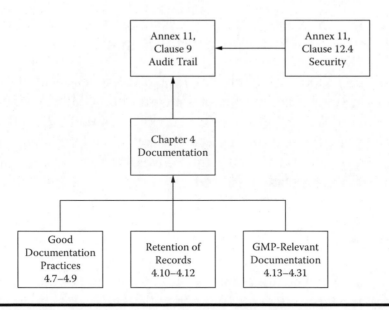

Figure 12.1 **Relationship between Clause 9 for audit trail and other parts of EU GMP.**

* EudraLex, Volume 4, "EU Guidelines to Good Manufacturing Practice, Medicinal Products for Human and Veterinary Use, Annex 11–Computerised Systems," June 2011.
† EudraLex, "The Rules Governing Medicinal Products in the European Union Volume 4, Good Manufacturing Practice, Medicinal Products for Human and Veterinary Use, Chapter 4: Documentation," June 2011.

a computerized system, from which we can derive the following essential requirements:

- Record entries have to be clear and legible.
- Records must be indelible.
- Records must be recorded contemporaneously.
- Actions and the corresponding records must be traceable.
- Any alteration made to an entry should be signed and dated.
- The alteration should permit the reading of the original information.
- Where appropriate, the reason for the alteration should be recorded.

These documentation requirements have a direct impact on the requirements for audit trails contained in Annex 11 as follows:

- Entries in the audit trail have to be understandable.
- The old and new value for a change must be recorded along with who made the change.
- Entries must be date and time stamped. The format of this must be unambiguous and may also require the time zone, especially for multinational companies.
- A reason for changing data may be required.
- Audit trails need to be associated with the activities supported, and it must be possible to search the entries for specific events.
- Audit trails have to be retained for the record retention period (the minimum period is at least five years following release by a Qualified Person under Section 4.10 but could be much longer if the data are part of the marketing authorization as required under Section 4.12).
- Audit trails must be secure from change.

Security Section Clause 12.4

Before considering the audit trail requirements contained in Clause 9, we need to consider that in Clause 12 on security there is the following requirement:

12.4 Management systems for data and for documents should be designed to record the identity of operators entering, changing, confirming, or deleting data including date and time.

Thus, there is a basic requirement for computerized systems to record the individual who enters, modifies, reviews, or deletes data along with a date and time that the activity occurred.

As long as the requirements from Clause 12.4 are met, an audit trail is not essential to the operation of a computerized system. For example, if records can be managed by different versions created over time showing who created, modified, or deleted a version, then the intent of 12.4 is met and an audit trail could be justified as not required. However, systems like this are few, and an audit trail should be considered. We will discuss the requirements contained in Clause 9 and linked with relevant Chapter 4 sections. It is the personal view of the author that effective audit trails are essential when working electronically.

Annex 11 Audit Trail Requirements

The first point to consider in Clause 9 is that the incorporation of an audit trail in a computerized system should be based on a documented risk assessment.

> Consideration should be given, based on a risk assessment, to building into the system the creation of a record of all GMP-relevant changes and deletions (a system-generated "audit trail").

An audit trail is integral with the overall design of a compliant system and therefore needs to be built in from first principles rather than bolted onto an existing application. However, when purchasing a commercially available system, the decision about an audit trail has already been made, and you have to confirm that the way it has been implemented is consistent with an organization's interpretation of the regulations.

Often, laboratory systems have been designed with the audit trail included in the file containing the data generated by the system. This is not adequate, as the audit trail cannot monitor and record deletion of the file that contains it. Therefore, the audit trail must be built within the application itself to monitor not only the records being created but also the associated metadata that provide context and meaning for the actual data.

A further item of information that can be gleaned from the previous sentence is that the scope of an Annex 11 audit trail should cover GMP-relevant changes and deletions. Therefore, we need to consider what GMP-relevant data are. These are defined in Chapter 4 on documentation and covered in Sections 4.13 to 4.31 and include instructions such as specifications and recipes and the records generated by the execution of instructions such as laboratory records, production records, or evidence of SOP execution.

However, many commercial audit trails are a bucket containing everything that has occurred within the system. Examples of audit trail entries can include:

- Log-on and log-off events
- Log-on failures
- Account locking due to a user forgetting his or her password
- Changes to the configuration of the computerized system—these can be changes with attached equipment or instruments or changes to the software configuration of the application
- User account management changes, for example, creation or inactivation of an account or changes to a user's access privileges
- Creation of a record
- Modification of a record
- Deletion of a record
- Electronically signing a record

From this list, only the last four are GMP relevant; therefore, there is a very strong case for separating system-related events such as log-on and log-off from the GMP-relevant audit trail events in which the inspectors and QA are most interested.

Second, there is a requirement for a reason for change when modifying or deleting GMP-relevant data.

> For change or deletion of GMP-relevant data, the reason should be documented.

Audit trails implemented in many commercial applications have the ability for users to add free text entries if required. However, this is a slow and potentially error-prone method of entering information into an audit trail event. What is needed is the ability to enter user-defined reasons for change to speed entry to the audit trail. This would allow the system administrator to enter the agreed reasons for change as part of the application configuration. These reasons may be different throughout the application, for example, for creation, modification, or deletion of a record.

Moreover, the last section of Clause 9 contains three requirements:

> Audit trails need to be available and convertible to a generally intelligible form and regularly reviewed.

- Audit trails need to be available when a reviewer, auditor, or inspector wants to see the entries associated with an item of GMP-relevant data.
- If required, the audit trail needs to be capable of being reviewed on the screen, printed out, or converted to PDF or another format so that an inspector can review it. However, the point about "generally intelligible form" implies that the content of many audit trails is computer-speak and needs to be simple and understood easily.
- Finally, there is little point in having an audit trail in a system unless it is reviewed. The time period specified is "regularly," which under the requirements of Clause 1 (risk management) allows the company to define the period. For systems handling GMP critical data associated, say, with batch release, the review may be before release of the batch. For less critical systems, the frequency may be lower, say, monthly or quarterly.

There is a major problem with many commercially available computerized systems: Few have the functions available to make any audit trail review efficient or effective.

As the requirement for audit trails is to identify any change or deletion of GMP-relevant data, there should be a simple flag or traffic light that highlights for a given set of data if there have been any such changes or deletions. Providing that the system has been validated to demonstrate that the flags work, a review by exception process can be used. If there are no flags, no review is needed. If a flag or flags are raised, the reviewer can drill down into the detail and determine if an individual change is acceptable. This is illustrated in Figure 12.2, where the audit trail indicates that there were no deletions but two data sets have been modified and have the same result. The application should now allow the reviewer to access the underlying record and associated metadata to see what has occurred and to see if it complies with the company procedures.

When reviewing the audit trail, there is typically no mechanism to show that the entries have been reviewed and by whom. There is a basic tenant of GMP that if there is an instruction, there needs to be evidence that the audit trail entries for that set of GMP data have been reviewed. This needs

Item	Sample	Result	Modify?	Delete?
1.	Batch 479 – A1 – 01	0.492		
2.	Batch 479 – A1 – 02	0.480	✓	
3.	Batch 479 – A1 – 03	0.480	✓	
4.	Batch 479 – A1 – 04	0.481		

Figure 12.2   Audit trail entries indicating data that have been modified or deleted.

to be changed and made simple; for example, a review of all relevant entries for a data set can be documented as reviewed in a single action rather than acknowledging each entry individually.

However, in the short term, review of audit trails can be enforced only procedurally; therefore, SOPs have to make it clear that when the second person approves a record, his or her signature includes a review of the audit trail and associated metadata within the computerized system.

Additional Audit Trail Requirements

Unlike 21 CFR 11,* there are no explicit requirements for time and date stamping audit trail entries in Clause 9 of Annex 11. However, this is covered under Clause 12.4.

The requirement that audit trails should be secure is covered in Chapter 4 under the requirements for good documentation practices and record retention requirements as seen in Figure 12.1.

References

EudraLex, Volume 4, *EU Guidelines to Good Manufacturing Practice, Medicinal Products for Human and Veterinary Use,* Annex 11: Computerized Systems, June 2011.

EudraLex, "The Rules Governing Medicinal Products in the European Union," Volume 4, *Good Manufacturing Practice, Medicinal Products for Human and Veterinary Use,* Chapter 4: Documentation, June 2011.

---

* US FDA, 21 CFR Part 11, "Electronic Records; Electronic Signatures; Final Rule." *Federal Register* 62(54), 13429, March 1997.

McDowall, R.D., "Comparison of FDA and EU Regulations for Audit Trails,"
    Scientific Computing, January 2014.
US FDA, 21 CFR Part 11, "Electronic Records; Electronic Signatures; Final Rule." *Federal
    Register,* Vol. 62, No. 54, 13429, March 1997.

Chapter 13

Change and Configuration Management

EU Annex 11-10, Operational Phase

Any changes to a computerized system including system configurations should be made only in a controlled manner in accordance with a defined procedure.

Other References

4.2 Validation documentation should include change control records (if applicable) and reports on any deviations observed during the validation process.

12.3 Creation, change, and cancellation of access authorizations should be recorded.

Analysis

Similar to the operational phase, the maintenance phase applicable to computer systems covers the operational life period (refer to Figure 2.1).

The objective of the maintenance phase is to modify an existing computer system while preserving its integrity. This process includes, as applicable, the migration or retirement of each relevant system component. The process ends with the retirement of the computer system, including interfaces, infrastructure, and, as applicable, electronic records.

Operational procedures should be established to define the request, assessment, review, approval, and implementation of changes in computer systems and associated components.

In addition, changes can come to the software manufacturer, which modifies the software. The manufacturer should inform the regulated user of such changes.

The other source of possible modifications to the system is the incidents that are encountered during the execution of the computer systems. These incidents are recorded and entered into the problem resolution process (Annex 11-13). Refer to Chapter 16.

Computer systems modifications must be documented, validated, and approved prior to release of the product.

The maintenance phase is triggered when a "validated" computer system undergoes modifications to the application, infrastructure, or associated documentation due to a problem or the need for improvement or adaptation to new settings.

After the system is released to operations, the system is considered "validated." It indicates a status designating the computer system complying with all requirements established in the requirements document, the operators are effectively trained, and the applicable operational procedural controls are established.

Additionally, the "validated" status indicates that all documents (e.g., specifications, test procedures, user manuals, and so on) and products have been formally reviewed and agreed upon. These baseline documents and products serve as the basis for further development.

The "validated" status of computer systems performing GMP-regulated activities is subject to threat from modification in its operating environment, which may be either known or unknown.

Due to the complexity of some computer systems, a seemingly small local modification may have a significant impact to the "validated" status of the computer systems performing GMP-regulated activities. When any modification (even a small modification) is made to the computer system, the validation status of the computer system needs to be re-established.

The potential impact of the proposed modification must be evaluated to determine the revalidation extent. This extent following a modification should be examined on a case-by-case basis depending on the complexity of the computer system, associated interfaces, and all documents and products. A risk analysis should be taken as a basis for this decision.

Based on this impact analysis and risk analysis, the regulated user can then plan for the appropriate system development methodology, affected baselines, and an appropriate regression testing to show that unchanged but vulnerable portions of the system have not been adversely affected. The impact assessment, comprehensive requirements, applicable implementation, updates of specifications, and appropriate regression testing provide the confidence that the computer system is validated after a modification.[*]

Of special interest is the impact of the modification to the documentation. All documentation must be carefully assessed to determine which documents have been impacted by a modification. All approved documents that have been affected must be updated in accordance with configuration management procedures. Specifications must be updated before additional maintenance to the system is made.[†]

The maintenance of computer systems fails because of the lack of accurate documentation. This is one of the main reasons computer systems get out of GMP control and finish in a remedial action. The investment of the regulated users implementing computer systems is very high. However, the regulated users do not give the necessary effort to maintain computer systems in the state of GMP control after released to operations.

The change control process must cover or verify all the previous activities.

In addition, it is a good practice that each proposed modification, together with the risk and impact assessments and final implementation, be reviewed by qualified representatives of appropriate disciplines that might affect the validated status of the computer system. The intent is to determine the need for action to ensure and document that the system is maintained in a validated state.[‡]

Figure 13.1 provides a pictorial view of the high-level maintenance SIPOC (Suppliers, Inputs, Process, Outputs, and Customers).

---

[*] US FDA, "General Principles of Software Validation; Final Guidance for Industry and FDA Staff," January 2002.

[†] US FDA, "General Principles of Software Validation; Final Guidance for Industry and FDA Staff," January 2002.

[‡] EudraLex, "The Rules Governing Medicinal Products in the European Union," Volume 4, *EU Guidelines for Good Manufacturing Practice for Medicinal Products for Human and Veterinary Use*, Annex 15: Qualification and Validation, February 2014 (Draft Rev 1).

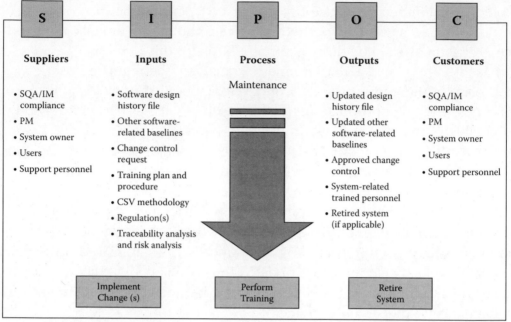

Note: "Implement Change(s)" requires the system life cycle to start all over from Concept to Go Life.

Figure 13.1   Maintenance SIPOC.

Types of Maintenance

Maintenance of a computer system consists of, among other things:

■ Perfective maintenance or the correction of the system due to new requirements or functions.

■ Adaptive maintenance, or the correction of the system due to a new environment, which could include new hardware, new sensors or controlled devices, new operating systems, or new regulations.

■ Corrective maintenance, or the correction of the system due to the detection of errors in the design, logic, or programming of the system. It is important to recognize that the longer a defect is present in the software before it is detected, the more expensive it is to repair. Refer to Table 2.1.

■ Preventive maintenance or the correction of the system to improve its future maintainability or reliability or to provide a better basis for future enhancements.

After the proposed modification is approved, the applicable SLC (Chapter 2) is re-executed to ensure that the proposed modifications are implemented correctly, all documentation is complete and up to date, and no undesirable changes have occurred during the implementation of the proposed modification.

It is important to acknowledge that the maintenance of existing application software can account for over 70% of all effort expended by a software organization. The computer hardware suppliers normally recommend minimum maintenance schedules including accuracy checks for their components.[*]

Data Migration

A migration plan is developed, documented, and executed. The planning activities shall include users. Items in the plan shall include the following:

1. Requirements analysis and definition of migration
2. Development of migration tools
3. Conversion of software product and data
4. Migration execution
5. Migration verification
6. Support for the old environment in the future

Users receive notification of the migration plans and activities. Notifications shall include the following:

1. Statement of why the old environment is no longer to be supported
2. Description of the new environment with its date of availability
3. Description of other support options available, if any, once support for the old environment has been removed

Parallel operations of the old and new environments may be conducted for smooth transition to the new environment. During this period, necessary training shall be provided as specified in the contract.

---

[*] FDA, "Guide to Inspection of Computerized Systems in the Food Processing Industry," Office of Regulatory Affairs (ORA), Division of Emergency and Investigational Operations (DEIO) and the Center for Food Safety and Applied Nutrition (CFSAN), http://www.fda.gov/ICECI/Inspections/InspectionGuides/ucm074955.htm.

When the scheduled migration arrives, a notification is sent to all concerned. All associated old environment's documentation, logs, and code should be placed in archives.

A postoperation review is performed to assess the impact of changing to the new environment. The results of the review shall be sent to the appropriate authorities for information, guidance, and action.

Data used by or associated with the old environment is accessible in accordance with the requirements for data protection and audit applicable to the data.

Retirement (If Applicable)

One main cause to retire computer systems is the maintainability issues of obsolete technology.

The retirement process starts with planning. A retirement plan, to remove active support by the operation and maintenance organizations, is developed and documented. The planning activities shall include users. The plan shall address the following items:

1. Cessation of full or partial support after a certain period of time
2. Archiving of the software product and its associated documentation
3. Responsibility for any future residual support issues
4. Transition to the new software product, if applicable
5. Accessibility of archive copies of data

Users are given notification of the retirement plans and activities. Notifications include the following:

1. Description of the replacement or upgrade with its date of availability
2. Statement of why the software product is no longer to be supported
3. Description of other support options available, once support has been removed

Parallel operations of the retiring and the new computer system may be conducted for smooth transition to the new system. During this period, user training shall be provided as specified in the training plan.

When the scheduled retirement arrives, notification shall be sent to all concerned. All associated development documentation, logs, and code should be placed in archives, when appropriate.

Data used or associated with the retired system shall be accessible in accordance with the requirements for data protection and audit applicable to the data.

References

ISO 13485:2012, "Medical Devices—Quality Management Systems—Requirements for Regulatory Purposes," Sections 4.2.3, 7.3.7, 7.5.2; February 2012.

ISPE GAMP 5: *A Risk-Based Approach to Compliant GXP Computerised Systems*, International Society for Pharmaceutical Engineering (ISPE), 5th ed., Operational Appendices O6 and O7, February 2008.

PI 011-3. "Good Practices for Computerised Systems in Regulated 'GXP' Environments," Pharmaceutical Inspection Cooperation Scheme (PIC/S), September 2007.

WHO, Technical Report Series, No. 937, 2006. Annex 4, Section 12, "Change Control," 2006.

Chapter 14

Periodic Evaluation
Independent Review to Ensure Continued Validation of Computerized Systems

R.D. McDowall
Principal, McDowall Consulting

EU Annex 11-11, Operational Phase

Computerized systems should be periodically evaluated to confirm that they remain in a valid state and are compliant with GMP. Such evaluations should include, where appropriate, the current range of functionality, deviation records, incidents, problems, upgrade history, performance, reliability, security, and validation status reports.

Analysis

Annex 11 requires that periodic evaluations or reviews be carried out throughout the operational phase of a computerized system's life cycle to ensure that the system remains in a validated state.

This requirement needs to be combined with applying risk management principles from Annex 11 Clause 1.* Therefore, the frequency of the periodic review will be based upon the criticality of the computerized system: Critical systems will have more frequent periodic reviews compared with lower risk systems that will have longer intervals between reviews.

Interpretation of Annex 11 Clause 11 for periodic reviews includes the following:

- Periodic reviews of computerized systems must be conducted.
- There are no exceptions to this regulation (i.e., only critical systems should be evaluated) as all systems must be reviewed.
- The frequency of the review is determined by the company's policies and justified where necessary to an inspector.
- The aim of any periodic review is to ensure that the system is compliant with the applicable regulations and that it remains in a validated state over the time since the last review.

Although Annex 11 does not say who should carry out the periodic review, any periodic review should fall under self-inspections described in Chapter 9 of EU GMP,† the main requirements of which are

- Regulated activities should be examined at intervals to ensure conformance with regulations.
- Self-inspections must be preplanned.
- Self-inspections should be conducted by independent and competent persons.
- Self-inspections should be recorded and contain all the observations made during the inspections.
- Where applicable, corrective actions should be proposed.
- Completion of the corrective actions should also be recorded.

A periodic review needs to be performed by an independent and knowledgeable person to ensure an objective and not subjective approach to

---

* The Rules Governing Medicinal Products in the European Union. Volume 4: Pharmaceutical Legislation—Medicinal Products for Human and Veterinary Use—Good Manufacturing Practices, including Annex 11–Computerised Systems, January 2011.

† EudraLex, Volume 4, Good Manufacturing Practice (GMP) Medicinal Products for Human and Veterinary Use, Part I—Basic Requirements for Medicinal Products, Chapter 9: Self Inspections, 2001.

evaluating a computerized system. Therefore, independence and impartiality of the person conducting a periodic review are of prime importance.

Overview of a Periodic Review

As noted in EU GMP Chapter 9, a periodic review is a planned and formal activity. Thus, the first requirement for conducting a review is an SOP covering the whole process, which is shown in Figure 14.1.

1. **The planning phase** (covering all systems). This links the inventory of computerized systems with a risk classification of each system (the figure suggests critical, major, or minor, but this is only a suggestion) to the SOP for periodic reviews and audits and the self-inspection schedule. Therefore, the principle is that the critical systems are reviewed more frequently than major or minor, and major systems are reviewed more frequently than minor ones. The frequency of review for each type of system will be determined by your company.
2. **The execution phase** (for each system reviewed). For each system selected for review, there is a common process that consists of planning and preparation for the review; the opening meeting; performing the audit, including a check on the effectiveness of corrective actions from a previous review; the reviewer's closed meeting, where the observations are examined to determine if there are any findings or noncompliances; the closing meeting, where findings and observations are discussed; and finally the writing of the review report and an action plan for any corrective or preventative actions.

Objectives of a Periodic Review

There should be two main aims of a periodic review of a computerized system:

1. To provide independent assurance to the process owner and senior management that controls are in place around the system being reviewed and are functioning correctly. The system is validated and controls are working adequately to maintain the validation status.

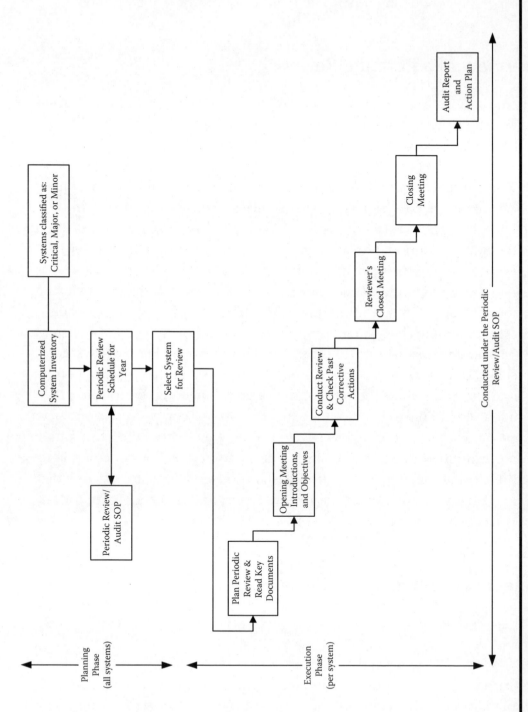

Figure 14.1 Flowchart for a periodic review or audit of a computerized system.

2. To identify those controls that are not working and to help the process owner and senior management improve them and thus eliminate the identified weaknesses. The impact of a finding may be applicable to a single computerized system or all systems in a facility.

The second objective is the most important in the author's opinion. Moreover, it is an important outcome from any periodic review for senior management to realize that some controls may require systematic resolution: If a problem is found in a procedure that is used for all systems, the resolution of this may impact all computerized systems used in a facility rather than just the one being reviewed.

An alternative way of reducing the workload could be to perform a periodic review of common services shared by multiple computerized systems such as:

■ User account management
■ Incident management
■ Change control
■ Backup and recovery

In this way, a single periodic review can cover many computerized systems.

Reviewer Skills and Training

There are a number of requirements necessary for a person to conduct a periodic review effectively:

■ Knowledge of the current GMP regulations and the associated guidance documents issued by regulatory agencies or industry bodies. At a minimum, this knowledge needs to be in the same good practice discipline to which the facility works, but knowledge of the requirements of other good practice disciplines is an advantage because where one discipline can be vague on a specific point another may have more detail. For example, in GMP there are no regulatory agency guidelines for the SOPs required for a computerized system, but the FDA has issued one for clinical investigations[*] where a minimum list of procedures can be found in Appendix A of this US FDA Guidance.

■ Note that the knowledge of regulations above said "current." This is because the regulations and guidance are changing at an increasing rate especially in the EU, where it is easier and quicker to change the regulations as we have seen with Annex 11 itself.[†]

■ Experience of working with computerized systems and knowing where (noncompliance) bodies can be buried and where bad practices could occur.

■ Understanding of the current procedures used by the company, division, or department for implementing and operating validated computerized systems. This is the interpretation of the regulations and guidance for the users to work with, which need to be both current and flexible.

■ Open and flexible approach, coupled with the understanding that there are many ways of being in control. Therefore, the reviewer's ways of validating a computerized system and maintaining its validated state—or indeed those in the GAMP guide[‡] and GAMP Good Practice Guide: Risk Based Approach to the Operation of GXP Computerised Systems[§]—are not the only way of working.

■ Finally, good interpersonal skills coupled with a hide as thick as an elephant's. The reviewer needs to ask open questions to understand what process is being carried out and investigate with pertinent questions to identify if the work performed is adequate or there are non-compliances. Persuasion may be required to change ways of working, as would a hide as thick as an elephant's to ignore any personal remarks or insults that may come your way.

How Critical Is Your System?

The starting point is the facility's inventory of computerized systems contained that should be categorized according to risk. Some of the risk

---

[*] US FDA, FDA Guidance for Industry, Computerized Systems in Clinical Investigations, May 2007.
[†] The Rules Governing Medicinal Products in the European Union. Volume 4: Pharmaceutical Legislation—Medicinal Products for Human and Veterinary Use—Good Manufacturing Practices, including Annex 11–Computerised Systems, January 2011.
[‡] GAMP Guide, version 5, 2008, Appendix O8, Periodic Reviews.
[§] GAMP Good Practice Guide: Risk-Based Approach to Operation of GXP Computerised Systems, 2010, Section 12: Periodic Reviews.

categories may be critical, major, minor, no GXP impact, or high, medium, low. You will want to focus effort on the most critical systems to be reviewed most often, as they pose the highest risk, and the lowest priority systems will be reviewed less frequently, as they pose the lowest risk. Most of the computerized systems that are featured in FDA warning letters are networked systems with multiple users because they have the greatest impact.

From the inventory, there will be a listing of the most critical systems: These will have the most frequent reviews to ensure that they are in control with decreasing frequency for the major and minor systems. A review schedule of all computerized systems in the facility would be drawn up for the coming year. Typically, the schedule for the year will be written by the person responsible in QA late the previous year, which lists all systems due to be reviewed and the months in which this will happen.

When to Perform a Review?

In the author's opinion, there are three times to consider a review of a computerized system:

- Before operational release of system. This is to ensure that the system development has been undertaken according to corporate standards and the validation plan. You may think that with all the planning and documentation produced in a validation, this is the last time to perform a review. However, the author believes that this is the right time for the simple reason that if something has been missed from the validation of a critical system, such as checking that a calculation works correctly, do you really want to operate a system for a year or so and then discover it?
- Periodic review. To ensure that the operational system still remains validated, this will be a planned and scheduled activity and will be carried out on a regular basis for each computerized system in the facility in which it is operational. There may be occasions where the review schedule is changed to link to a planned upgrade of the system, but this is typically performed after the system has gone live and is in operation.
- Prior to an inspection. Occasionally, some companies may review a system before an inspection to ensure that there are no major compliance issues. However, if this approach is taken, ensure that there is sufficient time between the periodic review and the inspection to ensure that the remedial activities are implemented and actually work

before the inspection. Personally, if a computerized system is so critical, it will be reviewed on a frequency that does not require a special review such as this.

Although you can conduct a periodic review at these times during the lifetime of a computerized system, the principles of what a review consists of and the way one is conducted are the same.

Types of Periodic Review

We now have the scope of the audit defined in terms of breadth and depth. Now we have to decide how we will approach the review. There are three basic ways you could conduct a periodic review or audit as shown in Figure 14.2; these are the horizontal, vertical, or diagonal approach, which will be explained in more detail.

- ■ **Horizontal audit or review.** This review is conducted across the breadth of the system documentation. It attempts to cover all areas but at a low depth. It is typically undertaken if there is little time available to perform the review or the system has not been reviewed before. The aim of this type of review is to give the confidence that all the major computer validation requisites are in place but, typically, there may not be enough time to look in depth at how the various areas are

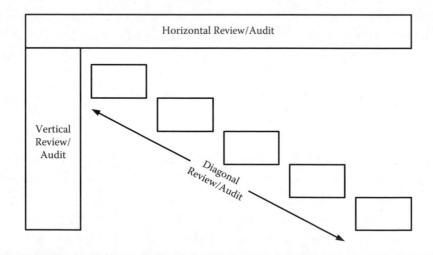

Figure 14.2 Types of audit or periodic review.

integrated. Note that a horizontal audit can turn into a vertical audit if a problem is found during the review and the problem is required to be investigated in more detail.

■ **Vertical audit or review.** In contrast to the horizontal audit, the vertical audit takes a very narrow perspective selecting one or more areas to review but goes into a lot of detail checking, for instance, that the controlling procedure has been followed. An example of a vertical review could look at the change control procedure and all the change requests for a specific system. This could be examined in much more detail than possible with a horizontal audit.

■ **Diagonal audit or review.** As the name suggests, this is a mixture of horizontal and vertical audits. The purpose is to see that all the major validation elements are in place, they operate correctly, and all applicable processes work and are integrated. Therefore, when examining defining user requirements in the horizontal portion of a review, the diagonal audit will assess the traceability of requirements from the URS to the rest of the life-cycle documents. In addition, the review can also take a test script and trace it back to the URS. As you can see, the diagonal audit examines the system more thoroughly than a horizontal audit.

In practice, all three types of auditing can be used effectively during a periodic review depending on how much time is available.

Writing the Periodic Review Plan

Returning to the execution phase outlined in Figure 14.1, we will look at the various tasks in order, starting with writing the plan for the periodic review. This consists of a number of activities that cumulate in the plan.

■ **Agree on the Date for the Review**. When a system is due to be reviewed, the reviewer will contact the process owner to agree on dates for the review to take place. How long the review will take depends on the size and complexity of the computerized system, but it typically takes between one and three days. It is important that when dates are agreed on, key personnel will be available to discuss their specialist subject areas with the reviewer. Otherwise, the benefit of the review could be lost, as noncompliances could be missed due to the lack of specialist knowledge. For example, smaller systems can be audited in one day, but if the IT Department is to be included or it is a larger system, then more likely two to three days may be required.

■ **Agree on the Scope of the Review.** The reviewer should ask for information about the system (if not known already) to determine the scope of the review. This is particularly important for systems where the users and IT have responsibilities, as two departments need to be coordinated. If the IT department is outsourced, then the outsourcing company needs to be contacted to ensure that its staff are available for the review.

■ **Write the Periodic Review Plan.** A review plan is written that contains the name of the system to be reviewed, agreed dates of the review, the department and location where the system is sited, and the regulations and procedures upon which the review will be based that will be cited, for example, GMP or GLP regulations or industry guidance documents. Included in the plan should be a timetable of activities of when the reviewer wants to discuss specific subjects. It is important to inform staff when they will be required, and this helps them plan their own work. This will avoid people hanging around, waiting.

■ **Approval of the Review Plan.** The periodic review plan is a formal document that needs to be signed by the reviewer as the author as well as an approver. Depending on the company policies, the process owner may also need to sign the plan to acknowledge that he or she approves the plan and to implement any corrective actions if there are any findings or noncompliances.

Preparation for a Periodic Review

From the perspective of the reviewer, the individual needs to read about the system and refresh his or her knowledge on any relevant SOPs under which the system is and under which the system operates. Key documents to be read include the following:

■ Computerized system validation SOP
■ Validation plan for the last full validation of the system to be reviewed and the corresponding validation summary report
■ User requirements specification for the current version of software that is installed

- Organizational charts
- List of applicable procedures as a minimum and copies of some of the key SOPs, if possible, for example, change control SOP, user SOPs, etc.

This allows you to have an understanding of the system and procedures before you arrive to perform the review and to be able to do some research if required before the review starts. A reviewer could ask for more documents than listed above, but there is always a balance between the quantity of material and time used to prepare for the review and the time on site.

Equally so, the users who will be subject to the audit need to prepare. At the most basic, if not already done, tidy up the location (you will be surprised how many people do not do this). Also, check that all documents are current and approved. If there are any unapproved or unofficial documents, ensure they are removed from desks and offices and destroyed. There are other areas where the users can prepare; for example, read the current procedures and ensure that training records are up to date.

Activities during the Periodic Review

After the review plan has been written and approved and the reviewer has done his or her preparation, the great day dawns and the review takes place. As can be seen in Figure 14.1, the activities that take place consist of:

- **Opening Meeting.** This should be the shortest part of the periodic review where the reviewer and the users and, where appropriate, IT and QA staff who will be involved with the audit are introduced to each other. The reviewer will outline the aims of the review along with a request for openness, as this is an internal audit designed to identify if the system is under control and remains validated. It is important that the head of the department attend both the opening and closing meetings to see if there are any issues to resolve. The importance of the head attending must not be underestimated. If this key individual is not present, it sends a subliminal message to all, including the reviewer, that the individual has no interest in the validation status of the computerized systems. I certainly would document his or her absence in the review report.
- **How Do We Work Here?** I mentioned earlier that the person conducting a periodic review should not have fixed views of how a computer

validation should be conducted, as there are many ways to be compliant. The key point in a periodic review is to keep asking the question "Are you in control?" To orientate me for an audit or periodic review after the opening meeting, I prefer if the auditees give a short presentation of how validation was conducted for the system. This approach is very useful because it allows the person conducting the periodic review (i.e., me) to understand the terminology used by the facility and the overall validation strategy used for the system under review. In the end, it helps avoid misunderstandings and miscommunication between the two parties.

■ **Carry Out the Periodic Review.** This is the heart of the periodic review where the last validation, organization, staff training records, change control, backup and recovery operation of the system and associated procedures, and so on will be assessed. We will look in more detail in the second part of this chapter.

■ **Reviewer's Private Meeting.** This is the time for the person conducting the review to review his or her notes and documents provided by the department to see if any observations are identified as findings or non-compliances. In addition, some outline notes for the closing meeting are prepared; these must include all major issues to be discussed with the process owner—the reviewer should not omit bad news and then add these little gems to the report so that it comes as a surprise to the process owner.

■ **Closing Meeting.** This is where the reviewer's initial findings are presented and discussed so that there should be no surprises when the draft report is issued for comment. All findings should be based on objective evidence, for example, noncompliance with a procedure or regulation. There may be occasions when a difference comes down to interpretation of regulations; then the auditor should seek information in industry guidance documents to support the finding.

■ **Write and Approve Periodic Review Report and Action Plan.** At the conclusion of the on-site portion of the review, the reviewer now has to draft the report, which will contain what the reviewer saw and the findings or noncompliances. Either contained in the report or as a separate document will be the action plan for fixing the noncompliances.

■ **Implementing Corrective and Preventative Actions.** Any findings and their associated corrective or preventative action plans are implemented and monitored, ready for review when the system comes due.

Who Is Involved and What Do They Do?

Who should be involved with a periodic review, apart of course, from the person who is conducting the review? Here is a list of potential people. Depending on the size of the system being reviewed, some of these roles may be combined, especially if the users are responsible for the whole system including the IT support, the system is relatively small, or there are only a few users.

- **Management.** Although the individual may not be directly responsible for the system itself, it operates in the department for which he or she is responsible and accountable. At a minimum, the individual should be present at the opening and closing meetings to introduce him- or herself, and listen to the review conclusions and discuss any findings.
- **Process Owner.** This individual in the department is responsible for the system. For a stand-alone system, this may be the user who runs the system. For larger networked systems, it may be that the process owner is the department manager.
- **System Owner.** The system owner is the person responsible for supporting the system from an IT perspective. The process owner can take this role if the system is stand-alone where IT support comes from within the department or an individual in the IT department if the system is networked. In the latter situation, the system owner could be from an external company if the IT operations have been outsourced.
- **Power User/System Administrator and User.** Depending on the size of the system, a single person or many individuals could take these roles. However, the reviewer needs to have access to somebody within the department who knows the system in depth from a technical perspective (the power user or system administrator) and may require an experienced user to discuss procedures and use of the system.
- **Computer Validation.** Because the periodic review will examine the last validation of the system, there needs to be a person available to answer the reviewer's questions on this topic. Depending on how the work was performed, this could be the system administrator from the user base or a member of the computer validation group within the organization.
- **Quality Assurance.** A member of QA who is responsible for the department may also be involved with the periodic review. Depending on their depth of knowledge, their involvement may range from interested observer to a full participant.

Here is where the timetable for the periodic review comes in. Instead of having everybody waiting to be called, a timetable for the review should state what topic will be covered and, roughly, when it will take place. This allows individuals to carry out their normal jobs and turn up at an appointed hour. There may be some variation in the timetable depending on the reviewer findings, so be prepared to be flexible with the timings.

Review of the Last System Validation

It is ironic that computer systems that are supposed to automate operations and streamline processes often generate mountains of paper. Therefore, if a system, subject to a periodic review, has been validated since the last review, the current review should start with the last system validation (if not reviewed in the last system review). Depending on the size and complexity of the computerized system, this could take a short time or last at least a day. So, where do we begin?

Rather than list my ideas, the GMP inspectors who do this for a living have written their approach in Sections 23 and 24 of PIC/S guide PI-011, called computerised systems in GXP environments.* Section 24 of this guide, entitled Inspector's Aide Memoires, contains six checklists for inspecting a computerized system, although the main focus of these checklists is on the application. There is little on the IT infrastructure and services supporting it. Section 23, entitled Inspection Considerations, is more interesting from the perspective of a periodic review and how to conduct one, although Clause 23.4 notes that this guidance, much the same as any checklist, should not be used as a blunt instrument when inspecting a computerized system but used selectively to build up an understanding of how computerized systems are validated and operated by a company. However, we can learn and adapt the approach outlined here.

Preparation before the Review. As mentioned in the first part, the reviewer needs to do a little homework by reading some key documents before he or she starts the periodic review. The PIC/S guide suggests starting with the validation summary report; however, in my view this is only adequate, and a better approach is to read the following documents:

---

* PI 011-3. "Good Practices for Computerised Systems in Regulated 'GXP' Environments," Pharmaceutical Inspection Cooperation Scheme (PIC/S), September 2007.

- Validation Plan—The last full validation plan of the system will detail the activities and documented evidence that were intended to be performed and written, respectively.
- Validation Summary Report—to see what was actually done and understand the reasons for the differences and the justification for the changes made to the plan.
- User Requirements Specification—to define the intended use of the system and to assess the quality of the requirements: Are they testable or verifiable?

The rational for reading these documents is shown in Figure 14.3. It checks the quality of the validation control by comparing both the intent and delivery of the validation effort and asking if they match. This provides a good foundation to begin the review of the validation of the system. If the validation is suspect, then the quality and accuracy of the results produced by the system will be suspect as well. Reading the URS determines how well the intended purpose of the system has been defined and hence how well the rest of the validation, shown with dotted boxes in Figure 14.3, is likely to have been performed.

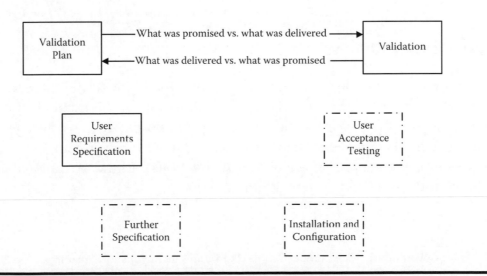

Figure 14.3 Preparatory reading before a periodic review.

Reviewing Requirements: Role of Traceability

Traceability is a regulatory requirement in Clause 4 of Annex 11* and, typically, traceability is achieved using a traceability matrix. A traceability matrix should allow a reviewer to trace requirements from the URS to where the requirement is either verified or tested later in the life cycle or vice versa (test or verification back to the requirements). This key validation document demonstrates that user requirements have been met in later phases of the life cycle. It also provides confidence to the reviewer that the validation team has done a good job. This is then confirmed in the periodic review by selecting several requirements and following them through the life cycle via the traceability matrix.

Other Areas for Review

There is insufficient space to cover some other aspects of the review of the validation such as:

- Configuration of the software: Is it the same as installed or has it been changed? If changed, where is this documented and how is it tested?
- Reviewing vendor documentation critically.
- Installation documentation for the IT, instrument, and software components of the system.

Operational Review

In this section of the periodic review, we will be looking at the different types of users, the system security (e.g., Look closely at the number of characters in a user's password as he or she logs on; do the access privileges on paper match those in the system?), the procedures for the system, and use of the system in operation. Typically, you will get out into the operational area and talk with users and system administrators.

---

* The Rules Governing Medicinal Products in the European Union. Volume 4: Pharmaceutical Legislation—Medicinal Products for Human and Veterinary Use—Good Manufacturing Practices, including Annex 11–Computerised Systems, January 2011.

Depending on the scope and use of the system, this part can vary from relatively simple to very extensive, so advice here is generic rather than detailed. Check that users' training records are current and that the users have been trained on the current versions of procedures. Furthermore, do the procedures for the system describe how to use it in sufficient detail or are they vague?

IT Department Involvement

For a networked system, it will be inevitable that at some stage you will need to include the IT department in a periodic review to see how some activities such as backup and change control are carried out. Again, IT will need to be notified and have staff available according to the schedule in the review timetable. If the IT department activities are outsourced, then agreement with the outsourcing company may also have to be sought.

The principles here are the same for the users: Is there a procedure, is it followed, and is there evidence of this? One issue is that some IT procedures may be written under sufferance and may be basic and never read from the day they were written. However, look at the procedure to see what is written and ask the IT staff to talk about or demonstrate what is done and where the records are to demonstrate it was followed: Do they match? If yes, this is fine; if not, then you have findings to consider.

Reviewer's Closed Meeting

This is the time at the end of the review for the observations to be reviewed, determine if there are any findings, and grade them according to severity as outlined in the next section. The optimist in me thinks that if I allow an hour for the closed meeting, I can take my time; review what I have seen; identify the findings; and, if time allows, classify them as to their severity. The pessimist in me knows that regardless of the timetable, I will overrun the review, and this will reduce the time for my closed meeting. However, this is a quiet period where the review notes and observations can be reviewed and any findings identified and classified as outlined in the following.

Observations, Findings, and Recommendations

What's in a word? The heading above lists observations, findings, and recommendations; what do they mean? Again, each company will have its own definitions, but these are mine:

- Observations: These are what the reviewer saw during the periodic review. Depending on the company requirements, these can be detailed or summarized. However, consider that the same reviewer may not conduct the next periodic review of this system and there needs to be sufficient detail to enable another person to follow what was done in the current review. For example, a reviewer should list an SOP with its version number so that the next reviewer can see what has changed since the last review. Note that observation as used here is not in the same context as an FDA 483 observation; it is simply what the reviewer saw.
- Findings: A noncompliance with regulations or procedures, these would be equivalent to a 483 observation where there is a noncompliance with the regulations or company procedures. However, are all findings or noncompliance findings the same? For example, is a missing signature from a document the same as not validating a computerized system? No; therefore, we need to have a classification scheme, and one that could be used is presented in Table 14.1, where each finding is classified in ascending order of severity from 1 to 4.
- Recommendations: This is something that I am occasionally asked to do by some clients. Recommendations are not noncompliances but simply nonbinding recommendations to the process owner by the reviewer that a working practice or way of performing a task could be improved. Whether the recommendation is implemented is the choice of the process owner.

Closing Meeting

After the reviewer's closed meeting, the review is concluded by the closing meeting. Here, all involved with the audit will be present. The reviewer will lead the meeting by presenting the conclusions of the audit and the findings, which should be done without interruption. One problem with reviews and audits is that the highest level of praise is "adequate," which means little to the people on the receiving end. The reviewer should include areas where

Table 14.1   A Classification of Findings or Noncompliances

Rank	Grade	Meaning
0	—	• No finding
1	Minor	• Does not impact data or product quality, data integrity, or patient safety
2	Moderate	• Small impact on data or product quality, data integrity, or patient safety • A procedure is not followed • A single-event GXP deviation that does not appear to be systems based and does not impact safety, identity, strength, quality, efficacy, or purity of the product or component and therefore should not result in a regulatory action
3	Major	• A system-based deviation that does not impact safety, identity, strength, quality, efficacy, or purity of the product or component and therefore should not result in a regulatory action • Data integrity issues that affect determining the quality of a product • A deficiency has produced or may produce a product that does not comply with its marketing authorization or indicates a major deviation from GXP regulations • A combination of several "other" deficiencies in the same area, none of which on their own may be major, but which together may represent a major deficiency and should be explained and reported as such
4	Critical	• A system-based deviation that is likely to impact safety, identity, strength, quality, efficacy, or purity of the product or component and therefore may result in a regulatory action • A deficiency that has produced or leads to a significant risk of producing either a product that is harmful to the human or veterinary patient or a product that could result in a harmful residue in a food-producing animal

good work has been done and say so. If there are findings, then the major ones as a minimum need to be covered. If the reviewer has been open, the users will know where the problems are before the meeting but not necessarily the classification.

After the reviewer has presented his or her initial observations and findings, the meeting is open for comment. This is important, as the reviewer may have misinterpreted something that can be corrected while he or she is on site by going through the procedures or other documented evidence. It is important for the reviewer to cover all major findings and issues face to face with the users so that there are no surprises in the report; otherwise, they will feel aggrieved that bad news was not passed on face to face.

Documenting the Periodic Review

A draft report of the review is the formal outcome that will present the observations and findings as we have discussed earlier in this chapter. The users have an opportunity to comment on the report and feed these back to the reviewer. Associated with the report is a corrective action plan where the findings (moderate and above) are listed and the process owner is asked to complete the corrective and preventative actions against the findings. Once the report and corrective action plan are agreed upon, then they are finalized.

To demonstrate that a review has taken place, some organizations produce an audit certificate signed by the reviewer, and this is shown to an inspector.

References

EudraLex, Volume 4, "EU Guidelines to Good Manufacturing Practice, Medicinal Products for Human and Veterinary Use, Annex 11–Computerised Systems," June 2011 http://ec.europa.eu/health/files/eudralex/vol-4/annex11_01-2011_en.pdf.

EudraLex, Volume 4, "Good Manufacturing Practice (GMP) Medicinal Products for Human and Veterinary Use, Part I – Basic Requirements for Medicinal Products," Chapter 9: Self Inspections, 2001.

GAMP Good Practice Guide: Risk Based Approach to Operation of GXP Computerised Systems, 2010, Section 12: Periodic Reviews.

GAMP Guide, version 5, 2008, Appendix O8, Periodic Reviews.

McDowall, B., "Maintaining Laboratory Computer Validation—How to Conduct Periodic Reviews?", European Compliance Academy (ECA), April 2012, http://www.gmp-compliance.org/pa4.cgi?src=eca_new_news_print_data.htm&nr=3085.

PI 011-3. "Good Practices for Computerised Systems in Regulated 'GXP' Environments," Pharmaceutical Inspection Cooperation Scheme (PIC/S), September 2007.

US FDA, FDA Guidance for Industry, Computerized Systems in Clinical Investigations, May 2007.

Chapter 15

Security*

EU Annex 11-12, Operational Phase

12.1 Physical and/or logical controls should be in place to restrict access to computerized system to authorized persons. Suitable methods of preventing unauthorized entry to the system may include the use of keys, pass cards, personal codes with passwords, biometrics, restricted access to computer equipment and data storage areas.

12.2 The extent of security controls depends on the criticality of the computerized system.

12.3 Creation, change, and cancellation of access authorizations should be recorded.

12.4 Management systems for data and for documents should be designed to record the identity of operators entering, changing, confirming, or deleting data including date and time.

Related References

2.0 All personnel should have the appropriate level of access to carry out their assigned duties.

---

* This chapter was written based on O. López, *Computer Technologies Security Part I—Key Points in the Contained Domain*, Sue Horwood Publishing Limited, 2002.

4.3 For critical systems, an up to date system description detailing the physical and logical arrangements, data flows, and interfaces with other systems or processes, any hardware and software pre-requisites, and security measures should be available.

7.1 Data should be secured by both physical and electronic means against damage.

11.0 Computerized systems should be periodically evaluated to confirm that they remain in a valid state and are compliant with GMP. Such evaluations should include, where appropriate, the current range of functionality, deviation records, incidents, problems, upgrade history, performance, reliability, security, and validation status reports.

Analysis

To create a trusted digital environment within an enterprise, it must be ensured that both the application and infrastructure components are truly secure. Annex 11 addresses the subject of security for computer systems in Item 11-12.

It is the responsibility of the system owner* to provide the suitable controls over the application and network components to ensure that only authorized personnel can make changes to any component of the computer system and the security of the data residing on the system.

In its Chapter II, Article 9(2), the Commission Directive 2003/94/EC, setting out the legal requirements for EU GMP, establishes the basic principles of security to the computer systems performing GMP functions:

> The electronically stored data shall be protected, by methods such as duplication or back-up and transfer on to another storage system, against loss or damage of data, and audit trails shall be maintained.

The first step to search for the extent of the security controls (11-12.2) applicable to the computer systems is during the initial system risk assessment. This assessment is performed at the initial phase of the SLC and performed again as part of each change assessment. The identified risks

---

* The person responsible for the availability and maintenance of a computerized system and for the security of the data residing on that system (EU Annex 11).

are used to support the development of the computer system requirements document, including the security-related requirements.

The controls that are implemented resulting from the security-related requirements are intended to build a trusted digital environment. The attributes relevant to a trusted digital environment are

- Accurate
- Legible
- Contemporaneous
- Original
- Attributable
- Complete
- Consistent
- Enduring
- Available when needed

Trustworthy records must also be considered as part of the requirements for record retention, archiving, and retrieval. Refer to Chapter 26.

A vital factor necessary to achieve trustworthy records is the implementation of electronically based solutions with comprehensive security features. Regardless, the requirements document must contain the aspects of information security and data protection.

A guarantee that the infrastructure, application software, and the regulated electronic records are maintained in a secure environment is critical to the validated status of a computer system, particularly if it is an enterprise-level system.

Security must be instituted at several levels (Annex 11-2). Procedural controls must govern the physical access to computer systems (*physical security*). The access to individual computer system platforms is controlled by network-specific security procedures (*network security*). Finally, application-level security and associated authority checks control the access to the computer system applications (*applications security*).

Physical Security

The following items are the key practices that are applicable for the security of the physical environment of a computer system:

1. Limit physical computer access to authorized individuals (Annex 11-12.1).
2. The power sources for computer equipment must be controlled in order to prevent an accidental uncontrolled loss of power and fluctuations in voltage levels, which could potentially damage equipment, software files, and data files.
3. The power supplies for all computer equipment must meet both the manufacturers' requirements and national safety requirements for wiring, grounding, and radiation.
4. Critical environmental parameters, which include but are not limited to relative humidity and temperature, must be maintained within the computer equipment manufacturers' requirements. In cases where there are a number of requirements, the most stringent should be utilized.
5. Critical environmental parameters must be monitored on a regular periodic schedule in order to ensure that they continue to meet the manufacturers' requirements.
6. The facility where the computer equipment resides must be equipped with the appropriate fire extinguishing systems or equipment.
7. The computer operations support, personnel facilities maintenance, and all other personnel who need access to the physical environment must be responsible for knowing where and how to obtain the applicable operational procedures, understanding their contents, and accurately performing their execution.
8. Use authentication checks at physical access points in order to establish that the machine-readable codes on tokens and PINs are assigned to the same individual. These checks must be performed on the controlled access locations where the computer hardware is resident.
9. Use "time-outs" for underutilized terminals in order to prevent unauthorized use while unattended.

Network Security

The following items are the key practices that are applicable for the security of the network environment:

1. Network resources have a qualified authentication mechanism for controlling access (Annex 11-12.1). Access control decision functions are

defined using access right lists,* such as Access Control Lists (ACLs), and these allow the allocation of use, read, write, execute, delete, or create privileges. Access controls enable a system to be designed in such way that a supervisor, for example, will be able to access information on a group of employees, without everyone else on the network having access to this information. The access controls are an element of the authority check security features.

2. The process for setting up user access to a network is the responsibility of the appropriate network security administration personnel. The technical preparation, education, and training for personnel performing administration tasks are fundamental. The determination of what is required and the provision of documented evidence of technical preparation, education, and personnel training is a key regulatory requirement (Annex 11-2).

3. Procedural controls, which specify the manner in which network security is administered, must be established and documented. Network users must be trained in the policies, practices, and procedures concerning network security (Annex 11-2).

4. The management of network user accounts is a key procedural control. This process includes the request for the addition, modification, and removal of access privileges. The request must be approved by the appropriate manager, documented, and submitted to the network security administration for implementation (Annex 11-12.3).

5. There must be a procedure for granting controlled temporary network access for personnel (Annex 11-12.1).

6. In the event that a user leaves the company, there must be a process for notifying the appropriate security administration as soon as the employee departs (Annex 11-12.1).

7. Provisions must be made for the regular monitoring of access to the network.

8. There must be an escalation procedure for defining the actions to be taken if unauthorized access to the network is discovered (Annex 11-13).

---

* An access control list (ACL) is a list of security protections that apply to an entire object, a set of the object's properties, or an individual property of an object. Each Active Directory object has two associated ACLs. The *discretionary access control list* (DACL) is a list of user accounts, groups, and computers that are allowed (or denied) access to the object. A DACL consists of a list of access control entries (ACEs), where each ACE lists the permissions granted or denied to the users, groups, or computers listed in the DACL. An ACE contains a security identification with permission, such as Read access, Write access, or Full Control access. The *system access control list* (SACL) defines which events (such as file access) are audited for a user or group.

9. A documented record of security administration activities must be retained (Annex 11-12.3).

10. Procedures must be established to control remote access to the network (Annex 11-12.1). Systems that have connections to telephone communications through modems should have strict access controls and restrictions. Access restrictions on these systems should be designed to prevent unauthorized access or change. One possible method for controlling remote access is telephone callback.

11. Use time-stamped audit trails (Annex 11-9) to record changes, to record all write-to-file operations, and to independently record the date and time of any network system administrator actions or data entries/changes.

12. Unauthorized modification of the system clock must be prevented (Annex 11-12.4).

13. Systems that are connected over the Internet should be protected by a suitable firewall.

14. Antivirus and firewall software should be updated on a regular basis.

Applications Security

The following items are key practices that are applicable for the security of applications. These practices are applicable to both networked and stand-alone applications:

1. All applications must have a qualified authentication mechanism to control access (Table 15.1).

2. There must be procedural controls for passwords covering the length, used symbols/characters, period of validity, and their reuse (Annex 11-12.1).

3. Software "virus checking" must take place periodically for the protection of the application and data.

4. For each application, procedural controls must be established that specify the manner in which application security is administered (Annex 11-12.1).

5. The process for setting up access to applications must be defined and executed by the appropriate application-specific security administration personnel. The technical preparation, education, and training for personnel performing administration tasks are fundamental. The determination of what is required and the documented evidence of

Table 15.1   Authentication

Requirement	Implementation
The following features must be implemented: • Automatic log off • Unique user identification In addition, at least one of the other listed implementation features must be a procedure to corroborate that an entity is who it claims to be.	• Automatic log off • Biometrics • Password • PIN • Telephone callback • Token • Unique user identification

the technical preparation, education, and training of personnel is a key regulatory requirement (Annex 11-2).

6. The management of the user application accounts is a key procedural control. This process includes the request for the addition, modification, and removal of application access privileges (Annex 11-12.3). The request must be approved by the appropriate manager, documented, and submitted to the application security administration for implementation.

7. There must be a procedure for granting controlled temporary application access for personnel (Annex 11-12.1). As in the regular access, temporary access must follow security best practices.

8. In the event that a user leaves the company, there must be a process for notifying the appropriate security administration as soon as the employee departs (Annex 11-12.1).

9. There must be an escalation procedure for defining the actions to be taken if unauthorized access to the application is discovered (Annex 11-13).

10. A documented record of security administration activities must be retained (Annex 11-12.3).

11. Procedures must be established to control remote modem access to applications (Annex 11-12.1).

12. If data input or instructions can come from only specific input devices (e.g., instruments, terminals), the system must check the source of the input, and the use of the correct device should be verified by the operator.

13. Use time-stamped audit trails (Annex 11-9) to record changes, to record all write-to-file operations, and to independently record the date and time of any application-specific operator actions or entries.
14. Use time-stamped audit trails (Annex 11-9) to keep track of any record modifications carried out by the database administrator.
15. Use operational checks to enforce sequencing.
16. Use authority checks (Annex 11-12.1), when applicable, to determine if the identified individual has been authorized to use the system and has the necessary access rights to operate a device or to perform the operation required.
17. Unauthorized modification of the system clock must be prevented (Annex 11-12.4).
18. Security procedures must be established limiting access to confidential information. In addition, access to data should be limited so that inadvertent or unauthorized changes in data do not occur.
19. Access rights are assigned to user groups only, especially acceptable for read-only access rights.
20. Regular backups of all files and data should be made and stored in a secure location to prevent intentional or accidental damage (WHO, 2006). Security should also extend to devices used to store programs, such as tapes, disks, and magnetic-strip cards. Access to these devices should be controlled.

Database Security/Integrity

1. The design and implementation of security-related procedural and technological controls applicable to a database are based on a security risk assessment (Annex 11-1, Annex 11-5, Annex 11-6, Annex 11-7.1, and Annex 11-12.2).
2. A database is valid during the time of use if the maintenance, including security management of the database, is guaranteed.
3. During the qualification of database-based/inclusive systems, considerations should be given to the following*:
   - Implementing procedures and mechanisms to ensure data security and keeping the meaning and logical arrangement of data

---

* European Medicines Agency, Q&A: Good Manufacturing Practice (GMP), http://www.ema.europa. eu/ema/index.jsp?curl=pages/regulation/q_and_a/q_and_a_detail_000027.jsp#section8.

- Load testing taking into account future growth of the database and tools to monitor the saturation of the database
- Precautions for necessary migration of data (Annex 11-17) at the end of the life cycle of the system

4. Readability tests must take into account the aging process of the data storage devices and the disk drives used. Periodic control of readability is essential. The database must be checked regularly for database integrity and e-recs availability and integrity (Annex 11-7.1).

5. For business continuity purposes (Annex 11-16), the electronic records (e-recs) associated with data management systems must be periodically backed up (Annex 11-7.2). Audit trails (Annex 11-9) to these systems must be required (Annex 11-12.4). Other technological and procedural controls may be required for data management systems.

6. The activity of entering data, changing or amending incorrect entries, and creating backups should all be done in accordance with written, approved SOPs (WHO, 2006).

References

ICH Harmonised Tripartite Guideline, "Good Clinical Practice, E6," Section 5.5.3(d), June 1996.

ISPE GAMP 5: "A Risk-Based Approach to Compliant GXP Computerised Systems," International Society for Pharmaceutical Engineering (ISPE), 5th ed., Management Appendix M9 and Operational Appendix O11, February 2008.

O. López, *Computer Technologies Security Part I—Key Points in the Contained Domain*, West Sussex, UK: Sue Horwood Publishing Limited, 2002.

PI 011-3. "Good Practices for Computerised Systems in Regulated 'GXP' Environments," Pharmaceutical Inspection Cooperation Scheme (PIC/S), September 2007.

US FDA, 21CFR Part 58.51, "Specimen and Data Storage Facilities," April 1999.

US FDA, 21CFR Part 58.190(d), "Storage and Retrieval of Records and Data," April 1999.

WHO, Technical Report Series, No. 937, Annex 4, Appendix 5, Section 4, 2006.

Chapter 16

Incident Management

EU Annex 11-13, Operational Phase

All incidents, not only system failures and data errors, should be reported and assessed. The root cause of a critical incident should be identified and should form the basis of corrective and preventive actions.

Analysis

The malfunctions or failures of computer system components, incorrect documentation, data errors, improper operation, or interface errors illustrate some of the incidents that can affect the correct operation of a computer system. These system incidents are also nonconformances.[*]

Effective monitoring of the operation of a computer system also involves user or operator training in proper operation. This facilitates their ability to recognize unexpected responses and outputs and to fully document such incidents to aid in the evaluation and debugging process.

System outputs, including reports, should be periodically examined for accuracy and evident discrepancies. When new or unusual circumstances occur in the software's environment or related processes, the necessity for

---

[*] Nonconformance—A departure from minimum requirements specified in a contract, specification, drawing, or other approved product description or service.

increased or additional monitoring should be considered. Periodic maintenance schedules should include provision for verification that software and hardware remain as defined in the specification of the current revision.

All incidents related to computer systems must be identified, recorded, traced, investigated, assessed, and prioritized, and corrective and preventive measures must be adopted. The SME should conduct a root cause analysis or any similar method in order to determine the nature of the incident. This assessment should include the criticality of the incident and category. Based on these two factors, handling the incident may be different.

> "An appropriate level of root cause analysis should be applied during the investigation of deviations, suspected product defects and other problems. This can be determined using Quality Risk Management principles. In cases where the true root cause(s) of the issue cannot be determined, consideration should be given to identifying the most likely root cause(s) and to addressing those. Where human error is suspected or identified as the cause, this should be justified having taken care to ensure that process, procedural or system based errors or problems have not been overlooked, if present. Appropriate corrective actions and/or preventative actions (CAPAs) should be identified and taken in response to investigations. The effectiveness of such actions should be monitored and assessed, in line with Quality Risk Management principles."[*]

In order to mitigate incidents quickly or to avoid introducing additional system errors, appropriate procedural controls must be applied to enable the early identification of a breakdown and the initiation of an appropriate preventive action. The effectiveness of these procedural controls must be verified.

Monitoring procedural control includes methods for:

- Identifying and documenting incidents, errors, and improvements requests
- Incident validity assessment
- Response priority assignment
- Scope and frequency monitoring after fixing the incident

---

[*] EudraLex, The Rules Governing Medicinal Products in the European Union Volume 4, EU Guidelines for Good Manufacturing Practice for Medicinal Products for Human and Veterinary Use, Chapter 1, Pharmaceutical Quality System, Section 1.4A (xiv) , January 2013.

The solution to an incident may take technological or procedural controls and may need the partial/total revalidation of the computer system.

The following sections suggest a course of action to identify, record, trace, investigate, assess, and prioritize corrective measures to adopt computer system incidents. In all cases, a root cause analysis or an equivalent method is used to identify the malfunction.

Process Equipment-Related Malfunction

The personnel responsible for managing the process equipment causing the malfunction must:

■ Record a problem description, incident, or an initial error analysis and specify the modification needed to fix the malfunction.
■ Check any stored data and, if applicable, reconstruct the malfunction.
■ As applicable, fill out the appropriate change control or maintenance forms, and submit for approval.
■ Fix or replace the process equipment causing the malfunction.
■ Perform applicable regression testing, including the interfaces between the equipment and the computer system.
■ Release the system for use.

Software/Infrastructure Component Malfunction

The personnel responsible for managing the software component malfunction must record a problem description, incident, or an initial error analysis.

If the analysis demonstrates an infrastructure component malfunction, proceed as above.

Specify the software modifications needed to fix the malfunction and an impact analysis of the modification to the system.

Fill out the appropriate change control forms and submit these for approval. Include the root cause analysis report, modifications needed, and impact analysis.

If the software modification does not constitute an emergency change, wait until the change control form is approved; carry out the corrective actions identified; perform applicable regression testing in the applicable environment before the system is returned to the operational environment; and, as applicable, update the system documentation and/or user's manual.

If the user's manual was impacted by the modification, update the user's manual and conduct user training on the changes. Release the system for use.

Incorrect Documentation or Improper Operation

If the analysis demonstrates incorrect documentation, the personnel responsible for managing the documentation must update the system documentation and/or user's manual.

If the user's manual was impacted by the modification, conduct user's training on the revised documentation.

If the analysis demonstrates improper operation, update the system documentation and/or user's manual to address the improper operation issue.

Perform a user refresher training on the correct operation of the system.

On completion of the implementation, the original report and associated documentation must be filed in the site document retention center or with the change control documentation for the computer system.

Emergency Incidents

If the system modification or replacement part constitutes an emergency change:

- Carry out the initial error analysis and corrective actions identified.
- After the modifications have been made, perform applicable regression testing.
- Return the system to production.
- Follow the steps for the appropriate documentation updates.

References

ICH Harmonised Tripartite Guideline, "Good Manufacturing Practice Guidance for Active Pharmaceutical Ingredients, Q7," November 2000.
ISO 13485, "Medical Devices—Quality Management Systems," Sections 8.5, 8.5.1, 8.5.2, 8.5.3; July 2012.

ISPE GAMP 5, A Risk-Based Approach to Compliant GXP Computerised Systems, International Society for Pharmaceutical Engineering (ISPE), 5th ed., Operational Appendices O4, O5, O7, February 2008.

Chapter 17

Electronic Signatures
Electronic Signing Requirements

R.D. McDowall
Principal, McDowall Consulting

EU GMP Annex 11-14, Operational Phase

Electronic records may be signed electronically. Electronic signatures are expected to:

a. have the same impact as hand-written signatures within the boundaries of the company,
b. be permanently linked to their respective record,
c. include the time and date that they were applied.

Introduction

The first use of electronic signatures in a GMP environment came with the release in 1997 of the FDA regulation for electronic records and signatures, 21 CFR 11.[*] This regulation allowed for the first time the use of fully electronic work, provided the other requirements of Part 11 were met to ensure

---

[*] FDA, 21 CFR Part 11, "Electronic Records; Electronic Signatures; Final Rule," *Federal Register,* 62(54), 13429, March 20, 1997.

the trustworthiness and integrity of the electronic records generated by the computerized systems.

In the intervening years, Part 11 has been joined by the Japanese electronic signature and electronic records regulation in 2005[*] and in 2011 by the EU GMP regulations.[†]

In this chapter, we will focus on the electronic signature requirements of EU GMP Annex 11[‡] contained in Clause 14. For the documents and records to sign, the reader should look at EU GMP Chapter 4;[§] and when electronic signatures are used for batch release, the reader is referred to EU GMP Annex 16[¶] and Annex 11 Clause 15, which are discussed in Chapter 18 in this book. The relationships for batch release in EU GMP are shown in Figure 17.1.

In writing this chapter, the author has considered only electronic signatures used by systems that are fully electronic and has excluded hybrid or heterogeneous systems (electronic records with handwritten signatures on linked paper printouts).

Annex 11 Clause 14 deals specifically with electronic signatures. When you read this clause, you will be surprised to see how short and simple the regulation is when compared with the 21 CFR 11 requirements. In fact, there

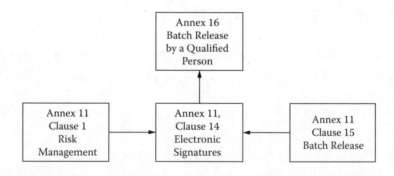

Figure 17.1   Relationship of Clause 14 with other Annex 11 clauses and Annex 16 for batch release.

---

[*] Use of Electromagnetic Records and Electronic Signatures, Pharmaceutical and Food Safety Bureau, Notification number 0401022, 2005.

[†] EudraLex, Volume 4, EU Guidelines to Good Manufacturing Practice, Medicinal Products for Human and Veterinary Use, Annex 11–Computerised Systems, June 2011.

[‡] EudraLex, Volume 4, EU Guidelines to Good Manufacturing Practice, Medicinal Products for Human and Veterinary Use, Annex 11–Computerised Systems, June 2011.

[§] EudraLex, The Rules Governing Medicinal Products in the European Union Volume 4, Good Manufacturing Practice, Medicinal Products for Human and Veterinary Use, Chapter 4: Documentation, Revision 1, June 2011.

[¶] EudraLex, Volume 4, EU Guidelines to Good Manufacturing Practice, Medicinal Products for Human and Veterinary Use, Annex 16–Certification by a Qualified Person and Batch Release, 2001.

are 40 words to describe how electronic signatures can be applied in Annex 11, and this compares with 745 words to describe all electronic signature requirements throughout Part 11, excluding the definitions.*

Clause 14 also has to be interpreted via Clause 1 of Annex 11, which states that risk management needs to be applied throughout the life cycle of a computerized system. Therefore, the electronic signature regulations can be interpreted via a documented risk assessment for an individual system to comply with Annex 11 or a global interpretation for all systems.

Interpretation of Annex 11 Electronic Signature Regulations

As noted above, the requirement for electronic signatures is relatively short and brief, and therefore the regulation needs to be interpreted carefully.

The first part of Clause 14 simply states:

Electronic records may be signed electronically.

This has two points that are of interest. The first is explicit and the second is derived from the wording of the clause.

The first point is that the use of electronic signatures is an option that is not compulsory or mandatory because an organization can still use handwritten signatures on paper records if required. However, in the author's view, business drivers will force companies to implement electronic signatures with electronic working practices to avoid delays in releasing products or to have data available electronically for preparing regulatory submissions, annual quality reviews, etc. In addition, the issues of data integrity are such that electronic working avoids issues with hybrid systems (managing signatures and records across two incompatible media types) and the relative ease of falsifying records with a hybrid system.

The second point is that unlike 21 CFR 11, there is no mention in Annex 11 of the technologies that can be used to implement electronic signatures. This allows an individual company the ability to assess and implement different technologies as they become available for electronic signing of records or to standardize on a single type of signature technology. It also future-proofs the regulation in comparison with the approach taken by 21 CFR 11,

---

* FDA, 21 CFR Part 11, "Electronic Records; Electronic Signatures; Final Rule," *Federal Register*, 62(54), 13429, March 20, 1997.

which specifies three approaches: electronic signature (password and user identity), biometric, and digital signature. Note that the glossary in Annex 11 does not define electronic signature.

The remaining sections of Clause 14 look at the requirements of electronic signature implementation and the minimum requirements for ensuring data integrity. Note that the regulation is written in simple terms from which an organization will perform a risk-based assessment to interpret how it will implement the regulation in practice.

There are three subclauses to consider, which will be covered in the remainder of this section, that electronic signatures must:

> a. Have the same impact as handwritten signatures within the boundaries of the company.

From this part of the regulation, a number of points can be derived or interpreted, such as:

- Who is the person signing?
- Has this individual been trained in the role for which he or she is signing?
- Has the individual been trained to use the electronic signature function of the computerized system he or she is using?
- Does the individual understand that electronic signatures are equivalent to handwritten signatures?
- Is the signer's name legible? I hope that as we are dealing with a computerized system it will be.
- Is the meaning of the signature stated, for example, author, reviewer, and so on?
- Is there an order of signing? For example, the technical author is first and technical reviewers and approvers follow.
- Are there controls to prevent the same individual from authoring and approving his or her own work?
- A person cannot deny signing a document, and implicit in this is that users must not share user identities and passwords for whichever technology is being used to sign the records.
- E-signature integrity must be maintained outside of application but inside the company (company in this context can vary from a single site to multiple sites throughout the world). This has implications in the design of computerized systems used in a regulated environment that we will discuss later.

Many of these interpreted or inferred requirements are similar to those mandated under 21 CFR 11 regulations.[*]

b. Be permanently linked to their respective record.

The second part is involved with linking an electronic signature with the corresponding electronic records. This is important for ensuring data integrity and reliability of the output of a computerized system operating in a regulated environment.

Interpretation needs to consider questions such as:

■ Is the signature attached to the record or records to be signed or a report of data interpretation? If a report of work is performed, the report needs to link to the records and the associated metadata within the system.
■ Is the signature secure and unable to be deleted?
■ If a signature is deleted, does the signed record indicate that the report has been altered?
■ If the underlying electronic record and associated metadata have been changed, does the electronic signature become invalid?
■ Does the system allow a supervisor to revoke an electronic signature if a report has been superseded?
■ There is no statement in Annex 11 of how records should be linked to the respective electronic signatures, which decouples the regulation from technology and, again, makes it future proof.

There is one implicit requirement, however, in that the signature must be attached to the record to which it relates and not hidden away in the audit trail of the system.

c. Include the time and date that they were applied.

The last part of Clause 14 is important for establishing the sequence of signing electronic records and the integrity of the time and date stamp. The following elements can be inferred from this section of the regulation:

■ Has the time and date stamp been taken from a reliable source?

---

[*] FDA, 21 CFR Part 11, "Electronic Records; Electronic Signatures; Final Rule," *Federal Register*, 62(54), 13429, March 20, 1997.

■ How is the network time server synchronized to a trusted time source, for example, Network Time Protocol (NTP), national laboratory atomic clock, Global Positioning System (GPS) network, and so on?

■ How accurate is the time stamp?

■ Who has access to the computer clock and who can change it? (This is especially important for stand-alone systems and requires a procedure with associated records.)

■ What is the format of the time stamp? Will a 12- or 24-hour clock be used?

■ Is the time zone indicated on the signed record, especially for multinational companies?

■ If applicable, will the clock be automatically adjusted for summer and winter time changes?

■ Is the date stamp unambiguous, especially in multinational companies, for example, DD MM YYYY?

Impact of Annex 11 Electronic Signature Requirements on Software Design

Looking solely at Clause 14, there are a number of issues concerning electronic signatures that directly impact the design of software used in GMP-regulated environments.

The first is the direct impact that Clause 14 has on the design of many computerized systems used in regulated GMP laboratories. Clause 14 requires that signed electronic records or a report of an analysis must be available outside of the computerized systems. This is not an unreasonable requirement because the users of the information generated by a system could typically reside outside of the department in development, regulatory, or manufacturing. After the data have been interpreted by an analyst, a report will be prepared with an electronic signature attached to the report. Therefore, the electronic signature must be applied to a representation of the records to which it pertains and should not be stuffed as an afterthought by a vendor's software engineers into the audit trail, where it is difficult to see that the record has been signed. In short, the record and the signature must be together.

Furthermore, the linkage between the signature and the record interpretation must be permanent as required by Annex 11. How this is to be achieved is left to interpretation, but some options are to have a secured PDF, file check sums, encryption, or another means to prevent falsification of laboratory results. Thus, if an attempt were made to replace a signature or to change the results on a signed report, the attempt would be recognized and the report invalidated or corrupted to indicate tampering. This is especially important outside of the system because there will be no audit trail available to monitor unauthorized attempts at falsification.

References

EudraLex, "The Rules Governing Medicinal Products in the European Union Volume 4, Good Manufacturing Practice, Medicinal Products for Human and Veterinary Use, Chapter 4: Documentation," June 2011.

EudraLex, Volume 4, "EU Guidelines to Good Manufacturing Practice, Medicinal Products for Human and Veterinary Use, Annex 11–Computerised Systems," June 2011.

EudraLex, Volume 4, "EU Guidelines to Good Manufacturing Practice, Medicinal Products for Human and Veterinary Use, Annex 16–Certification by a Qualified Person and Batch Release," 2001.

FDA, 21 CFR Part 11, "Electronic Records; Electronic Signatures; Final Rule," *Federal Register*, 62(54), 13429, March 20, 1997.

Use of Electromagnetic Records and Electronic Signatures, Pharmaceutical and Food Safety Bureau, Notification number 0401022, 2005.

Chapter 18

Batch Certification and Release

Bernd Renger

Director, Bernd Renger Consulting

EU Annex 11-15, Operational Phase

When a computerised system is used for recording certification and batch release, the system should allow only Qualified Persons to certify the release of the batches and it should clearly identify and record the person releasing or certifying the batches. This should be performed using an electronic signature.

Related References

11-2, Personnel—There should be close cooperation between all relevant personnel such as Process Owner, System Owner, Qualified Persons, and IT. All personnel should have appropriate qualifications, level of access, and defined responsibilities to carry out their assigned duties.

Introduction

This chapter describes how the Qualified Person (QP) according to EU Directive 2001/83 and his legal responsibility for batch certification and subsequent release as laid down in the revised version of EU GMP Annex 16 links to the requirements and expectations as expressed in EU GMP Annex 11.

This linkage may be the case when directly working with IT systems to document certification or applying release status to batches in an Enterprise Resource Planning (ERP) system or relying within the PQS on computerized systems as part of quality decision-making processes.

Legal and Regulatory Background

The European institution of the QP goes far beyond the responsibilities as described in 21 CFR 210 & 211 for the Quality Unit and thus are summarized below for readers not familiar with the complex European pharmaceutical regulations.

The Qualified Person

The institution of a QP was introduced in the EEC (European Economic Area, now European Union) in 1976 by the 2nd Pharma Directive.

Since then, two requirements are basic pillars of the European Pharmaceutical Legislation, having been transposed into national laws of each of the 28 Member States of the European Union as well as the three member states of the European Free Trade Association that have adopted the European Regulations to form the European Economic Area (EEA):

- An applicant for a manufacturing or import authorization must have at his disposal the services of at least one QP in order to obtain an authorization in the European Union
- Each batch of a pharmaceutical product manufactured in or imported into the EEC has to be certified and released by a QP. Whereby the release step that is following the official act of certification may be delegated to another function within or outside the company, based on an SOP or contract.

This institution of a QP was introduced significantly earlier than the Common European GMP Regulations that were introduced in 1991. Responsibilities have been laid down in a European Directive that had to be transferred into National Law in the Member States. Therefore, the legal and personal responsibilities and liabilities of the QP are correspondingly higher than the responsibilities of any other key functions within a Pharmaceutical Quality System as described in the EU GMP.

After introducing the Common European GMP Regulations, the role of the QP was also described in the EU Guidelines for Good Manufacturing Practice for Medicinal Products for Human and Veterinary Use, Part I (Basic Requirements for Medicinal Products), and to further clarify and specify the process of certification and batch release by the QP within the European Union (plus the three states forming the EEA) a more detailed, specific Annex 16 to the European GMPs was issued and came into operation in January 2002.

The recently issued Directive 2011/62 EU ("Falsified Medicines Directive") amending the codified Pharma Directive 2001/83 EC has defined various requirements and delegated acts to prevent the entry of falsified medicines into the legal supply chain in the European Union or EEA. Consequently, all chapters of the EU Guidelines for Good Manufacturing Practice for Medicinal Products for Human and Veterinary Use, Part 1 (Basic Requirements for Medicinal Products) have been revised or are under revision to reflect this new paradigm. Annex 16 (Certification by a QP and Batch Release) is one of the documents mostly impacted by these new regulations and therefore subject to major revision.

Certification, Confirmation, and Certificates

The basic responsibilities of a QP are to certify:

- in case of medicinal products manufactured within the European Union that each batch has been manufactured and checked in compliance with the laws in force in the corresponding member state, in accordance with requirements of the marketing authorization, and following GMPs
- in case of medicinal products coming from third countries that each production batch has undergone a full analysis within the corresponding member states to ensure the quality of the medicinal products

This has to be documented in a register or equivalent document.

The act of certification relates to the finished product before a batch is released for sale or distribution.

In case of partial manufacturing, the QP of manufacturers performing manufacturing steps prior to finished products has the responsibility to issue a QP confirmation, stating that the partial manufacturing or testing has been performed under the laws in force of the corresponding member state, in accordance with the manufacturing authorization, and following GMPs.

Assigning release status to the finished batch of product may be done by the QP as an integral part of certification or it may be done afterward by another person via an arrangement delegated by the QP in an SOP or contract.

IT Systems and QP Certification/Confirmation

As mentioned previously, EU legislation requires a manufacturer to have at least one QP at its disposal, but a site or manufacturer may have more than one QP who may certify batches. Due to the personal liability and responsibility associated with this activity, identification of the person performing the official certification and release (or confirming of a partial manufacture of a batch) is essential for the system.

Therefore, any documentation of QP activities and finished product certification in particular must clearly be attributed to the QP in charge. In case electronic systems are used—either as stand-alone systems controlling the certification (or confirmation) activities or ERP systems that manage not only batch status but also the process of batch release—they must comply with the requirements of Annex 11, item 15:

> When a computerised system is used for recording certification and batch release, the system should allow only Qualified Persons to certify the release of the batches and it should clearly identify and record the person releasing or certifying the batches. This should be performed using an electronic signature.

The new revision of Annex 16 "Batch Certification and Release by a Qualified Person" clearly differentiates between the act of certifying a batch that has to be performed by a QP personally and the subsequent assigning of release status to the finished batch of product or release for shipment in case of a confirmation of partial manufacturing that may be delegated within or outside the pharmaceutical company based on an SOP or contract to appropriately trained and responsible persons.

Therefore, this paragraph of the revised Annex 11 does not fully correspond to the more differentiated view of Annex 16, and requirements may be more complex to follow and implement in case companies are using various different hybrid systems, for example:

1. Paper-based certification documents, paper-based entry into a certification/release register with subsequent transferring of the release status into an IT-based ERP system. In that case, the signature of the QP is a personal signature, and there is no need for implementing an electronic signature. However, the manual transfer of the release status and its peer review may be performed by technical staff, not the QP himself, based on an SOP describing the process and its supervision. In that case, the requirement of Annex 11 must be interpreted in a way that access control, authorization, and audit trails must allow to unambiguously identify who has performed any entry or change of data.
2. Paper-based certification documents but an electronic file as certification/release register—possibly even already as a module of an ERP system—with subsequent automatic transfer of the release status into an IT-based ERP system. In that case, the signature of the QP is still a personal signature on the certificate, but an electronic one is in the register, requiring the implementation of an electronic signature system.

Because the entry in the register is one of the responsibilities of the QP that cannot be delegated, there is no step that may be performed by technical staff.

In that case, the requirement of Annex 11 fully applies.

In case an electronic signature is used by the QP, the requirements of item 14 "Electronic Signature" must be fulfilled:

Electronic records may be signed electronically. Electronic signatures are expected to:

a. have the same impact as handwritten signatures within the boundaries of the company,
b. be permanently linked to their respective record,
c. include the time and date that they were applied.

The QP Relying on the Pharmaceutical Quality System

According to the revised version of Annex 16 "Batch Certification and Release by a Qualified Person," the QP has to fulfill the following operational responsibilities prior to certification of a batch for release to market or for export personally:

■ Certification is permitted under the terms of the manufacturing/importation authorization (MIA).
■ Any additional duties and requirements of national legislation are complied with.
■ Certification is recorded in a register or equivalent document.

In addition, the revised Annex lists numerous points for which the QP carries the responsibility for ensuring they have been covered and been properly dealt with. However, these may be delegated to appropriately trained personnel or third parties.

Annex 16 recognizes that in these cases the QP will need to rely on a quality management system. However, the QP should have ongoing assurance that this reliance is well founded.

> The QP who certifies a finished product batch before release may do so based on his personal knowledge of all the facilities and procedures employed, the expertise of the persons concerned and of the quality system within which they operate…

These are especially the Head of Production and the Head of Quality Control.

Therefore, it is the QP's duty prior to release of a batch to ensure that certain prerequisites are fulfilled as described in Annex 16 to the EU GMP Guide:

> Before certifying a batch prior to release the QP doing so should ensure, with reference to the guidance above, that at least the following requirements have been met:
>
> a. the batch and its manufacture comply with the provisions of the marketing authorization (including the authorization required for importation where relevant);

   b. manufacture has been carried out in accordance with Good Manufacturing Practice or, in the case of a batch imported from a third country, in accordance with good manufacturing practice standards at least equivalent to EC GMP;

   c. the principal manufacturing and testing processes have been validated; account has been taken of the actual production conditions and manufacturing records;

   d. any deviations or planned changes in production or quality control have been authorized by the persons responsible in accordance with a defined system;

   e. any changes requiring variation to the marketing or manufacturing authorization have been notified to and authorized by the relevant authority;

   f. all the necessary checks and tests have been performed, including any additional sampling, inspection, tests, or checks initiated because of deviations or planned changes;

   g. all necessary production and quality control documentation has been completed and endorsed by the staff authorized to do so;

   h. all audits have been carried out as required by the quality assurance system;

   i. the QP should in addition take into account any other factors of which he is aware that are relevant to the quality of the batch.

Interestingly, the revision of Annex 16 does not differentiate between:

■ Data that have to be supplied to the QP on a batch-by-batch basis; for example, test results and release status of starting materials used, test results and compliance of the finished product, batch record review data, deviations associated with this batch (see Figure 18.1).

■ And those data that might not be checked on a batch-by-batch basis but would be reported as a result of Quality Management Reviews of selected Quality Systems ensuring the requirements as defined in Annex 16 are complied with—training of staff, procedures comply with marketing authorization, equipment is qualified or calibrated, processes are validated, and ongoing stability data of the product are compliant.

Although it may be possible to run manufacturing and testing operations (especially in smaller companies) totally paper based and thus provide the batch-related data to the QP prior to confirmation or certification also in

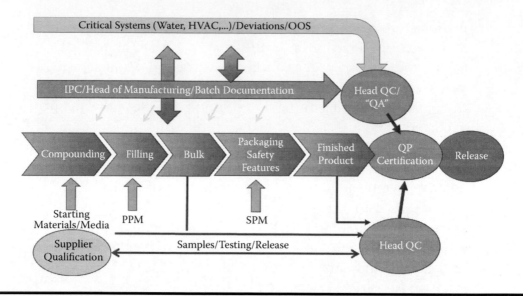

Figure 18.1 Pharmaceutical quality system—data flow to the QP prior to batch certification and release.

paper format, it is rather unlikely that a paper system is capable of providing the "system related" data including an alarming function in the event of any deviation from expectations or failures.

Therefore, these data should be supplied in electronic format to facilitate their transfer, evaluation and processing, and visibility for the QP if considered necessary for ensuring compliance.

Systems that should be considered a resource of information are laboratory LIMS; Deviations and CAPA systems; monitoring systems for surveillance of manufacturing conditions including temperature, humidity, non-viable particle count; risk management tools; stability databases; training databases; supplier management; audit and contract databases; and so on.

Annex 11 applies to all forms of computerized systems used as part of GMP-regulated activities. This is a wide scope statement and includes all computerized systems including the in-house developed spreadsheets and databases.

This requires these systems must comply and fully correspond to the requirements of the revised Annex 11. Whereas established systems like TrackWise® may easily comply with this expectation, it will not be easy to cope with these requirements in case companies use simple spreadsheet applications, for example, for tracking of deviations, change control, or corrective and preventive actions.

Control of Batch Release

Whereas the certification and subsequent release decisions are essentially limited to a QP, the assigning of the release status to the batch may be delegated within or outside the pharmaceutical company based on an SOP or contract and performed by appropriately trained and responsible staff.

In that case, if release is controlled via IT (ERP or warehouse management) systems, these must be accordingly configured and validated as requested by Annex 16:

> Safeguards to ensure that uncertified batches are not released should be in place and may be physical (via the use of segregation and labeling) or electronic (via the use of validated computerised systems). When uncertified batches are moved from one authorized site to another, the safeguards to prevent premature release should remain.

This paragraph makes two very important and pertinent statements:

1. The requirement of segregating batches and products with different status is not justified in case validated computerized systems are in place—a requirement unfortunately still considered essential by various conservative authorities and inspectorates.
2. Unreleased batches of finished products (and therefore also unreleased semifinished or bulk batches) may be transferred and transported, however, only between authorized sites, which implies that there are QPs on each site of this supply chain that must ensure the appropriate controls are in place to absolutely exclude any release prior to final certification.

Usually, companies will allow downgrading the status of a batch to a larger segment of persons, including key personnel in quality, supply chain, or logistics, to allow the shortest reaction to any incident or observation that needs to ensure the batch in question is no longer free to be shipped to customers and patients.

In that case, too, any lifting of the ban and re-releasing the batch or parts of it are exclusively to be performed by a QP, requiring again the full application of the requirements of Item 15 of Annex 11.

Chapter 19

Business Continuity

EU Annex 11-16–Operational Phase

For the availability of computerized systems supporting critical processes, provisions should be made to ensure continuity of support for those processes in the event of a system breakdown (e.g., a manual or an alternative system). The time required to bring the alternative arrangements into use should be based on risk and appropriate for a particular system and the business process it supports. These arrangements should be adequately documented and tested.

Introduction[*]

Business continuity refers to the prepared measures that will secure business operations in case of system failure or trouble.

Business continuity, including a disaster recovery procedural control, should ensure minimal disruption in the case of loss of hardware, software, and data files.

At the lowest level, the business continuity applies to the accidental deletion of a single file, in which case a procedure should be in place for

---

[*] O. López, "Maintaining the State of Validation," in *21 CFR Part 11: Complete Guide to International Computer Validation Compliance for the Pharmaceutical Industry,* West Sussex, UK: Sue Horwood Publishing and Boca Raton, FL: Interpharm/CRC, 2002, 111–115.

restoring the most recently backed-up copy. At the other extreme is a disaster such as a complete destruction of the hardware, software, and data files. For this situation, a procedure addressing the following should be in place:

- Specification of the minimum replacement hardware and software requirements to obtain an operational system and their source
- Specification of the period within which the replacement system should be back in production, based on business considerations
- Implementation of the replacement system
- Steps to restore the data so that processing activities may be resumed as soon as possible
- Steps to revalidate the system to the required standard

The disaster recovery procedural control employed to restore the system should be tested regularly, and all relevant personnel should be made aware of its existence and trained to use it. A copy of the procedure should be maintained off-site.

Analysis

The regulated user should establish a plan that is enabled when a computer system fails or is interrupted. The plan references the procedure that would be followed in the event of a system failure and include, as applicable, the restoration of data.

Disaster recovery procedural control should be available for the most common disasters—often power failure or hard disk failure. In addition, the disaster recovery procedures provide the alternatives to the systems that are in operation, in the case of incidents in their operation.

In case of complete destruction of the hardware, software, and data files, the backups and documentation of the system should be available to build up a complete new system. It should be documented whether and, if so, how the process is continued in case of a disaster (unavailability of the system).

In case of a power breakdown or other failures in which the recovery of the system includes recuperating data, it is necessary to ensure that the integrity of the data is not compromised during the return to normal operation. The integrity and accuracy of the data must be verified.

The timeliness of enabling the business continuity plan should be associated with the urgent level of the need of use of the program. For example, the impact of the product recall should be able to have timely access to relevant information.

Necessity of business continuity will be determined after consideration of risk assessment results of the relevant operations.

In order to maintain the validated status of computer systems, these measures should also be verified in advance. Any faults and corrective measures adopted must be registered.

In summary, based on risk assessments, it is required to have accessible plans ensuring continuity of support for critical processes as well as knowing the time required to bring alternatives into operation. Annex 11 explicitly requires that these arrangements need to be documented and tested adequately before use.

Business Continuity Plan*

The content of a business continuity plan should include:

- Description of possible failures, situations, and reporting
- Reporting procedure should contain:
  - Error/fault classification or description of disaster situation with impacts on the related process
  - Determination of responsible persons for corrective actions, trouble shooting, error diagnostics, and preventive actions
- Explanation of alternative systems available, if applicable
- Process description in case of failures and outage situations
- Instructions for the required documentation and, if applicable, maintenance of alternatively recorded data into the computerized system
- Description of the boot-up process of the computerized systems after bug fixing
- Naming of authorized persons for the recommissioning process

The integrity and accuracy of the data should be verified after recommissioning. If data of the alternative process will be re-entered manually into the (initial) system, these data should be verified (Annex 11-6).

The business continuity plan should be reviewed periodically and the responsible persons defined.

---

* Aide-mémoire of German ZLG regarding EU GMP Annex 11, September 2013.

References

Aide-mémoire of German ZLG regarding EU GMP Annex 11, September 2013.
ISPE GAMP 5, A Risk-Based Approach to Compliant GXP Computerised Systems,
    Operational Appendix O10, International Society for Pharmaceutical
    Engineering (ISPE), 5th ed., February 2008.

Chapter 20

Archiving

EU Annex 11-17–Operational Phase

Data may be archived. This data should be checked for accessibility, readability, and integrity. If relevant changes are to be made to the system (e.g., computer equipment or programs), then the ability to retrieve the data should be ensured and tested.

Analysis

Data archiving is the process of transferring e-recs that are no longer actively used to a separate records storage device for long-term retention, often disabling it from any further changes.

This transfer can be locally to either near-line (e.g., to removable media in an automated device, such as CD-Rs in a jukebox), off-line (e.g., to a local or remote storage area) or to another record repository. A tracking feature is needed to record the change of location for both ease of access and to meet regulatory requirements (e.g., control of changes).

In addition to Annex 11-17, Annex 11-4.8, 10, and 11 are applicable.

To account and record the transfer of e-recs to the archiving environment, a change control must be requested. The implementation plan and the records to be archived must be documented and approved. After transferring the e-recs from the active storage device to the inactive archived device, the verification to be performed to the e-recs includes that the e-recs are not altered in value, links, and meaning.

After the e-recs are migrated to the archiving environment, checks and control are required to ensure the preservation of data and records content and meaning throughout the required retention period. These checks and controls are discussed under Storage in Chapter 10.

If changes are proposed to the storage-related computer infrastructure (hardware and software) and the application accessing the archived e-recs, accessibility, readability, and accuracy checks must be performed as part of the qualification of the new components.

The person who owns the archived e-recs will be responsible for adequacy of archiving and associated controls of these records.

When an outside agency is used to provide a data archiving service, there should be a formal agreement including a clear statement of the responsibilities of that outside agency (Annex 11-3).

Method of Archival

Each system is analyzed to determine its disposition and the method of archival to be used. There are five types of disposition:

- Extract/migrate—Data is extracted from the current system and moved to another location or the entire instance is migrated elsewhere.
- Host—These are single-instance database systems that are not typically managed by the site and are hosted elsewhere.
- Archive—Will contain the following two types:
  - Report—In this case, the official record is considered to be in hard copy currently or the most effective end state will become hard copy.
  - Physical to Virtual (P2V) (encapsulate)—In order to be able to access the data effectively, in some cases it is necessary to have both the application and the database in a virtual environment. In this case, software will be used to encapsulate the data and application and the product housed in a server designated for this purpose.
- Transition—This is used where there is a need to transition the application or documentation to a new site because of the new site taking over responsibility of the business or to transition the application to a new company due to site sale.

- No Retention—Where there is no need to keep or delete data and the system can be shut down.

Retirement

The purpose of the retirement process is to replace the archived media or eliminate the archived media or archived e-recs. If the archived e-recs are backed-up accordingly, the retirement of the archiving media or the archived e-recs is not a critical process. The e-recs are no longer actively in use.

To account and record the retirement of archived e-recs or archiving media, a change control must be requested. The retirement implementation plan and the records to be archived must be documented and approved.

At the end of the retirement process, the e-recs may be physically erased for all media. E-recs retention requirements are discussed in Chapter 10.

References

GAMP® Good Practice Guide, "Electronic Data Archiving," 2007.
ISO 11799: 2003(E) "Information and Documentation—Document Storage Requirements for Archive and Library Materials."
ISPE/PDA, "Good Practice and Compliance for Electronic Records and Signatures. Part 1 Good Electronic Records Management (GERM)," July 2002.
MHRA, "Good Laboratory Practice: Guidance on Archiving," March 2006.

Chapter 21

SLC Documentation

Related References

4.1 The validation documentation and reports should cover the relevant steps of the life cycle. Manufacturers should be able to justify their standards, protocols, acceptance criteria, procedures, and records based on their risk assessment.

4.4 User Requirements Specifications should describe the required functions of the computerised system and be based on documented risk assessment and GMP impact. User requirements should be traceable throughout the life cycle.

4.7 Evidence of appropriate test methods and test scenarios should be demonstrated. Particularly, system (process) parameter limits, data limits, and error handling should be considered. Automated testing tools and test environments should have documented assessments for their adequacy.

Analysis

The computer SLC-related documentation (computer documentation) means instructions, records, and reports that relate to the computer system implementation, operation, maintenance, and retirement, from high-level design documents to end-user manuals. Table 21.1 illustrates some typical computer documentation.

Table 21.1 System Documents Grouping

SLC	Document[a]	Group[b]	Subgroup[c]
Initial requirements	Job descriptions with predefined roles and responsibilities on those areas related with manufacturing (Annex 11-2)	Instructions	Specification[d]
	Requirements specification (Annex 11-4.4, 11-3.3), data migration requirements (Annex 11-4.8), interfaces requirements (Annex 11-5), e-sig requirements (Annex 11-14)	Instructions	Specification
	Risk management plans (Annex 11-1)	Instructions	Procedure[e]
	Risk analysis (Annex 11-1)	Instructions	Specification
	Risk results and final conclusions (Annex 11-1)	Records/reports	Reports[f]
	Validation plans (Annex 11-4.3)	Instructions	Procedure
	Security requirements (Annex 11-12.4)	Instructions	Specification
	Job descriptions with predefined roles and responsibilities on those areas related with manufacturing (Annex 11-2)	Instructions	Specification
	Supplier suitability and requirements	Records/reports	Reports
	Supplier assessment and audit reports (Annex 11-3.2, 11-3.4, and 11-4.5)	Records/reports	Reports
	Quality and service agreements (Annex 11-3.2)	Instructions	Specification
Design	System specification	Instructions	Specification
	User manuals	Instructions	Procedure
	Design specification	Instructions	Specification
	Design reviews	Records/reports	Records[g]

Programming	Programming standards		Instructions	Procedure
	Source/configuration code files		Instructions	Procedure
	Source/configuration code reviews		Records/reports	Records
Testing	Testing plans		Instructions	Procedure
	Data migration checklists (Annex 11-4.8)		Instructions	Protocol[h]
	FAT and SAT plans		Instructions	Procedure
	Interface test plans (Annex 11-5)		Instructions	Procedure
	FAT and SAT results		Records/reports	Reports
	Qualification plans		Instructions	Procedure
	Testing reports		Records/reports	Reports
	Verification (executed) checklist (Annex 11-3.3)		Records/reports	Records
	Technical review reports		Records/reports	Reports
Installation	IQ, OQ, and PQ (Annex 11-4.7)		Instructions	Protocol
	Executed IQ, OQ, and PQ		Records/reports	Records
	Validation/qualification results and summaries		Records/reports	Reports
	Traceability analysis report (Annex 11-4.4)		Records/reports	Reports

(continued)

Table 21.1   System Documents Grouping (continued)

SLC	Document[a]	Group[b]	Subgroup[c]
Operation	Standard operating procedures (SOPs) (refer to Chapter 22) including system life cycle (Annex 11-4.5), data migration (Annex 11-4.8), data access (Annex 11-7), data storage (Annex 11-7), backup and restore (Annex 11-7.2), printouts generation and verification (Annex 11 8.1), periodic reviews (Annex 11-11 and 11-9), audit trail requirements (Annex 11-9), configuration management (Annex 11-10), security (Annex 11-12 and US 21 CFR Part 11.10(g) – authority checks), access management (Annex 11-12.2), incident management (Annex 11-13), archiving (Annex 11-17), contingency (Annex 11-16), training (Sections 2.10-2.14, Volume 4 EU Guidelines GMP, Part 1 Chapter 2)	Instructions	Procedure
	Incident (Annex 11-13) and deviation (Annex 11-4.2) reports	Records/reports	Reports
	Periodic review results and metrics reports (Annex 11-11)	Records/reports	Reports
	Self-inspection[i] reports	Records/reports	Reports
	Computer systems inventory (Annex 11-4.3)	Records/reports	Reports
	Periodic review results and metrics reports (Annex 11-11)	Records/reports	Reports
	Inventory listing(s) (Annex 11-4.3)	Records/reports	Reports
	Periodic archiving verification report (Annex 11-17)	Records/reports	Reports
Maintenance	Periodic archiving verification (Annex 11-17)	Instructions	Protocol
	Data migration plans (Annex 11-4.8)	Instructions	Procedure
	Data migration checklists (Annex 11-4.8)	Instructions	Protocol
	Remediation plans (Annex 11-11)	Instructions	Procedures

	Change control records (Annex 11-4.2, Annex 11-10)	Records/reports	Records
	Change control reports (Annex 11-4.2, Annex 11-10)	Records/reports	Reports
	Access authorization records (Annex 11-12.3)	Records/reports	Records
	Audit trail records (Annex 11-12.4)	Records/reports	Records
	Personnel training records (Annex 11-2)	Records/reports	Records
	Internal quality audits reports	Records/reports	Reports
	Incident (Annex 11-13) and deviation (Annex 11-4.2) reports	Records/reports	Reports
Retirement	Retirement plans	Instructions	Procedure
	Data migration checklists (Annex 11-4.8)	Instructions	Instructions
	Retirement summary reports	Records/reports	Reports

a. M. Roemer, "New Annex 11: Enabling Innovation," *Pharmaceutical Technology*, June 2011.
b. EudraLex, The Rules Governing Medicinal Products in the European Union, Volume 4, "Good Manufacturing Practice, Medicinal Products for Human and Veterinary Use, Chapter 4: Documentation," Revision 1, June 2011.
c. EudraLex, The Rules Governing Medicinal Products in the European Union, Volume 4, "Good Manufacturing Practice, Medicinal Products for Human and Veterinary Use, Chapter 4: Documentation," Revision 1, June 2011.
d. Specification: Describes in detail the requirements the computer system or component have to conform. A specification serves as a basis for quality evaluation.
e. Procedures: Give directions for performing certain operations.
f. Reports: Document the conduct of particular exercises, projects, or investigations, together with results, conclusions, and recommendations.
g. Records: Provide evidence of various actions taken to demonstrate compliance with instructions.
h. Protocol: Give instructions for performing and recording certain discrete operations.
i. EudraLex, Volume 4, "Good Manufacturing Practice (GMP) Medicinal Products for Human and Veterinary Use, Part I–Basic Requirements for Medicinal Products, Chapter 9: Self Inspections."

Life Cycle

"All phases in the life of the system from initial requirements until retirement including design, specification, programming, testing, installation, operation, and maintenance."

EU Annex 11—Glossary

In addition, records should document the outcome of the activities carried out and parameters measured. The system should provide a means of gathering information, confirmation of performance, and traceability.[*]

In the software-engineering context, computer documentation is regarded as software. The application software and system-level software are considered a set of instructions to the computer infrastructure, input devices, and output devices. It is like a procedural control to a regulated user. All regulatory provisions applicable to software are also applicable to its documentation. The configuration management (Annex 11-10) in Annex 11 is the essential control applicable to the computer documentation.

There are two types of documentation used to manage and record GMP compliance: instructions (directions and requirements) and records/reports. Refer to Table 21.1.

The instructions and records/reports are generated during the SLC of the computer system. The computer documentation may be either printed material or electronic records, such as computer files, storage media, or film. The more added documents written, the higher the cost of managing them due to the increasing difficulty of keeping the documents consistent with the "as is" computer system.

SLC computer documents are submitted for retention to the appropriate document control area and retained for a period at least as long as specified by the predicated regulations applicable to the system. They must be ensured to the appropriate version control and, as any record, integrity of the document throughout the retention period. The documentation retention period of computer systems supporting manufacturing areas should be until the retirement of the system plus the storage period required for the last batch of finished drugs processed by the computer system. Until the

---

[*] TGA, "Australian Code of Good Manufacturing Practice for Human Blood and Blood Components, Human Tissues and Human Cellular Therapy Products," Version 1.0 April 2013.

retention period is achieved, the computer system's documentation must be available for inspection by a regulatory agency or competent authority in a timely fashion. Obsolete information must be archived or destroyed in accordance with a written record retention plan.

All computer system–related documentation must be rigorously controlled (Annex 11-10) to ensure that it is consistent with the system in operation and to ensure that the computer system can be properly operated and maintained. This control includes an inventory list.*

If the computer documentation is managed by a computer system (e.g., Electronic Document Management System [EDMS]), only authorized persons (Annex 11-12.1) should be able to enter or modify electronic files representing documents in the computer, and there should be a record of changes and deletions (Annex 11-9); access should be restricted by passwords or other means (Annex 11-12.1) and the result of entry of critical data should be independently checked (Annex 11-6).†

The e-recs in the EDMS represent computer documentation and must comply with the data integrity guidelines established by Annex 11. Refer to Chapter 26.

Specific validation issues of most EDMSs include:

- continuity readability following software upgrades
- integrity of the document during conversion
- production, storage, and retrieval of multiple renditions of a document
- storage of signatures associated with documents

The quality attributes, which are applicable to any type of document, are unambiguous, appropriate, comprehensive, available, accessible, followed, and periodically reviewed. The content of the computer system documents must be consistent with the type of software developed and the risk of the computer system. In addition, documentation must satisfy five basic elements: they are written, appropriate, clear, verified, and approved.

Test scripts and test results, which are part of a formal inspections and testing activity, should contain appropriate information that clearly identifies them. This information may include an identification number that is

---

* EudraLex, The Rules Governing Medicinal Products in the European Union, Volume 4, "Good Manufacturing Practice, Medicinal Products for Human and Veterinary Use, Chapter 4: Documentation," Section 4.32, Revision 1, June 2011.
† TGA, "Australian Code of Good Manufacturing Practice for Human Blood and Blood Components, Human Tissues and Human Cellular Therapy Products," Version 1.0 April 2013.

traceable to a requirement identification number, the revision number of the document, the test execution or review date, and the name and signature of the person who conducted the test or review.

Summary*

The following documentation and records for the computer system should be available:

- a written protocol for the initial verification and prospective validation of the computer system
- a general description (including diagrams as appropriate) of the system, its components, and operating characteristics
- a list of programs with a brief description of each
- diagrams of hardware layout and interaction, system logic, or other schematic forms for manufacturing systems software packages (excluding Operating Systems and similar)
- a review of hardware and software "start-up" and "normal run" fault logs during development and subsequent ongoing use of the computer system
- records of evaluation data to demonstrate that the system is operating as stated (verification stage and ongoing monitoring)
- range of limits for operating variables
- details of access security levels/controls
- details of formal change control procedures
- procedure for ongoing evaluation
- records of operator training

References

EudraLex, The Rules Governing Medicinal Products in the European Union, Volume 4, "Good Manufacturing Practice, Medicinal Products for Human and Veterinary Use, Chapter 4: Documentation," Section 4.32, Revision 1, June 2011.

M. Roemer, "New Annex 11: Enabling Innovation," *Pharmaceutical Technology*, June 2011.

---

* TGA, "Australian Code of Good Manufacturing Practice for Human Blood and Blood Components, Human Tissues and Human Cellular Therapy Products," Version 1.0 April 2013.

TGA, "Australian Code of Good Manufacturing Practice for Human Blood and Blood Components, Human Tissues and Human Cellular Therapy Products," Version 1.0 April 2013.

Chapter 22

Relevant Procedural Controls

Introduction

The integrity of the information managed by a computer system is protected by procedural controls more than by the technology used to apply the controls.

Procedural Controls

"Give directions for performing certain operations."

EudraLex, Volume 4, Chapter 4: Documentation, Revision 1, June 2011

Procedural controls provide instructions for essential activities of each aspect of the computer system development: operations; maintenance; retirement; and, overall, the validation of computer systems. They address all aspects of software engineering, software quality assurance, and operations of computer systems.

The European Compliance Academy (ECA) published a list on EU-GMP SOPs (Standard Operating Procedures) needed in a GMP environment.[*] SOPs required by EU-GMP are mainly defined in the EU Guidelines to Good

---

[*] http://www.gmp-compliance.org/enews_4431_Which-SOPs-are-required-by-GMP_8382,9074,Z-QAMPP_n.html, GMP News, 20/08/2014

Manufacturing Practice of EudraLex Vol. 4 (EU-GMP Guide). There is no comprehensive list provided, but Chapter 4 of Part 1 (Documentation) of the Guide gives some examples:

> There should be written policies, procedures, protocols, reports and the associated records of actions taken or conclusions reached, where appropriate, for the following examples:
>
> > Validation and qualification of processes, equipment and systems
> > Equipment assembly and calibration
> > Technology transfer
> > Maintenance, cleaning and sanitation
> > Personnel matters including signature lists, training in GMP and technical matters, clothing and hygiene and verification of the effectiveness of training
> > Environmental monitoring
> > Pest control
> > Complaints
> > Recalls
> > Returns
> > Change control
> > Investigations into deviations and nonconformances
> > Internal quality/GMP compliance audits
> > Summaries of records where appropriate (e.g., product quality review)
> > Supplier audits

Chapter 4.30 requires that operating procedures "should be available for major items of manufacturing and test equipment."

From the above list it can be determined the procedures covering computer technologies may include System Life Cycle (Annex 11-4.5), Risk Management (Annex 11-1), Programming Standards, Data Migration (Annex 11-4.8), Data Access (Annex 11-7), Data Storage (Annex 11-7), Backup and Restore (Annex 11-7.2), Printouts Generation and Verification (Annex 11-8.1), Periodic Reviews (Annex 11-11 and 11-9), Audit Trail (Annex 11-9), Configuration Management (Annex 11-10), Security (Annex 11-12 and US 21 CFR Part 11.10(g) – Authority Checks), Access Management (Annex 11-12.2), Incident Management (Annex 11-13), Archiving (Annex 11-17), Remediation (Annex 11-11), Signature Lists (Annex 11-2), Supplier Audits (Annex 11-3.2), ongoing monitoring, personnel responsibilities, retirement, and so on.

Many of the above procedures are discussed in this book. Chapter 23 discusses the procedural controls applicable to maintenance and operation.

One of the most important procedures to be established for computer systems in GMP-regulated activities is the procedure applicable to keeping the integrity of the critical electronic records (refer to Chapter 27). There is no requirement in the EU GMPs to maintain electronic copies of records in preference to other media such as microfiche or paper. If the regulated user decides to maintain regulated records in electronic format, Annex 11 provides the regulatory agencies or competent authority expectations to generate, maintain, retain, and retire critical records for the period established by the applicable predicate rule.

Each procedural control applicable to a computer system must contain the pertinent GMP controls. If the regulated user does not have complete instructions or does not understand what he needs to do, the outcome can be unexpected results or operational or maintenance failures.

Fixing each unexpected result or failure will imply a costly remediation project without counting the paperwork tracing the remediation with plans, specifications, testing, and effectiveness (Annex 11-13).

As any GMP document, the quality attributes applicable to all procedural controls are appropriate, clear, and consistent with related procedures; adhere to regulatory, industry, and company standards; and are approved, available, accessible, followed, controlled, and periodically reviewed. The SLC process must be consistent with the applicable computer system's validation procedural controls.

Table 21.1 depicts some sample procedures that are mapped to Annex 11. To summarize Table 21.1, procedural controls for computer systems should be available for the following activities:

- Development and maintenance of computer systems
- Operation of computer systems
- Management of the access to computer systems and management of the records
- Retention and storage of data
- Prevention of unauthorized access to the data
- Loss management procedures to de-authorize lost, stolen, missing, or otherwise potentially compromised tokens, cards, and other devices
- System restart and the recovery of data
- Management of electronic signatures

All procedural controls must be reviewed periodically in order to ensure that they remain accurate and effective. Where appropriate, a number of topics may be combined into a single written procedure. Wherever possible, procedures should be established at a level that allows them to be utilized across a number of implementation and maintenance projects and systems. When new procedures should be needed, existing written procedures are reviewed to determine if they can be upgraded to include new requirements or processes. Redundant procedures must be avoided.

The project team and the system owner should determine which procedures are appropriate for a particular system development, validation, or maintenance activity.

The effectiveness of these procedural controls must be periodically verified.

Reference

EudraLex, The Rules Governing Medicinal Products in the European Union, Volume 4, "Good Manufacturing Practice, Medicinal Products for Human and Veterinary Use, Chapter 4: Documentation," Sections 4.22-4.32, Revision 1, June 2011.

Chapter 23

Maintaining the Validated State in Computer Systems

Introduction*

In the regulated life science industries, plenty of attention is paid to the validation of new computer systems and associated infrastructure.

Def: Validated

It is used to indicate a status to designate that a system or software complies with applicable GMP requirements.

After the release of the computer systems to support operations, the Annex 11 Operational Phase of these systems initiates. This is the period of time in which relevant processes are in place to operate, monitor for satisfactory performance, modify as necessary to conform to user and regulatory requirements, and correct identified faults and failures.

Computer systems maintenance and operations create a treat to the validated state of the systems by altering the delivered validated computer systems or baseline to meet the changing needs of users or intended use.

---

* This chapter is an update of a paper published in August 2013 by the Institute of Validation Technology, http://www.ivtnetwork.com/article/maintaining-validated-state-computer-systems.

The primary reasons a system development is not complete without the operational phase are the presence of latent defects in the computer system and changes that occur in its operational environment. Over 67% of the relative cost of the system will be accounted to the computer system's maintenance.[*] A percentage of this budget will be assigned to the revalidation effort.

It is very common in our industry to observe that a few years after deploying a computer system, deficient operational supporting processes or the incorrect implementation of such processes nullify the validated state of the computer system, rousing remediation activities. This situation is a typical one across multiple computer systems, provoking a remediation project across the company and adding cost to the operational life of many computer systems.

This chapter provides a brief description of the typical operational life activities and processes in support to preserve the validated state of computer systems performing regulated operations.

Operational Life

After the system has been released for operation, the computer system operational life activities take over.[†]

The Operational Phase is governed by two key processes: operation and maintenance.

The operation defines the activities of the organization that provides the service of operating a computer system in its live environment for its users.

The maintenance defines the activities of the organization that provides the service of managing modifications to the software product to keep it current and in operational fitness. This process includes, as applicable, the migration and retirement of the computer system.

To maintain uniformity during the maintenance period, the maintenance activities must be governed by the same procedural controls followed during the development period.

Written procedural controls must be available for the operation and maintenance of computer systems.[‡]

---

[*] Zelkowitz et al., 1979.

[†] López, O. *21 CFR Part 11: Complete Guide to International Computer Validation Compliance for the Pharmaceutical Industry,* CRC Press, Boca Raton, FL, 2004, 111–115.

[‡] ICH, *Good Manufacturing Practice Guide for Active Pharmaceutical Ingredients,* Q7, Section 5.44, November 10, 2000.

Operational Activities

Routine use of computer systems during the operational life requires procedural controls describing how to perform operational activities. These operational procedural controls must be in place and approved by the appropriate individuals. The execution of these procedural controls should be monitored by the regulated user to verify the accurate implementation and adherence.

These procedural controls should be reviewed on a periodic basis as in line with the local retention policy.

In addition, it is vital that management ensure that the relevant regulated users are trained accordingly.

Key operational procedural controls are

■ *Archiving.* In the context of the regulated user, archives consist of records that have been selected for permanent or long-term preservation on the grounds of their evidentiary value. All computer system baselines should be archived in an environmentally controlled facility, as applicable, that is suitable for the material being archived, and that is secure and, where possible, protected from environmental hazards. A record of all archived materials should be maintained. Periodically, the archived records "should be checked for accessibility, readability, and integrity" (Annex 11-17).

■ *Backups.* A backup process must be implemented to allow for recovery of the system following any failure that compromises its integrity.* Integrity and accuracy of backup data and the ability to restore the data should be checked during validation and monitored periodically (EU Annex 11.7.2). The frequency of backups depends on data criticality, amount of stored data, and frequency of data generation. The procedural controls establishing the backup process must be in place for ensuring the integrity of backups (secure storage location, adequately separated from the primary storage location, and so on). This may be part of a more general disaster recovery plan.

■ *Business Continuity.* Business continuity (Annex 11-16) procedural controls, including disaster recovery procedural controls, ensure minimal disruption in the case of loss of data or any part of the system. It is necessary to ensure that the integrity of the data is not compromised

---

* OMCL Network/EDQM of the Council of Europe. *Validation of Computerized Systems—Core Document,* July 2009.

during the return to normal operation. At the lowest level, this may mean the accidental deletion of a single file, in which case a procedural control should be in place for restoring the most recently backed-up copy. At the other extreme, a disaster such as a fire could result in loss of the entire system. The procedural control employed should be tested regularly, and all relevant personnel should be made aware of its existence and trained to use it. A copy of the procedural controls should be maintained off-site.

■ *Infrastructure Maintenance.* The procedural controls applicable for the preventative maintenance and repair of the infrastructure provide a mechanism for anticipating problems and, as a consequence, possible loss of data. In addition to the typical infrastructure elements such as system-level software, servers, wide area network, local area manager, and the associated components, the infrastructure includes UPSs and other emergency power generators. Modern infrastructure hardware usually requires minimum maintenance for the reason that electronic circuit boards, for example, are usually easily replaced and cleaning may be limited to dust removal. Diagnostic software is usually available from the supplier to check the performance of the computer system and to isolate defective integrated circuits. Maintenance procedural controls should be included in the organization's procedural control. The availability of spare parts and access to qualified service personnel are important for the smooth operation of the maintenance program. Annex 11 Principle 2 governs the maintenance of infrastructure.

■ *Problem Reporting.* The malfunction or failure of computer system components, incorrect documentation, or improper operation that makes the proper use of the system impossible for an undetermined period characterize some of the incidents that can affect the correct operation of a computer system (Annex 11-13). These system incidents may become nonconformances. In order to remedy problems quickly, a procedural control must be established to record by the users of the system any computer system failures. This enables the reporting and registration of any problems encountered by the users of the system.

■ *Problem Management.* Reported problems can be filtered according to whether their cause lies with the user or with the system itself and can be fed back into the appropriate part of the supplier's organization. In order to remedy problems quickly, a procedural control must be established if the system fails or breaks down. Any failures, the results of the analysis of the failure, and, as applicable, any remedial actions taken must be documented (Annex 11-13). Those problems that require a remedial action involving changes to any baseline are then managed through a Change Control process (Annex 11-10).

■ *Retirement.* The retirement of computer systems performing regulated operations is a critical process. The purpose of the "Retirement Period" is to replace or eliminate the current computer system and associated interfaces and, if applicable, ensure the availability of the data that has been generated by it for conversion, migration, or retirement. The applications listing shall be updated accordingly after the application listed in the approved Retirement Final Report. The update should include that the system is no longer in production and retired (Annex 11-4.3).

■ *Restore.* A procedural control for regular testing of restoring backup data (Annex 11-7.2), to verify the proper integrity and accuracy of data, must be in place.

■ *Security.* Computer systems security (Annex 11-12) includes the authentication of users and access controls. Security is a key component for maintaining the trustworthiness of a computer system and associated records. Security is an ongoing element to consider and is subject to improvement. In particular, after a system has been released for use, it should be constantly monitored to uncover any security violations. Any security violation must be followed up and analyzed, and proper action should be taken to avoid a recurrence. The security includes access, including adding and removing authorized users; virus management; password management; and physical security measures. The level of access is to be based on the assigned duties (Annex 11-2).

■ *Training.* All staff maintaining, operating, and using computer systems that perform GMP-regulated activities must have documented evidence of training in the area of expertise. For users, the training will concentrate on the correct use of the computer system and how to report any failure or deviation from the normal operating condition and security. The training must be based on defined responsibilities and must include GMPs. The training records must be kept.*

---

* EudraLex, The Rules Governing Medicinal Products in the European Union, Volume 4, "Good Manufacturing Practice, Medicinal Products for Human and Veterinary Use, Chapter 2: Personnel," Sections 2.10–2.14, Revision 1, August 2013.

Maintenance Activities

The validated status of computer systems performing regulated operations is subject to threat from changes in its operating environment, which may be either known or unknown.

The January 2011 EudraLex Volume 4, Annex 11—Computerised Systems establishes in Item 10 that "any changes to a computerised system including system configurations should only be made in a controlled manner in accordance with a defined procedure."

The above statement is consistent with other regulations and guidelines such as US FDA 21 CFR 211.68, 820.30(i), 820.70(i), 820.40, 11.10(d), 11.10(e); WHO–Technical Report Series, No. 937, 2006, Annex 4, Section 12; and PIC/S PI 011-3 (Part Three).

Explicitly, Section 3.3 of the World Health Organization (WHO)* stipulates three events to cover during the maintenance of computer systems:

■ *Verification and revalidation.* After a suitable period of running a new system, it should be independently reviewed and compared with the system specification and functional specification. The periodic verification must include data checks, including any audit trail. Computer systems used to control, monitor, or record functions that may be critical to the safety of a product should be checked for accuracy at intervals of sufficient frequency to ensure that the system is under control. If part of a computerized system that controls a function critical to the safety of the product is found not to be accurate, then the safety of the product back to the last known date that the equipment was accurate must be determined.

■ *Change control.* Modifications to the computer systems shall be made only in accordance with a defined procedural control, which includes provision for checking, approving, and implementing the modification or adjustment (Annex 11-10). Each modification should be reviewed, impact and risk assessed, authorized, documented, tested, and approved before implementation.

■ *Checks.* Data should be checked periodically to confirm that they have been accurately and reliably recorded or transferred. These checks include the following EU Annex 11 items: Data (11.5), Accuracy Checks (11.6), and Data Storage (11.7).

---

* WHO, *Validation of Computerised Systems*, Technical Report 937, Annex 4 in Appendix 5, 2006.

Summary

The GMP-regulated applications and infrastructure must be well maintained during the Operational Phase ensuring that the systems remain in a validated state and providing cost savings to the maintenance of the computer systems.

The Operational Phase consists of:

- Ensuring that system changes are performed according to the approved change control procedure
- Maintaining training records for users and technical support personnel
- Controlling user access
- Conducting periodic reviews based on established criteria
- Ensuring that data are backed up and archived in accordance within established schedules
- Identifying and tracking system problems and related corrective actions
- Maintaining configuration items

The above activities must be outlined in written and approved procedural controls.

References

EudraLex, The Rules Governing Medicinal Products in the European Union, Volume 4, "Good Manufacturing Practice, Medicinal Products for Human and Veterinary Use, Chapter 2: Personnel," Sections 2.10–2.14, Revision 1, August 2013.

EudraLex, The Rules Governing Medicinal Products in the European Union, Volume 4, "Good Manufacturing Practice, Medicinal Products for Human and Veterinary Use, Chapter 4: Documentation," Sections 4.22–4.32, Revision 1, June 2011.

López, O. *21 CFR Part 11: Complete Guide to International Computer Validation Compliance for the Pharmaceutical Industry,* Boca Raton, FL: CRC Press, 2004, 111–115.

Chapter 24

Annex 11 and the Cloud

R.D. McDowall
Principal, McDowall Consulting

Yves Samson
Director, Kereon AG

Overview of the Chapter

This chapter is unlike most of the others in this book, as it requires several interlinking strands in Annex 11 and the general chapters of EU GMP to be presented and discussed. In addition, some readers may not be familiar with the concept of the cloud or the regulatory implications of cloud computing. Therefore, this chapter will be structured as follows:

- Regulatory requirements of Annex 11 and some of the other EU GMP general chapters
- A definition of cloud computing and the focus on the main types for pharmaceutical companies
- Requirements for IT infrastructure qualification as per the Principle of Annex 11
- Selection of a hosting company including the benefits of an audit
- Main elements of the agreement between the company and the service provider
- Operational and monitoring phase of the work

EU GMP Annex 11

The requirements for GMP-compliant cloud computing are contained in several sections of EU GMP Annex 11[1] as shown in the following:

Principle:
IT Infrastructure shall be qualified.

1. Risk Management:
   Risk management should be applied throughout the life cycle of the computerized system taking into account patient safety, data integrity, and product quality. As part of a risk management system, decisions on the extent of validation and data integrity controls should be based on a justified and documented risk assessment of the computerized system.
2. Personnel:
   There should be close cooperation between all relevant personnel such as Process Owner, System Owner, Qualified Persons, and IT. All personnel should have appropriate qualifications, level of access, and defined responsibilities to carry out their assigned duties.
3. Suppliers and Service Providers:
   3.1 When third parties (e.g., suppliers, service providers) are used, for example, to provide, install, configure, integrate, validate, maintain (e.g., via remote access), modify, or retain a computerized system or related service or for data processing, formal agreements must exist between the manufacturer and any third parties, and these agreements should include clear statements of the responsibilities of the third party. IT departments should be considered analogous. (Note that this requirement should also take into consideration the applicable requirements in EU GMP Chapter 7 on Outsourcing[2]).
   3.2 The competence and reliability of a supplier are key factors when selecting a product or service provider. The need for an audit should be based on a risk assessment.
7. Data Storage
   7.1 Data should be secured by both physical and electronic means against damage.
   7.2 Regular backups of all relevant data should be done. Integrity and accuracy of backup data and the ability to restore the data should be checked during validation and monitored periodically.

10. Change Control

Any changes to a computerized system including system configurations should be made only in a controlled manner in accordance with a defined procedure.

12. Security

12.1 Physical or logical controls should be in place to restrict access to computerized systems to authorized persons. Suitable methods of preventing unauthorized entry to the system may include the use of keys, pass cards, personal codes with passwords, biometrics, restricted access to computer equipment, and data storage areas.

13. Incident Management

All incidents, not only system failures and data errors, should be reported and assessed. The root cause of a critical incident should be identified and should form the basis of corrective and preventive actions.

16. Business Continuity

For the availability of computerized systems supporting critical processes, provisions should be made to ensure continuity of support for those processes in the event of a system breakdown (e.g., a manual or alternative system). The time required to bring the alternative arrangements into use should be based on risk and appropriate for a particular system and the business process it supports. These arrangements should be adequately documented and tested.

Note that this chapter also needs to be read in conjunction with Chapter 6 and Chapter 25 in this book.

The relationships between the various clauses of Annex 11 through a cloud-computing life cycle are shown in Figure 24.1. We will discuss three main phases in this chapter:

1. Selection of an appropriate cloud provider that includes the assessment of the quality management system, qualification of the IT infrastructure, and training of all staff involved with operating it including GMP awareness as it relates to their work
2. Negotiating the contract to include measurable levels of service and backup of the data
3. Operation and monitoring phase

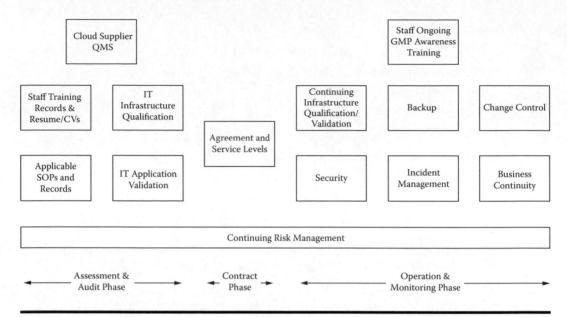

Figure 24.1 Relationship between the applicable Annex 11 requirements and the life cycle of cloud computing.

A fourth phase of the life cycle is de-clouding, which is the orderly migration of data from the cloud to another provider, application, or archive, which will not be discussed in this chapter and the reader is referred to the article by Stokes.[3] However, de-clouding must be considered when selecting a supplier and negotiating the contract for services with a supplier.

Legal Requirements

In addition to GXP regulations on the IT infrastructure, there may also be legal requirements to consider; these impact three main areas of a pharmaceutical company:

- Data privacy
- Intellectual property
- Physical location of the server

Data Privacy

When a company is considering moving data to external cloud-based solutions, it should be aware that the data stored into the cloud are implicitly available for and readable by third parties, for example, NSA. Furthermore, if a pharmaceutical company wants to store patient-related data, there are mandatory requirements regarding the confidentiality of patient-related data that must be followed; therefore, the decision to work with a cloud service provider must be made carefully.

There is also European Directive 95/46/EC[4] on the protection of personal data to consider. The United States has developed the Safe Harbor agreement,[5] which is intended to be compliant with the directive. Unfortunately, the NSA has gotten around this using PRISM. The US Patriot Act[6] requires a service provider to hand over data to the US government without requiring a court order or even informing the data owner. See Table 24.1.

Intellectual Property

Moving to a company external cloud-based solution implies that the data confidentiality will be more limited than for data stored internally, as long as the company maintains a reasonable level of information security.

During the past 25 years, several companies made bad—sometimes fatal—decisions in cases of disregarded nondisclosure agreements. Such troubles were possible because such agreements cannot supersede the local law. If intellectual property is weakly protected in a specific country, no nondisclosure agreement can improve the situation. This specific scenario applies in case of cloud-based data located in such countries, too.

Table 24.1 GXP and Legal Considerations for Cloud Computing

Area	Key Questions
GXP Requirements	What GXP constraints apply on the data stored in an external cloud?
	In particular, are these constraints compatible with the legal requirements applying on a company external cloud?
Legal Requirements	What laws can apply to the data stored into a company external cloud?
	What are the applicable legal constraints in case of litigation?
Knowledge Management	How business critical are the data that should be stored into a company external cloud?
	Could the future business development of the company be significantly jeopardized if the stored data were accessed by unauthorized users?

Physical Location of the Server

Although any system running in the cloud will be virtualized, the question is where is the system physically located? From a GXP perspective, this is very important because the data contained in a system could be subject to impounding or sequestration by a regulatory agency.

Additionally, in case of litigation, it will be necessary to identify clearly where, at which location, and on which physical servers and infrastructure storage data are stored to ensure that local authorities can have access to the data or that data sequestration can be directly performed.

Summary of GXP and Legal Requirements

Making a long story short, the applicable constraints and requirements should be considered on several levels as shown in Table 24.1. It should be clear that today no state or country can provide warranty that, from a legal point of view, data stored into a company external cloud remain confidential without any unauthorized access by a third party.

What Is Cloud Computing?

The best definition of cloud computing is found in National Institute of Standards and Technology (NIST) SP800-145.[7] This is a very short document of about seven pages in length that describes the three main elements of cloud computing. From this document, one can derive Figure 24.2 to show the permutations that are possible with the cloud. Moving from left to right across the top of Figure 24.2, we can look at the elements of cloud computing in more detail to make more sense of the technology and approaches used. In essence, three elements comprise the cloud:

■ Customer requirements
■ Service model
■ Delivery model

All three elements need to be considered, but as we summarize at the end of this section, in our opinions we can narrow down many of the options to consider just one or two simply from the perspective of mitigating regulatory risk.

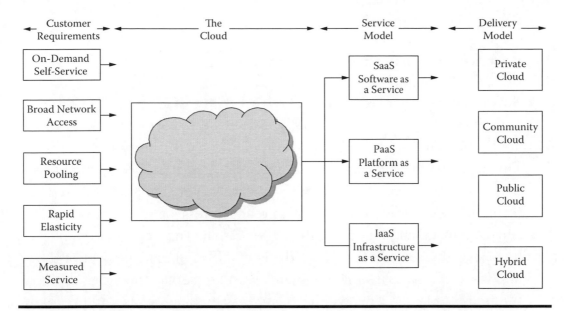

Figure 24.2 Major elements of cloud computing derived from NIST SP800-145. (Interpreted from P. Mell and T. Grance, *The NIST Definition of Cloud Computing*, NIST Special Publication 800-145, National Institute of Standards and Technology, Gaithersburg, MD, 2011.)

Customer Requirements for Cloud Computing

According to NIST, there are five main customer requirements for cloud computing:

- **On-demand self-service.** The customer has the ability to expand computing capabilities (e.g., server time, data storage) automatically without requiring discussion with the service provider.
- **Broad network access.** Services and capabilities are available over the network and are accessed mainly via a browser.
- **Resource pooling.** A provider's computing resources are pooled to serve multiple consumers using a multi-tenant model, with different physical and virtual resources dynamically assigned and reassigned according to consumer demand.
- **Rapid elasticity.** IT capabilities can be agreed and released, in some cases automatically, to accommodate customer demand.
- **Measured service.** Resource usage can be monitored, controlled, and reported, providing transparency for both the provider and user of the utilized service.

Cloud Service Models

Three service models can be provided by a hosting company:

- **Software as a Service (SaaS).** Perhaps the most common cloud computing service model is SaaS, which is the provision of one or more applications to a pharmaceutical customer to meet its business needs. This can vary from e-mail, office applications such as word processing, to GXP applications. Typically, the applications will be delivered through a web browser (thin client architecture) to reduce additional software installation costs for the organization. The important point to note with the SaaS service model is that overall management of the application and environment remains with the service provider and not the registered user. This will have issues with some quality and regulatory requirements, as we will discuss later in this chapter. However, the user usually will be responsible for user account management and possibly application configuration depending on the delivery model used, which we will discuss in the next section.

- **Infrastructure as a Service (IaaS).** This service model provides computer infrastructure via the Internet allowing an organization to expand computer infrastructure on demand. Typically, the IaaS provider has large physical servers on which virtual machines are created on demand for each customer to use and install its own operating systems and applications. If required, data storage facilities can be added. In this service model, the consumer has control over the operating systems, applications, and data storage but does not control the underlying cloud infrastructure.

- **Platform as a Service (PaaS).** The third cloud computing service model is really for software developers and is the provision of infrastructure and a development environment to create, test, and deploy applications. The provider's development environment can include programming languages, libraries, services, and utilities, which are all supported by the provider. The customer does not manage or control the underlying cloud infrastructure including network, servers, operating systems, or storage but has control over its own developed and deployed applications.

Cloud Services Delivery Modes

Having discussed the service models that can be found under the banner of cloud computing, we need to consider how it will be delivered. According to NIST[3] there are four models:

- **Private cloud.** Here the cloud infrastructure is provided solely for a single organization. The private cloud can be owned, managed, and operated either by the organization or a third party provider and can be located on or off site, but this is typically owned by the provider and is located off site.
- **Community cloud.** This delivery model is the provision of a cloud specifically for a defined community of companies with shared aims, for example, regulatory compliance. Similar to the private cloud, it can be owned by one or more members of the community or a third party and can be located on or off site.
- **Public cloud.** Access to the cloud infrastructure is for anybody, and because of the open access, this delivery model will not be considered further as it can be uncontrolled.
- **Hybrid cloud.** This is a combination of two separate cloud infrastructures (private, community, or public) that are linked to allow data and application portability (e.g., cloud bursting for load balancing between clouds).

Managing and Mitigating Regulatory Risk

Clause 1 of Annex 11 requires that the risk management measures should take into account the impact of the computerized system on patient safety, data integrity, and product quality.[1] Furthermore, this risk assessment needs to be documented. Because moving to the cloud means that several key functions (e.g., security, change control, and backup) are now in the hands of a third party, this places prime importance on managing these risks.

SaaS Service Cloud Options

For the purposes of this chapter, we will limit our discussions to the SaaS service model with delivery via a private cloud. The rationale is twofold: If an organization is storing intellectual property, this needs to be protected; if the focus is development or manufacturing, the data and information generated from these activities need to be protected, and you do not want to run the risk of compromising them with data from another company, regardless of which industry it is in.

Owing to the nature of the cloud, the users are physically and logically separated from the application and the hosting site where the computing resources are located. Business applications such as Enterprise Resource Planning (ERP), Quality Management System (QMS), or Laboratory Information Management System (LIMS) could be operated using cloud computing because the latency of the Internet (delay between entering data and receiving a response from the software) is usually acceptable. However, because the Internet is a public service and out of the laboratory's control, there can be no guarantee of acceptable levels of service unless the company has a dedicated line to the hosting site.

The great advantage of SaaS from the perspective of the company is that the potential financial cost model moves from a capital cost one (purchase of the software and associated licenses) to a revenue cost one (hire of user accounts and the software). However, we need to go into more detail about how an SaaS service can be delivered, and we have two main options to consider.

Single or Multi-Tenant Options

The single tenant option is shown in Figure 24.3. Here the cloud service provider has the computing resources, and each customer has its own version

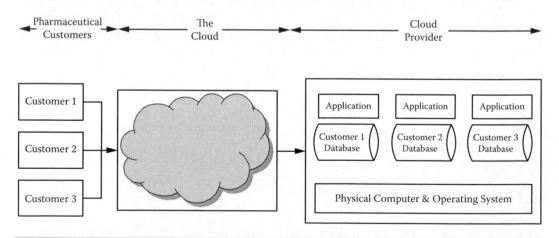

Figure 24.3   An SaaS cloud architecture illustrating isolated installations of an application (single tenant).

of the application with a separate database in separate virtual machines. Separate running instances of an application have a number of advantages:

- Configuration of the application, if available, is possible to meet a company's specific business needs and processes rather than a generic process.
- Your data is in a separate database.
- You set up and control the user account management for the whole of your application instance.
- It is easier to convince an inspector or auditor that you are in control and data integrity is not compromised. (If required, your application can sit on a separate virtual server.)
- Change control is easier and can be phased as each instance of the application is separated. Indeed, specific updates may be omitted if there is no business benefit to an organization.

However, the potential cost savings may not be as great as you think because this approach is similar to running the system in house on your own servers; therefore, a supplier may require a company to purchase the software rather than lease it.

In contrast, the second version of the SaaS is shown in Figure 24.4. This is where the service provider offers a single instance of the application with a single database. Here each company's operations and data are separated logically within a single database (setting up of company-specific user groups) and there is the logical separation of each company's data. Some comments about this approach are as follows:

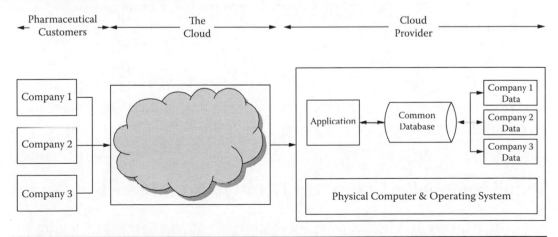

Figure 24.4 An alternative SaaS cloud architecture with a single application with database instance (multi-tenant).

- Costs should be less expensive than with single company instances of the application.
- The application will usually be a one-size-fits-all approach. Because there is only a single instance, it will be difficult to configure the software to an individual laboratory's business processes. Therefore, it will be a take-it-or-leave-it option: There is typically no configuration other than user account management. This means that your business process will need to conform to the application's mode of operation.
- Validation of some elements of data integrity (e.g., shared application and database) can be difficult because accessing another user's portion of the system will not be allowed. However, there could be a good case for having a basic validation that is then confirmed by each regulated company. However, the basic validation may not meet every company's CSV policies and procedures, so there would be some additional work needed.
- Each laboratory's data is separated logically in the database. However, how will you convince an inspector or auditor that one laboratory cannot change the data in a second laboratory's portion of the database?
- Change control will be difficult: Does each company delegate change control to the cloud company? This would be very unlikely because the service provider could issue service packs and application software updates with no consultation with the client companies. There could be a situation where simple patching of the operating system with security patches could be delegated to the service provider who had an appropriate procedure. However, no changes could be made to the application without agreement of all parties involved or a company has a month to evaluate upgrades before there is a universal installation for all customers.

Therefore, for the reasons given above, the single tenant SaaS approach shown in Figure 24.3 is much more preferable to that of the multi-tenant approach illustrated in Figure 24.4.

Requirements for Compliant IT Infrastructure

From the regulations above, there are three basic requirements for IT infrastructure operating in a regulated GXP environment, which can be located within an organization, outsourced to a third party, or in the cloud:

■ IT Infrastructure—physical, virtual, and software elements—must be specified and qualified to show that it works as intended and be kept under change control throughout the operational life. This is to comply with the specific requirements of EU GMP Annex 11 that IT infrastructure be qualified[1] and the expectation of the pharmaceutical industry as evidenced by the GAMP Good Practice Guide on IT Control and Compliance[8] of which the authors of this chapter were contributors.

■ Written procedures (instructions) must be in place and when executed have records to show that the activities actually occurred. Records generated in this and the item above must comply with GXP regulations, for example, documented contemporaneously with the activity and you can identify the individual who performed the work and to comply with the requirements of EU GMP Chapter 4 on documentation.[9]

■ Staff operating the infrastructure must be trained to do their work and additionally in the principles of GXP compliance, especially change control. This is especially important when the cloud provider with which you are contracting has only a few employees and may subcontract large parts of the work to third parties of which you may not be aware. EU GMP Chapter 7 on outsourcing[2] and contract agreements is applicable here.

IT Infrastructure Elements

It is important to understand the scope of IT infrastructure before we go much further in this discussion. From the perspective of GAMP, it consists of category 1 infrastructure software and category 1 hardware.[10]

The category 1 software consists of two types:

■ Established or commercially available layered software (e.g., operating systems, databases, programming languages, etc.)

■ Infrastructure software tools (e.g., network monitoring software, help desk, backup and recovery software and agents, security software, antivirus software, configuration management utilities, etc.)

The software applications, tools, and utilities are installed on category 1 hardware, which is equated to equipment under the GMP regulations that has to be appropriate design, adequate size, and suitably located for its intended purpose.[11, 12] When these qualified components are integrated together, they form the IT infrastructure.

However, care has to be taken with some of the infrastructure tools, for example, help desk depending on how the application is used (help desk tickets develop into change control records). In this case, the application needs to be validated because it contains GXP records.

The basic element of a computerized system is the IT infrastructure that allows any application to run on it. Although it has been a regulatory expectation since the mid-1990s, qualification of IT infrastructure has been a regulatory requirement only since 2011 with the issue of the new version of EU GMP Annex 11 on computerized systems.[1] In the Principle of the Annex, it states simply, *The application should be validated; IT infrastructure should be qualified.* Therefore, regardless of where the IT infrastructure is located—in-house, outsourced to the ends of the globe, or in the cloud—the infrastructure must be qualified in order to run GXP applications. Therefore, one of the prime requirements when selecting a cloud provider is to ensure that both the underlying physical infrastructure and the virtual environments created on it are qualified and kept under control.

What do we mean by qualified and kept under control?

Qualification is defined in the EU GMP glossary as *Action of proving that any equipment works correctly and actually leads to the expected results.*[13] Implicit in this definition is that there must be a definition of what the equipment is to do so that when it is tested the results can be compared with the specification. When the results are compared with what is expected and they match, then the equipment is considered qualified. However, we also need to consider what the word *control* means as well.

Control means that there are procedures in place for carrying out work and, as a result of executing these procedures, records are created that can be reviewed, audited, or inspected at a later date. These procedures including the qualification documents must be preapproved before execution and reviewed after it. As noted above, staff must also be trained in awareness of the applicable GXP regulations because they impact the work within the IT infrastructure. This includes any sub-contracted staff.

Service Providers: Requirements for Audits and Agreements

There are also further requirements that impact a cloud computing solution. EU GMP Annex 11, Section 3.1 states[1]:

> When third parties (e.g., suppliers, service providers) are used, for example, to provide, install, configure, integrate, validate, maintain (e.g., via remote access), modify, or retain a computerized system or related service or for data processing, formal agreements must exist between the manufacturer and any third parties, and these agreements should include clear statements of the responsibilities of the third party. **IT departments should be considered analogous**.

Put simply, there must be an agreement between the IT service provider such as a hosting company and the regulated user (i.e., the pharmaceutical company, contract manufacturer, contract research laboratory, or clinical research organization). This agreement must cover the roles and responsibilities of the people involved and the services offered.

However, before the pen hits the paper, a more important consideration must be taken into account. Do we audit the cloud provider? Annex 11 provides some guidance in this respect.

■ Clause 1 states that risk management should be applied throughout the life cycle of the computerized system taking into account patient safety, data integrity, and product quality.[1]
■ More specifically, Clause 3.2 states: The competence and reliability of a supplier are key factors when selecting a product or service provider. The need for an audit should be based on a risk assessment.[1]
■ However, the audit reports must be shown to an inspector on request as noted in Clause 3.4: Quality system and audit information relating to suppliers or developers of software and implemented systems should be made available to inspectors on request.[1]

Therefore, from a regulatory perspective, have you done demonstrable due diligence? This expected due diligence should not be considered only from a regulatory point of view but also from a business perspective because in many cases the decision to move to a cloud-based solution will impact many

Table 24.2   Additional 21 CFR 11 and Annex 11 Regulations Applicable to IT Infrastructure

Annex 11 Requirements for IT Infrastructure	21 CFR 11 Requirements for IT Infrastructure
• Staff and training records (Annex 11 item 2): Qualifications and CVs/resumes	• GXP predicate rule requirements, e.g.: Qualifications and CVs/resumes of staff
• Training records including initial and ongoing GXP awareness and competence	• Training records including initial and regular ongoing GXP awareness and competence
• Security (Annex 11 items 7.1 and 12)	• 11.10(b) Generate accurate and complete copies of records
• Backup and recovery (Annex 11 item 7.2)	• 11.10(c) Protection of records
• Change control and configuration management (Annex 11 item 10)	• 11.10(d) Limiting access to authorized individuals
• Periodic evaluation (Annex 11 item 11)	• 11.10 (e) Time stamped (audit trails)
• User account management (Annex 11 item 12)	
• Incident management (Annex 11 item 13) documented and linked to CAPA	

types of data, for example, GXP-relevant data and knowledge-related data as well. Table 24.2 shows further GMP related requirements, for example, 21 CFR 11[11] for IT infrastructure that need to be considered as part of an initial audit and included in the agreement between you and the hosting provider.

Although it may seem relatively easy to audit an API or a contract manufacturer, providing objective evidence with a reasonable degree of guarantee that a cloud service provider is delivering a compliant, reliable, and secure service can often be a challenge, as we will demonstrate.

Auditing a Cloud Provider

With the exception of the rare cases of cloud service providers dedicated to the pharmaceutical industry or to the related services, auditing a cloud service provider could represent a challenge. Although the regulated user is focused on a middle- to long-term approach, relying on some certainty, a typical cloud service organization will act with agility, not specifically related to locations, often with rapidly changing personnel, and focused on a best-effort approach. However, ensuring data integrity, accessibility, readability, and confidentiality requires some formal processes and controls, which need to be verified during an audit.

Audit Objectives

When auditing a cloud service provider, it is important not to lose sight of the main objective:

- Generate the confidence in the working capability and accuracy.
- The review of the service provider's Quality Management System (QMS) and the necessary openness and transparency during this review contribute to building the confidence for the future customer–provider relationship.

However, because no organization is perfect, usually the audit outcomes will be as follows:

- Provide rational evidence for confidence.
- Address areas of concerns, with related corrective measures (action plan).

Only if the audited organization accepts the audit findings and agrees to modify its approach through implementing appropriate corrective and improvement measures can an audit make sense for securing a future collaboration. Via this key topic, the clods can be separated from the clouds.

What Are We Auditing Against?

Based on the above explanations, Table 24.3 provides an overview of the main audit areas to be considered.

Does ISO 27001 Certification Provide Compliance with GXP Regulations?

Quality standard and certifications should be leveraged within the specific context of GXP because they represent—at least partially—a significant and

Table 24.3 Key Areas and Criteria for Auditing IT Hosting Providers (excluding the Quality Management System)

Area for Audit	Criteria
• Data integrity maintained throughout record retention period	• Data confidentiality • Data security • Access control and user management • Data retention measures
• Legal requirements placed on data stored in infrastructure	• Intellectual property claims • Patriot Act requirements/Safe Harbor agreements
• Qualified infrastructure	• Correctly designed and specified infrastructure • Correctly installed infrastructure • Verified operation • Qualified infrastructure applications • Authored and approved specifications and designs • Installation plans and records • Component verified/tested to show correct operation vs. the specification • Where appropriate, integration testing to the rest of the infrastructure • All infrastructure applications qualified, for example, network management software
• Data management	• Backup and restore processes • Business continuity and disaster recovery • Archiving
• Change management	• Does the change control procedure involve the data owner for changes to infrastructure? • Does the change control procedure involve the data owner for changes made to the system and application?
• GXP knowledge	• Does the service provider know the regulations and the need for records of activities? • Regulations require an appropriate combination of education, training, and experience • Knowledge of GXP regulations to enable them to perform their job

(continued)

Table 24.3 Key Areas and Criteria for Auditing IT Hosting Providers (excluding the Quality Management System) (continued)

Area for Audit	Criteria
	• There must be regular GXP update training (typically annually) • Formal training materials with assessment of competence
• QA oversight of IT activities is essential	• Knowledge of individual • Quality assurance regulatory requirements • Sufficient technical knowledge of IT infrastructure • Individuals can be either • Business QA with appropriate technical knowledge • Regulatory compliance within IT

reliable basement for the required good practices and for the regulated processes. The quality management system of an IT hosting company can be certified to one or more quality standards; for example:

■ ISO 27001[15]
■ COBIT (Control Objectives for IT)[16]
■ eSCM-SP (eSourcing Capability Model for Service Providers)[17]
■ PCI (Payment Card Industry) or other financial industry regulations

Note: Such quality standards and certifications *cannot* replace GXP regulations, which are mandatory requirements for a regulated user. This is not the place to agree or disagree with the GXP regulatory requirements; they have to be followed.

For example, Montrium has a white paper entitled Qualification Guideline for Microsoft Azure.[18] This document attempts to leverage the various certifications such as ISO 27001 that the Azure cloud platform for PaaS has for GXP compliance. This document is based on the reading and interpretation of audit reports. Using non-GXP standards for meeting regulatory compliance for a hosting company such as physical security, environmental controls, power supplies, and redundancy of these controls is an adequate approach. However, there are a number of basic problems in this document that are either omitted or glossed over:

- There is no mention of GXP awareness training for the Microsoft staff operating Azure (section 2.7.12).
- There is no mention of physical infrastructure qualification performed by Microsoft; the only mention is of the qualification of the customer's virtual environment in section 3.
- In many cases, there is a mention of "compliance" in the Microsoft procedures, but compliance with which standards? This is not mentioned.
- If staff do not have GXP awareness training, are they aware of the need for GXP regulatory documentation requirements outlined in EU GMP Chapter 4 on documentation?[9]

Therefore, the key question is how can a cloud solution be compliant with the GXP regulatory requirements?

Pharmaceutical auditors assessing cloud service providers need to know and understand the main IT quality standards above in order to avoid useless redundancies during audits and assessments. Understanding content and focus of such quality standard and certifications makes it possible to focus an audit on the areas of GXP requirements and procedures that are not really covered by the certification controls, such as GXP training as well as GXP documentation skills. A simple summary of the required approach for a service provider is as follows:

- Say what you do: Have a written procedure that staff are trained to follow.
- Do what you say: Follow the procedure always or document the rational for departing from it.
- Document it: Have records to show that the procedure was followed.

Particular attention should be given to the eSourcing Capability Model (eSCM)[17] because it covers both parties involved in an agreement:

- Service provider: eSCM-SP
- Client or customer: eSCM-CL

eSCM acknowledges that the conditions for a good, efficient, and compliant service delivery define and implement a consistent quality management approach. For this reason, auditing only the service provider based on eSCM-SP without auditing the regulated user (client) based on eSCM-CL is useless because such an approach would be inconsistent. That would be a novel approach for any GXP laboratory because usually the audits are one sided.

Methods of Auditing a Supplier

Given the fact that IT infrastructure is critical for any pharmaceutical company, it is surprising that many decisions are based on financial considerations. One reason for this is that IT generally reports through the finance group of an organization. However, it is important that IT infrastructure, regardless of how it is delivered, provides a reliable and compliant service. From the perspective of a user, much of this is hidden from view: Your workstation is plugged into a socket in the wall, and as long as the required services are provided, are you really worried about what happens at the end of the cable? You assume that IT is under control. Is this a valid assumption? Remember that the process owner (sometimes called the system owner) is responsible for the data generated that will be managed and supported by the IT infrastructure and systems.

Therefore, if outsourcing your IT services and infrastructure, sufficient due diligence needs to be performed to assure you that the service provider knows its job, follows written procedures, produces records, and has appropriately trained staff including all people who are sub-contracted by the service provider. There are three basic options for auditing a supplier, including a cloud service provider:

- Questionnaire only
- Questionnaire plus follow-up teleconference and review of documents
- Questionnaire plus on-site audit and verification of answers

We will consider the advantages and disadvantages of each approach.

Questionnaire

This is the option that is the quickest to perform but leaves you with the least confidence in the supplier. You are reliant on the supplier being honest and truthful when completing the questionnaire. Therefore, you must ensure that the questions asked are searching and, where appropriate, request supporting information, for example, a list of procedures or specifications and evidence of action for the qualification of a server.

When the completed questionnaire is received, it needs to be reviewed and assessed and not thrown in a drawer and forgotten. Are the answers acceptable, or do you need to ask the company for clarification? In the end, you need to make a decision whether to use this supplier, and the reasons for this should be documented in a summary report.

Questionnaire Plus Follow-Up

The next option for supplier assessment is to send the questionnaire and review the completed document as outlined above. Then the next task is to organize a web session/teleconference to review the answers and ask follow-up questions in addition to reviewing the documents. This addition to the questionnaire gives a company an opportunity to go into more detail and verify the answers in the questionnaire. Topic areas can be discussed in detail and approaches to compliance confirmed. One specific issue is the ability to see and check documentation that has not been provided in the questionnaire around the infrastructure: Some companies cite "intellectual property" reasons for refusing to disclose any design documentation. If this happens, then the hosting company should not be considered further.

Questionnaire Plus On-Site Audit

The questionnaire is completed and reviewed as the last two instances; however, in this option there is an on-site audit of the hosting facility or data center and the company offices. Note here that the audit may be in two parts because the offices may not be in the same location as the hosting facility. In fact, the two could be in different countries. The dates of the visit need to be planned and the schedule agreed including time to move between locations if needed. The offices will look at the quality management system including staff organization charts and training records, scope of accreditation—typically for ISO 27001[15]—and procedures with records of activities occurring. Key areas to spend time reviewing during the audit are the organization chart and the staff training records.

- The organization chart should show where sub-contracted staff are used. This is important for a number of reasons: Is there an agreement in place between the service provider and the sub-contracted organization detailing roles and responsibilities?
- Training records, resumes/curricula vitae, and position descriptions for service provider staff including sub-contractors must be reviewed to determine if they have a combination of education, training, and experience.

A problem with ISO standards is that they do not require current resumes or curricula vitae, which are required for the pharmaceutical industry.

■ A specific GMP requirement of US GMP and GLP in §211.25(a),[12] GLP in §58.29,[19] Part 11 in §11.10(i),[14] and EU GMP Annex 11 Clause 2[1] is shown in Table 24.4. Therefore, you must determine if there is sufficient GXP awareness training for the staff of your potential service provider including any sub-contracted personnel. If GXP training was given, then who was the trainer and what were his qualification/training or experience to give it? Failure to understand and probe here can have serious compliance problems later.

Table 24.4　Regulatory Requirements for Staff Training

Regulation	Regulatory Requirement
US GMP: 21 CFR 211.25(a)	Training shall be in the particular operations that the employee performs and in current good manufacturing practice (including the current good manufacturing practice regulations in this chapter and written procedures required by these regulations) as they relate to the employee's functions.
	Training in current good manufacturing practice shall be conducted by qualified individuals on a continuing basis and with sufficient frequency to ensure that employees remain familiar with CGMP requirements applicable to them.
US GLP: 58 CFR 29	(a) Each individual engaged in the conduct of or responsible for the supervision of a nonclinical laboratory study shall have education, training, and experience, or a combination thereof, to enable that individual to perform the assigned functions.
	(b) Each testing facility shall maintain a current summary of training and experience and job description for each individual engaged in or supervising the conduct of a nonclinical laboratory study.
US GMP: 21 CFR 11.10(i)	Determination that persons who develop, maintain, or use electronic record/electronic signature systems have the education, training, and experience to perform their assigned tasks.
EU GMP: Annex 11, Clause 2 Personnel	There should be close cooperation between all relevant personnel such as process owner, system owner, qualified persons, and IT.
	All personnel should have appropriate qualifications, level of access, and defined responsibilities to carry out their assigned duties.

How to Select an IT Service Provider

In this section, we use our experience to help you navigate the cloudy waters of service providers and select an adequate one. Specifically, we provide examples of responses from questionnaires and examples of on-site audits. Many hosting providers have ISO 27001 accreditation, but how many have the requisite GXP knowledge and training to be a suitable hosting provider for regulated healthcare organizations? The process to separate the clouds from the clods is shown in Figure 24.5 and consists of three stages.

Stage 1: Review Provider Websites

The first stage of the assessment process is a remote assessment of each potential hosting provider, which is achieved by looking on their website. You are looking for information about their customers and knowledge of GXP regulations for the pharmaceutical system. Specifically:

- Does the company know about the GXP regulations?
- Is their infrastructure qualified and can they provide a GXP-compliant service?
- Do they have any regulated pharmaceutical customers?

If the answers are no, you have identified the clods and no further action is required. The potential clouds then move to stage 2 of the process.

Case Study Example: A website search of about 20 websites of hosting providers identified only five potential hosting companies worthy of further consideration.

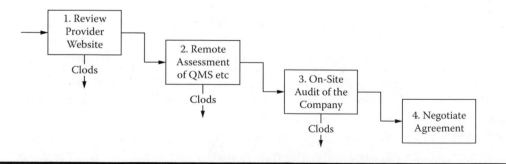

Figure 24.5   Process flow to help select an adequate cloud service provider.

Stage 2: Remote Assessment of the Quality Management System (QMS)

The remaining candidates are then sent a detailed questionnaire that asks questions about their accreditation schemes and their QMS such as quality manual, procedures infrastructure qualification, and staff training and knowledge of GXP regulations. Some potential service providers may state that because they are certified against a specific standard, for example, ISO 27001, that this is acceptable to the pharmaceutical industry. However, ISO 27001 cannot ensure compliance with pharmaceutical industry regulations because there are gaps, as you have seen from the earlier section in this chapter. Therefore, you need to ask specific questions to assess the hosting company's knowledge of pharmaceutical specific regulations. For example:

Question: Are specific controls in place for closed systems (i.e., availability and protection of records, audit trails, sequencing, access, training, documentation, and change control)?
Answer: 21 CFR Part 11 compliance is the responsibility of the customer on a solution-specific basis.

This is an interesting answer to a key question because it demonstrates no understanding of the Part 11 regulation or its interaction with the applicable predicate rule. Therefore, the company should be rejected without any further consideration.

Question: How do you qualify a server?
This question should also request evidence of the server specification and the execution of the installation.
Answer: These documents are confidential and are not disclosed to customers.

This answer to this question means that you have identified another clod and that the company must be rejected. Any service provider is acting as your agent, but you are still responsible for their work. The qualification of a server is important, and the documentation of the process needs to be available during the supplier qualification and for any inspection. We strongly recommend that the availability of any such material be documented in any agreement between you and the company.

You also need to focus on asking questions about backup and recovery, change control, and configuration management and incident management in the questionnaire to check that these functions are carried out in a compliant way.

Case Study Example: The five hosting companies were sent and returned questionnaires. Three companies were rejected because they responded with some of the examples cited above that demonstrated no knowledge of the GXP regulations.

Stage 3: On-Site Audit of the Service Provider

In our view, this stage is essential if GXP critical systems are being hosted externally to the organization and is also in compliance with Annex 11 Clause 3.2[1] because you may be allowed to view only some key documents at the supplier's site. This stage gives you much more detail and knowledge about a supplier than a questionnaire can ever provide. You should cover:

■ Details of the quality policy, quality manual, and procedures. Look at the services offered by the company within the QMS and how these are documented; for example:
  - Building and qualifying the physical infrastructure upon which the virtual systems will be installed
  - Building and qualifying virtual infrastructure components and their integration
  - Operating the infrastructure, both physical and virtual elements
  - Change control processes for physical and virtual infrastructure including the records associated with a sample of change requests— some of these may require requalification of a component
  - See that records are created according to GXP principles
■ Data center facilities. Many hosting companies may not build their own ISO 27001–certified facility but may hire space in one. Therefore, you need to understand where your virtual server is located in case of seizure, etc.

Case Study Example: The remaining two hosting companies were ranked with one as the preferred candidate for an on-site audit and the other held in reserve. Both companies claimed to have qualified IT infrastructure from the returned questionnaires plus any clarification questions. We will look at the audit findings from the preferred candidate together with the responses as shown in Table 24.5. Although the company claimed compliance, you will note that IQ/OQ documents are executed without approvals and that staff who are untrained in GXP awareness are let loose to work on the infra-structure until they have clocked 80 hours. Not an appealing thought. Is this provider classified as cloud or clod?

Because of this audit, the preferred supplier was rejected and the reserve supplier audited. The audit was satisfactory and confirmed qualified

Table 24.5   Audit Findings with Some Hosting Company Responses

Audit Finding	Hosting Company Response
• Installation qualification documents are not preapproved prior to execution.	• <Company> believes this is an inappropriate application of the GAMP standard, and that the standard has been misinterpreted in this case.
• IQ/OQ documents are not executed against equipment specifications to demonstrate fitness for intended use.	• <Company> product delivers qualified hardware, and so this is beyond the scope of the product.
• There is no specification and associated qualification testing, with associated quality assurance oversight, of the hypervisor layer.	• Acknowledged. A plan will be placed to qualify the hypervisor.
• GXP awareness training was given only to staff working greater than 80 hours per year on the qualified infrastructure.	• <Company> considers that staff working only for longer than 80 hours on the infrastructure should be trained in GXP compliance.
• Qualification documents are electronically signed in an EDMS. The electronic signatures are not compliant with the requirements of §11.50.	• <Company> utilizes EDMS as the predominant repository of documentation, and the deployment of EDMS is considered fit for purpose across our client base. Utilization of a different document repository or amendment of its deployment is out of scope of the product.
• The EDMS was incompletely validated by the vendor of the software because only two test cases, both designed to pass, were found in the validation documents. There were no test cases for security, audit trail, or other Part 11 functions.	• <Company> considers this system adequately validated.

infrastructure, GXP-compliant procedures and records, and adequately trained staff including GXP awareness training. They moved to the next stage in the process—the agreement.

What Do We Need in an Agreement?

In every business relationship, contracts are necessary, especially as we have noted under EU GMP Chapter 7 on outsourcing.[2] A service level agreement (SLA) is at first a contract between the user organization and a service provider, in this case a cloud or hosting company. EU GMP Annex 11, section 3.1[1] has been extensively quoted earlier in this chapter, setting the conditions for a formal collaboration between a regulated organization and third parties.

In order to be efficient and useful, an SLA should address some of or all the topics shown in Table 24.6 depending on the type of service required, for example, IaaS or PaaS. The different types of agreements and contracts are shown in Table 24.7.

Occasionally, there may be the need for an Underlying Contract (UC), which is a contract between an IT service provider and a third party. The

Table 24.6   Topics to Address in a Service Level Agreement

Service Level Agreement Content	
Service Delivery[a]	*Controls and Accountability*
• List of relevant (applicable) regulations and rules (policies)	• Controls, i.e., procedures and records of activities
• Specification and qualification of virtual infrastructure items	• Availability of all documents for an audit or inspection
• Change control procedure including regulated user sign-off for major changes	• Quality of service, quality attributes (acceptance criteria)
• Handling usage queries and questions	• Time to resolve issues before escalation
• Fault reporting and response, including feedback processes	• Corrective and preventive measures
• Prioritization of faults	• Underpinning contracts
• Escalation process	• Roles and responsibilities:
• Providing work-arounds	• IT supplier
• Software patching	• Regulated user

(continued)

Table 24.6   Topics to Address in a Service Level Agreement (continued)

Service Level Agreement Content	
Service Delivery[a]	*Controls and Accountability*
• Installation of software upgrades • Resolution and closure • Maintenance of spares and consumables • Software and data backup and recovery • System management, administration, and housekeeping • Support of underlying hardware and infrastructure • Software tools to be used • Routine testing	• Right of audit by regulated user • Right to audit by you • Commercial terms including end-of-contract terms and access to your data if company fails • Exit conditions from the contract including transfer of regulated user data/records

[a] According to GAMP 5 Appendix O2.[10]

Table 24.7   Types of Agreements between a Regulated User and a Service Provider

Agreement Type	Definition
Definitions—SLA vs. OLA	An SLA is an agreement/treaty between a service provider (IT) and the customer who is paying for the service. An OLA is an agreement made between the service provider of an organization and another functional body of the same organization.
Service Level Agreement—SLA	An SLA is legally binding whereas an OLA is a best-effort agreement within an IT infrastructure that defines the relationship among the internal support groups of an organization working to support the SLA.
Operation Level Agreement—OLA	An OLA is an outcome of a particular SLA. Once the SLA is agreed upon, the IT organization conducts sessions to find out what can fit an OLA to enable it to deliver the specified service.
Underlying Contract—UC	The contract is between the IT service provider and a third party to help the service provider deliver agreed services to a regulated customer.

third party provides goods or services that support delivery of an IT service to a customer. The UC defines targets and responsibilities that are required to meet agreed service level targets in an SLA. Such contracts should be clearly identified by elaborating an SLA or OLA because they finally impact the real scope of responsibilities as well as the possible access to the data of the regulated user. It is also important the GXP knowledge and procedures are sufficient within the third party of the UC.

Contract Management: How to Write a Contract

Before any contract can be established, the service provider's QMS and the associated activities must have been audited and the audit results must be considered acceptable. This allows the focus to shift from equipment qualification, which is covered by the QMS, to service delivery, which will be covered at first by the contract.

However, the definition of a service or operation contract requires expertise and a consistent approach. Failing to use the following recommendations can have fatal consequences for the service delivery and in particular for the service compliance. Successful contract management requires the following approach:

- Be careful.
- Be accurate.
- Be precise.
- Be as exhaustive as necessary.
- By reviewing agreements:
  - Be "critical."
  - Keep your eyes open.
- Avoid any assumptions and implicit (not formalized) requirements.

Contract management is a very specific activity with a major legal impact. For this reason, you should not hesitate to take the support of an IT lawyer, as appropriate, and to take advantage of such support. The experience shows regularly that large and global organizations try (and often succeed) to establish service delivery based on ambiguous and contradictory terms of service. Long written contracts with small text containing multiple and complex clauses put the "layman" in an unbearable position.

Particular attention must be given to the exit conditions and break points in the contract. Such conditions are very critical in terms of business capability and business continuity. The most appropriate moment for negotiating safe and acceptable exit conditions is before signing the first contract and before storing the first data in the cloud. The honeymoon period before the contract is signed and any money has changed hands is the best time to negotiate these items.

Operation and Monitoring Phase

The main requirements for the operating and monitoring phase of the cloud life cycle is to ensure that the service levels defined in the SLA are monitored, reviewed, and, where appropriate, updated. In addition, regular audits are essential to ensure that procedures are compliant especially for the areas outlined in Figure 24.1 under this phase of the life cycle: change control, backup, incident management, etc.

References

1. EudraLex, Volume 4, EU Guidelines to Good Manufacturing Practice, Medicinal Products for Human and Veterinary Use, Annex 11–Computerised Systems, June 2011.
2. EudraLex, The Rules Governing Medicinal Products in the European Union, Volume 4, "Good Manufacturing Practice, Medicinal Products for Human and Veterinary Use, Chapter 7: Outsourced Activities," Revision 1, January 2013.
3. D. Stokes, "Compliant Cloud Computing—Managing the Risks," *Pharmaceutical Engineering*, 33(4) 1–11, 2013.
4. Directive 95/46/EC of the European Parliament and of the Council of 24 October 1995 on the protection of individuals with regard to the processing of personal data and on the free movement of such data, http://eur-lex.europa.eu/LexUriServ/LexUriServ.do?uri=CELEX:31995L0046:en:HTML.
5. Safe Harbor US–EU Agreement on Meeting Directive 95/46/EC, http://www.export.gov/safcharbor/indcx.asp.
6. Uniting and Strengthening America by Providing Appropriate Tools Required to Intercept and Obstruct Terrorism Act (Patriot Act), 2001.
7. P. Mell and T. Grance, *The NIST Definition of Cloud Computing*, NIST Special Publication 800-145 National Institute of Standards and Technology, Gaithersburg, MD, 2011.

8. GAMP®, *Good Practice Guide: IT Control and Compliance*, International Society of Pharmaceutical Engineering, Tampa FL, 2005.

9. EudraLex, The Rules Governing Medicinal Products in the European Union, Volume 4, Good Manufacturing Practice, Medicinal Products for Human and Veterinary Use, Chapter 4: Documentation, January 2011.

10. ISPE GAMP®, *A Risk-Based Approach to Compliant GXP Computerised Systems*, International Society for Pharmaceutical Engineering (ISPE), 5th ed., February 2008.

11. EudraLex, The Rules Governing Medicinal Products in the European Union, Volume 4, Good Manufacturing Practice, Medicinal Products for Human and Veterinary Use, Chapter 3: Premises and Equipment, 2007. Note that a new version of Chapter 3 is in preparation, July 2014.

12. US Food and Drug Administration, 21 CFR 211, Current Good Manufacturing Practice for Finished Pharmaceuticals, 2008.

13. EudraLex, The Rules Governing Medicinal Products in the European Union, Volume 4, "Good Manufacturing Practice, Medicinal Products for Human and Veterinary Use: Glossary," 2007.

14. 21 CFR Part 11 – Electronic Records; Electronic Signatures; Final Rule. 1997.

15. ISO/IEC 27001: 2013, Information technology—Security techniques—Information security management systems—Requirements, International Standards Organization, Geneva, 2013.

16. COBIT 5 (Control Objectives for Information and Related Technology) version 5, Information Systems Audit and Control Association, 2012.

17. eSourcing Capability Models (eSCM-SP for service providers and eSCM-CL for client organizations); see http://www.itsqc.org.

18. Qualification Guideline for Microsoft Azure, Montrium Inc., June 2014, http://www.montrium.com/montrium-demonstrates-microsofts-continued-commitment-compliance-azure-cloud-life-sciences.

19. US FDA 21 CFR Part 58, Good Laboratory Practice for Non-Clinical Laboratory Studies.

Chapter 25

EU GMP Chapter 4– Documentation and Annex 11

Markus Roemer
Director, comes compliance services

EU Annex 11 FRONTPAGE for revision 1 – "Reasons for changes": the Annex has been revised in response to the increased use of computerized systems and the increased complexity of these systems. Consequential amendments are also proposed for Chapter 4 of the GMP Guide.

EU Chapter 4—Documentation "Reasons for changes": the sections on "generation and control of documentation" and "retention of documents" have been revised in light of the increasing use of electronic documents within the GMP environment.

Introduction

This chapter describes the surrounding conditions and related regulations around EU GMP Annex 11 so that the regulatory requirements toward computerized systems can be fully understood and properly interpreted. It is of major importance to understand the requirements for GMP documentation, especially if such instructions and records are kept in electronic format by a computerized system.

Thus, the focus must be set to EU GMP Chapter 4 defining GMP requirements for documentation, irrespective of whether documents or records are managed electronically or are paper based. The regulations do not define an ultimate standard for regulatory users, who hold sole responsibility to define how to establish, control, monitor, and record all activities that directly or indirectly impact the quality of medicinal products. From a regulatory point of view, a pharmaceutical company would be able to operate totally on paper-based processes. However, how would that work out in terms of efficiency and traceability, and would it be possible to ensure accuracy and integrity of documents and data?

An average pharmaceutical operation might have more than 200 change controls or deviations per year, 2,000 employees (trainings and qualifications), 1,200 procedures in place, and more than 300 suppliers and service providers (including audits and qualification) and comparable figures for batch numbers and releases, production orders, in-process controls, country-specific product licenses, laboratory measurements, and so on. There is the need to handle such "big data" volumes and how such data is affecting particularly or holistically processes and product quality, resulting in product and process knowledge. In addition, GMP compliance is based on documented evidence, and documents and records need to fulfill Good Documentation Practices.

The Inspector Working Group of Chapter 4 released in April 2008 the draft version of Chapter 4 for public consultation, stating: "The accuracy and integrity of documents is a fundamental pre-requisite and a 'document management system'* should be in place to ensure that proper controls are implemented over all categories of QMS documents to ensure compliance."

The referenced footnote (1) of the draft version was not taken over to the final version of Chapter 4; it states, "An 'electronic document management system' (EDMS) may be required for critical electronic records and other documents."

This was most probably because the phrase "may be required" is not worthwhile in a regulatory rule, but it might be recognized as an expectation by European inspectors because the amount and structure of data and the required time periods for research activities, for example, recall, investigation, trending, etc., should be efficient and pragmatic.

So-called Quality by Design approaches (refer to ICH Q11) can also be understood or interpreted as "Big Data" systems through the entire product life cycle, which starts at product development and might be a potential source of information including prior knowledge and development studies in order to establish a commercial manufacturing process.

---

* The Inspector Working Group of Chapter 4 released in April 2008 the draft version of Chapter 4.

Such processes should be validated (refer to EU GMP Annex 15), and "computerized systems/IT systems" are simply process elements or units of such a process. How development or manufacturing processes, applications, equipment and computers, critical quality attributes and quality target product profiles, control strategies, critical process parameters, quality risk and knowledge management, submission (eCTD) and marketing authorization, and finally GMP documentation and quality decisions relate to each other will be described on the next pages.

So, the realm of the basic "GMP documentation" topic must be extended to records and data management because such required principles and methods like Knowledge Management or Quality Risk Management provided by a Pharmaceutical Quality System (PQS) should be fully covered. Knowledge can or, in a scientific sense, should be gained from information, and such information is derived from valid data.

By understanding such an approach, turning theory into reality not only is limited to the result of GMP compliance (inspection readiness), but also it leads consequently to Operational Excellence.

One quintessence of Annex 11–Revision 1 from 2011 is to turn away from a classical or traditional validation approach, which might be a purely system-based one to a records-based, respectively, decision-based approach. In a wider view, validation based on ICH Q9–Quality Risk Management, for example, supports a scientific and practical decision-making approach and leads to knowledge management.

Annex 11 is divided into three sections or phases: General, Project Phase, and Operational Phase. Just by the number of headings, the Operational Phase contains most of the chapters, from 5 to 17, and each of them is technically oriented; for example, data storage, printouts, electronic signatures, security, change and configuration management, and so on. Except one heading, 15–Batch Release, is directly addressing a GMP-regulated activity; maybe a technical reader would stumble across this special clause first. In this context, Annex 11 refers also to Annex 16 of the EU GMP Guideline, and the relevance of the Qualified Person working with computerized systems as part of a quality decision-making process should also be taken into account.

First, the GMP Chapter 4 for Documentation should be introduced and then interpreted for electronic records regulated users and what this means for the validation approach according to Annex 11–Computerized Systems.

Overview EU GMP Chapter 4 Documentation

The European GMP rules governing medicinal products in the European Union is structured in three parts based on 9 chapters and 19 annexes, which can be found online at: http://ec.europa.eu/health/documents/eudralex/vol-4/index_en.htm.

In January 2011, the European Medicines Agency (EMA) announced the updated revisions of EudraLex Volume 4 (GMP)–Annex 11 "Computerised Systems" (short: Annex 11) and consequential amendment of EudraLex Volume 4–Chapter 4 "Documentation" because such documentation, especially managed as electronic records, correlates to the systems providing or containing such GMP records.

Chapter 4–Documentation and Annex 11 reference each other; refer to the "Reasons for changes" sections in each rule. Annex 11 and Chapter 4 versions of January 2011 have been revised simultaneously by the same Inspector Working Group; both documents were drafted, commented, announced, and became valid on the same dates.

Therefore, Annex 11 must be read always in combination with Chapter 4–Documentation but also for full understanding with other parts of the EU GMP rules; for example, Chapter 1–Pharmaceutical Quality Systems (referencing to ICH Q10), Chapter 2–Personnel, Chapter 7–Outsourced Activities, or Annex 15 (Qualification and Validation) or Annex 16 (Certification by a Qualified Person and Batch Release).

This chapter is not intended to describe each chapter of the EU GMP or other volumes in detail; for example, Annex 14 Manufacture of Medicinal Products Derived from Human Blood or Plasma, Part II for API production or EudraLex Volume 10 Clinical Trials Guidelines (European GCP rules). Also, the regulations or rules for Medical Devices in terms of the European Medical Device Directive (MDD) cannot be covered by this chapter, for example, for so-called combination products.

Chapter 2–Personnel covers the roles and responsibilities in a Pharmaceutical Quality System and will not be described in detail here. Although it should be important to keep the responsibilities in mind, especially for computerized systems where a process owner, system owner, and maybe a data owner (e.g., for external data storage—cloud or hosting services) should be considered.

However, the basic principles for document management within a Quality System (GMP PQS, ICH Q10, ISO 13485 or ISO 9001) and validation of computerized systems can be applied to all areas because it just covers Best Practice standards, which can or should be applied to all of them.

EU GMP Chapter 4 has the following structure:

- Principle
- Required GMP Documentation
- Generation and Control of Documentation
- Good Documentation Practices
- Retention of Documents
- Specifications
- Manufacturing Formula and Processing Instructions
- Procedures and Records

The *Principle* section defines basic requirements of GMP documentation. The two primary types of documentation used to manage and record GMP compliance are named to instructions (directions, requirements) and records/reports. The *Required GMP Documentation* section names the different types of documentation. It is the first time that the term *raw data* is mentioned, and electronic records regulated users should define which data are to be used as raw data. The requirements for the generation and control of documents apply equally to all forms of document media types, including paper-based, electronic, or photographic media. In addition, it is mentioned that documents (instructions or records) may exist in hybrid forms, and appropriate controls should be in place to ensure the integrity of records. In addition, the reference to the Marketing Authorization dossiers are mentioned for GMP documentation, the so-called *Good Documentation Practices* and *Retention of Documents* for GMP products (finished products and IMPs). The last three sections give some examples of required documents, which can be understood as minimum requirements. The concrete details of instructions and reports must be predetermined by the Quality System and Quality Risk Management principles.

Documentation—Basic Setup and Requirements

Chapter 4 defines two types of required GMP documentation, starting on the basis of the ultimate master document named to Site Master File (SMF) describing the GMP-related activities of the manufacturer. The Explanatory Notes for the SMF can be found in Part III of the EudraLex GMP Guideline and are based on the PIC/S guide PE-008-4. It should be noted that an SMF should already contain in Chapter 5 basic commitments regarding the documentation system, if these are managed on paper or electronically, and details if records are stored off site.

The two types are given as "instruction type" and "records/report types," where the instruction types represent input elements (directions or require-ments) and the records/reports types represent the output elements. Both elements represent a Pharmaceutical Quality System by predefined inputs and recorded outputs. Quality of products and process robustness are real-ized by a target-actual comparison. Such inputs are predefined specifica-tions or work instructions, and the outputs are required GMP documentation (protocols, records, CofA), which are proofing that the execution or quality targets met the specifications.

The most common and known standard for Quality Management Systems according to ISO 9001, also referenced in ICH Q10, defines these two types in Clause 4.2.3–Control of Documents and Clause 4.2.4–Control of Records.

Chapter 4 defines the instruction types as:

■ Specifications
■ Manufacturing Formulae, Processing, Packaging, and Testing Instructions
■ Procedures (otherwise known as Standard Operating Procedures, or SOPs)
■ Protocols
■ Technical Agreements (or Quality Agreements)

and the records/reports types as:

■ Records
■ Certificates of Analysis
■ Reports

Details of each required GMP document and record are defined in the following sections of EU GMP Chapter 4, for example:

■ Specifications
  – for starting and packaging materials
  – for intermediate and bulk products
  – for finished products

- Manufacturing Formula and Processing Instructions
- Packaging Instructions
- Batch Processing Record
- Batch Packaging Record
- Procedures and Records: Receipts, Sampling, Testing, and Others

For example, the Batch Processing Record (Clause 4.20) should be based on the relevant parts of the currently approved Manufacturing Formula and Processing Instructions, and Chapter 4 is naming details of the required information such as name and batch number of the product, records of the in-process controls, and approval by the person responsible for the processing operations (non-exhaustive listing).

This Batch Processing Record according to EU Chapter 4 is equivalent to US FDA 21 CFR Part 211; refer to Sec. 211.188 Batch Production and Control Records.

This Batch Processing Record is used (verified) by the Qualified Person for Batch Release according to Annex 16. This results to a quality decision according to Chapter 1, that no batch of product is released for sale or supply prior to certification by a Qualified Person. In addition, Annex 11 is also referring to the "Batch Release" in Clause 15, which is described in Chapter 18.

From a technical point, the Batch Processing Record must contain all relevant information (data) for the Qualified Person, who must ensure that all necessary steps have been completed through an agreed quality management system. This record is an important part of an entire supply chain of the medicinal product, which preferably should be in the format of a comprehensive diagram. It is based on instruction types such as the Manufacturing Formula and related Processing Instructions, which have been approved and were in a valid state at the point of the manufacturing time period or when the batch (production) order was started (version and status controlled data objects).

The EMA Guideline on process validation for finished products—Annex I (latest revision from January 15, 2014)—defines a so-called process validation scheme. It must be clear that performing the validation of a computerized system can be successful only if process design, knowledge (refer to ASTM E2500), and validation are applied. Basically "computer system validation" is the younger brother of process validation, and it is beneficial to combine qualification, computer system validation, and process validation activities (e.g., by a Validation Master Plan).

In today's modern operations, methods like continuous process verification (CPV) or just measurements within the process stream (IPC, PAT) linking product attributes and process parameters, including control and recording of such quality data up to an electronic batch record or data warehouse, are used and need to be understood. The EMA Guideline on process validation states, "Process validation should not be viewed as a one-off event"; the same applies to computer system validation including the surrounding conditions, which should also be acknowledged. Many computer system validation approaches are too strongly focused only on the technical aspects (e.g., like Software Categories according ISPE GAMP) instead of focusing on process- and product-relevant criteria as the starting point for any validation planning, requirements management, verification and testing activities, and well-balanced and concentrated efforts.

This leads us to the statement that in real terms we do not validate a computer system purely technically as an end in itself, like an ERP, MES, LIMS, DMS; validation should focus on the GMP-regulated activity (refer to Annex 11–Principles: "Systems Used As Part of GMP Regulated Activities"). Instead of saying "we should validate an ERP system," we should validate the regulatory activities of a system like batch number generation, materials tracking, master data management, supplier management, storage and transportation routing, and so on. On the other hand, the wording of Annex 11–Computer System Validation applies "where a computerised system replaces a manual operation."

Paper versus Electronic Records

A traditional full paper-based system would be to write the Processing Instructions and the corresponding Batch Processing Record using a typewriter (or text program), print them out, and sign them with handwritten signatures. The Batch Processing Record would be filled out by the operators.

A regulated user must define if the master documents are managed on paper or electronically (refer to Site Master File). Consequently, electronic records, if representing the unique master record, must be signed by an electronic signature. A printout of an electronic record signed electronically is just a copy of the master record, and it should be defined how the e-signature is displayed and printed on paper. In addition, Chapter 4 states that documents (instructions or records) may exist in hybrid forms, that is, some elements as electronic and others as paper. A hybrid form would be to have the electronic record following the printout of the record and then the printout is signed on paper. Then the master will be the paper record but should be linked to its respective electronic records to enable the work to be reassembled. It will be explained later how far a hybrid solution is beneficial or efficient.

The term of a so-called typewriter excuse may also come up in different discussions or situations. The idea was to define a computer system as not relevant to validation because it is purely used to generate the record, and the real record is the hard copy. Might this be ranked as a staunch statement or interpretation? For example, SOPs are written with Microsoft Word (text program), printed, and signed with a handwritten signature. The content of the SOP will be fully reviewed. Microsoft Word, as a "simple" text input processor and print functionality, must not be validated. Is it possible to fully review the result in the form of the written and printed SOP? According to Annex 11, Microsoft Office is a part of the infrastructure, which should be qualified. If we would enhance this perception to the level of systems like ERP or MES, the complexity, the applied logic and functions, as such plausibility, status, and boundary checks, would not allow us to define such a typewriter excuse, which would not be any more appropriate or even justifiable.

Even in a medium complex production, it is impossible not to work with any computerized system or laboratory/production equipment. In addition, EU GMP Chapter 1 defines the requirement of a complete history of a batch to be traced and retained in a comprehensible and accessible form.

Normally, the entire data objects on records are collected from several computerized systems, for example, monitoring, process control, production planning and execution, storage, sampling, maintenance, laboratory, training, deviation, market authorization, audit management systems, applications, or databases.

The entire supply chain of a medicinal product contains the material flow and the data flow from different data sources or even from different company sites, contractors, suppliers, etc. Such a data source might be any computerized system or equipment; therefore, data management and systems need to be analyzed in detail.

What Is a Computerized System?

Annex 11 defines a computerized system as a set of software and hardware components that together fulfill certain functionalities. The first part of the sentence, that a computerized system is a set of software and hardware components, is not really outstanding and new; however, by this definition, it covers all IT-related systems. The focus must be set on the fulfillment of certain functionalities when the computerized systems are used as part of a GMP-regulated activity. Maybe it should be noted that the initial revision of Annex 11 was written in 1992 and was titled "Computerized Systems." Today, basically centuries later in terms of IT periods, the title would be different and more related to IT systems and their interactions to the process. In addition, it might be discussed if the defined structure for Annex 11 and Annex 15 would be done again or a joined approach (and one single Annex document) would be more constructive and clear.

As we have realized, EU GMP Chapter 4 defines two documentation types: instructions and records/reports. One of the first questions might be if a system contains parts of instructions (directions), records/reports, or maybe both types. If so, the system is part of a GMP-regulated activity and should be validated. A computerized system is just a means to an end in the context of GMP compliance.

Very often, it makes sense during the initial phase of validation planning to define or analyze which records and reports should be created by the system. This is a records-based approach and might be very efficient to start the design or conception phase of an IT project based on the desired records (process outputs) and process steps. In addition, it can be avoided to lose track with complex systems and the high amount of modules, functions, and options.

What Is Software?

At first, this seems to be a simple or trivial question. However, it might be useful to analyze quickly our real validation object and mission. Just because we as the pharmaceutical industry validate computerized systems, we are not directly generating quality into a software product. A good-quality level of software can be created only by the software developers using well-defined development methods and standards. The problem is that a quality level of software cannot be easily measured or defined in an absolute number. It is not possible to measure the degree of validation or software quality as an absolute value. It remains as a relative term and even with boundless efforts there is no guarantee for a totally error-free operation. Due to the software and data complexity, validation can provide a high degree of assurance based on a risk-based approach. Even if two developers would solve the same development requirement (task) and program the code accordingly, both results would differ from each other. If two validation experts would validate this unit, both would also have at least slightly different validation approaches and results.

Typically, software can be defined as executable files, libraries, source code, and scripts structured into applications, modules, units, and databases. Normally, relational databases with database management systems (DBMS) might be used. Software or Source Code might be created in interpreted or compiled languages (high-level or low-level programming languages), and compiled language can be written in machine code or byte code (virtual machines). Software can be set up as source code and a separate application run-time (complied code); it might use graphical languages, configuration files, workflow engines or any other kind of platforms, middleware, or architecture (embedded systems, microcontrollers, etc.).

In any case, it should be clear that quality could be brought into a software or hardware product only by a defined software quality development life-cycle methodology (e.g., CMMI), selection of appropriate software development platforms and languages, and a release management/product and service policy. In other words, if today a new application would be developed, nobody would choose the language Turbo Pascal on an operating system of DOS with a database on dBase with a 486 PC. From a regulatory point of view, this might be possible, but modern programming platforms and languages might contain more built-in quality checks and verifications.

Software (source code) can be assigned to the GMP documentation type of instructions, so it is a part of our GMP-regulated activities. If a source code contains sequential instructions/directions, which means that it includes Manufacturing Formula and Processing Instructions according to Chapter 4–Documentation, such source code must be version and status controlled. Therefore, it is an ultimate prerequisite that software including programming languages and associated tools are fully under control even in an early development phase. For keeping systems in a validated status, processes like change, release, and configuration management are of major importance.

What Is Data?

Source code or software structures including interfaces are managing, collecting, displaying, and calculating data objects. Source code itself is useless if not provided with data inputs and other operational objects.

Simplified, the following data categories should be defined:

■ Master Data and Reference Data (e.g., units of measurements): Such basic data is often nontransactional. Master Data might be product names, items of a bill of material, routings, formula, or user names. Master Data and Reference Data belong to GMP documentation as an instruction type and are the corresponding meta-data in reports and records.

■ Transaction or Dynamic Data: This data category is often order or batch related and results out of a set of predefined Master Data and an activity to start any task (e.g., shop floor order for batch production). Transaction or Dynamic Data sets are based on single batch-specific instructions in an imperative mandatory style and recorded by logging mechanism, analytical measurements, or mathematical operations as the initial raw data sets.

■ Data Acquisition/Recorded Data: Based on a batch order, such data sets of a transaction with an end-to-end data protection during this time period of execution will be recorded, transformed, and archived. Proof of evidence is given by this data category as Records/Reports type, as defined and required by EU GMP Chapter 4. Typically, such data is stored in a rational database providing a secure consistency model over the entire retention period.

Meta-data is data information about other data sets. For example, a measured value by an analytic method on a batch record is given (e.g., pH value = 7.2). If this is a single measured value, it is defined as raw data. If it is the result of an average value out of 10 measured data points, each of these would be the raw data and the displayed value would be the calculated result. During the batch review, the value would be checked against its predefined specification (instruction), for example, 7.1 to 7.4 as an expected result. However, purely the value itself is not sufficient in terms of reproducibility and is not unambiguousness without meta-data of measuring devices and related status, methods and calculations used, executed and verified by whom, and so on. A part of such data is Master or Dynamic Data, some batch or order specific, or covered by the Pharmaceutical Quality System in a general procedural way.

Annex 11 (8. Printouts) states that it should be possible to create clear printed copies of electronically stored data. It is up to individual interpretation what a "clear" printout is and what electronically stored data are in terms of data types. It might be possible to print out a full SQL database table including all data types from master data, raw data, and reports, but it might not be very clear, transparent, or even useful.

Other expressions are also used, like true, full, or exact copy of data and records, but very often there is a clear and exact definition missing or hard to find. The US-FDA published a Question and Answer information in August 2013 stating that a printed chromatogram (HPLC system) would not be considered a "true copy" of the entire electronic raw data. This is correct, and not only would the raw data not be shown, but the meta-data around the measuring process would not be shown as well.

EU GMP Chapter 4 states that electronic records regulated users should define which data are to be used as raw data; at least, all data on which quality decisions are based should be defined as raw data. The magic words here are definitely the "quality decision." The documented rationale for the quality decisions are the GMP records and reports defined in EU GMP Chapter 4. The quality decision is done by a decision maker, as defined in EU GMP Chapter 2 by roles, duties, and responsibilities. The level of details of printed or displayed data should be the reasonable and defendable input and rationale for the decision maker at the time when the decision is made. Again, for a decision, the point of time (fourth dimension) is of major importance, which will be given in the following section.

Timelines and Life Cycles

It should also be clear that if we consider data chronology and periods, then validation of computerized systems might be a complex subject. Indeed, validation and data integrity must be understood together with the fourth dimension of time. This is also one of the reasons why release, change, and configuration management has such major importance to compliance. It might be useful to add something about the definition of the so-called *life cycle,* which is often used in the context of GMP compliance.

Not only source code, software defined as instruction type, but also all data categories are therefore status and version controlled. EU GMP Chapter 4–Generation and Control of Documentation states that the effective date should be defined. This effective date must take into consideration the different time bases of products, processes, systems, and records/data.

EU GMP Annex 11 (refer to Glossary section) uses the term of the life cycle regarding the computerized system from design to maintenance stages; Annex 15 defines a life cycle of the product and process and a validation life cycle.

EU GMP Chapter 1 (PQS) states that GMP applies to the life-cycle stages from the manufacture of investigational medicinal products (IMP), technology transfer, and commercial manufacturing through to product discontinuation.

Consequently, a data life cycle or record life cycle must also be mentioned. EU GMP Chapter 4 requires and states that appropriate controls should be in place to ensure the integrity of the record throughout the retention period, and batch documentation must be kept for one year after expiry of the batch to which it relates or at least five years after certification of the batch by the Qualified Person, whichever is the longer. For investigational medicinal products, the batch documentation must be kept for at least five years after the completion or formal discontinuation of the last clinical trial in which the batch was used.

Some misunderstanding and confusion can result from an IT validation project if the term "product life cycle" is used. A Qualified Person/pharmacist would understand the product as the finished pharmaceutical product; an IT person/supplier would understand the product as his or her computer system or application.

The different life-cycle types start with the product life cycle, as defined in EU GMP Chapter 1, including the entire life-cycle stages of a finished pharmaceutical product including Marketing Authorization. Products are produced with validated processes, so the second life-cycle type is the process life cycle. A computerized system or equipment is a part or element of a process, so the third life-cycle type is the system life cycle. Computerized systems contain instructions and create records based on data sets. Therefore, the last life-cycle type is the records/data life cycle.

So, why is it necessary to consider the different life-cycle types? The records/data life cycle is normally longer than the system life cycle when the system might be decommissioned. In addition, changes to the product by the marketing authorization holder or changes to the process (new process steps, product transfer to other sites or to a CMO, change of excipients) may also impact the system configuration and parameters. If a product is produced for 40 years, there will be several system life cycles used, and different data and records may be created. In addition, data itself is created along the entire product life cycle (clinical studies, submission, stability, manufacturing, distribution), which is also a part of Knowledge Management, for example, for new drug developments.

And Again Something about Audit Trails

EU GMP Chapter 4 states that suitable controls should be implemented to ensure the accuracy, integrity, availability, and legibility of documents. For electronic records, this brings up the special data category of Audit Trails, as per EU GMP Annex 11, "a system generated audit trail." Although Audit Trails are well known and very often discussed or even misunderstood/misinterpreted, it is worthwhile to define and analyze this special data set (meta-data) in more detail.

First, it is a technical function, which is automatically generated, consecutive on an event-trigged basis after the initial first change of an existing data object. It is a kind of logging function including watchdog behavior, recording changes of data or data status into a separate database table, when data sets under audit trail have been changed. The mechanism records the old and new value, date and time of change, reason of change, and which logged-in user performed the change, assuming that changes can be done only by users with the corresponding access rights and privileges. However, according to EU GMP Annex 11, all GMP-relevant data should be audit trailed.

As defined, there are different data categories such as master, transaction, and recorded data; and data objects are part of GMP records. Some GMP records are of the instructions type and some are of the records/reports type according to GMP documentation requirements. EU GMP Chapter 4 defines all GMP records with a given exemplary list of data objects with no claim to be complete.

For example (EU GMP Chapter 4–Documentation), the Manufacturing Formula (instruction type) should include:

1. The name of the product, with a product reference code relating to its specification
2. A description of the pharmaceutical form, strength of the product, and batch size
3. A list of all starting materials to be used, with the amount of each described; mention should be made of any substance that may disappear in the course of processing
4. A statement of the expected final yield with the acceptable limits and of relevant intermediate yields, where applicable

The corresponding Batch Processing Record (record type) should be kept for each batch processed. It should be based on the relevant parts of the currently approved Manufacturing Formula and Processing Instructions.

The required "data" given for the Manufacturing Formula are of the master and reference data category, there containing instructions and directions. The Batch Processing Record also includes transaction and finally recorded data sets. But besides that, both records contain meta-data/information, for example, name of records according to a unique naming convention, version of document, status of record, footer and header information like page number/total page numbers, measured value, and so on.

It might be helpful and required to separate and define the terms of data, records, and printouts. In addition, the term *audit trail* was mentioned. Now, an audit trail was purely described as a function previously, but it is also and mainly understood as a record. An audit trail, understood as a listing of all recorded audit trails, can be viewed on a computerized system. In addition, it can or should be printable. Let us assume the Batch Processing Record mentioned previously contains a measured value as raw data defined and a validated analytical method was used for the measurement, for example, version 27 of the method; then, the complete record as a printout should also contain all 26 changes (audit trail data) on the Batch Processing Record. Can this be true and correct?

This goes back to a much more fundamental question: Is it possible to create true, full, and exact copies of data and records on printouts? Technically yes; practically, no. However, is a decision maker also reviewing all last 26 changes of the method, which were approved by competent persons previously? Definitely not or only in the case of any irregularity.

Besides that, Quality Management incorporates Good Manufacturing Practice according to EU GMP Chapter 1 on two levels:

- System based: Periodic management reviews of the Pharmaceutical Quality System
- Product (Batch) related: Product Quality Reviews

Both activities should enable quality improvements appropriate to the current level of process and product knowledge.

Therefore, it might be immoderate if a report itself and its printout can provide proof of full GMP compliance.

Finally, what kind of data should be audit trailed and which data sets and objects should be printed out must be discussed with the relevant decision makers. If such a determination is missing, it can lead to missing quality oversight and metrics or alternatively too many data and even marginal data sets are recorded, which leads to unusable graveyard data.

Most of the computerized systems provide report or template designer tools. The report template is configured based on the database tables and fields. That means that data is assigned or configured as a record on a printout. Referring to the above-mentioned Batch Processing Record, this record is normally a selection and combination of data from several systems. The idea of a centralized data storage or data warehouse is not really a new one—but technology nowadays is able to provide such platforms and tools in an efficient cost and effort balance.

Most pharmaceutical companies operate on a hybrid approach, as EU GMP Chapter 4 states that many documents (instructions or records) may exist in hybrid forms, that is, some elements as electronic and others as paper. This also implies that a pharmaceutical company has to decide, finally, if the ultimate master/original records are electronic or on paper. This basic determination is very often forgotten or underestimated, but most of the problems and issues might be solved easily by such a general definition.

Quality of Decisions

It can be expected that a hybrid approach can be driven for the next years or maybe century. However, there is a certain limitation obviously inbound by this approach. For example, data integrity cannot be fully guaranteed because of manual inputs and transfers, which are always associated with higher risk compared with qualified interfaces. Other problems may come up with the completeness for the documented rationale toward the quality decision ("complete copy") or the linking of printouts to references in other electronic systems, the related access time to data, and much more.

By defining all the master records as electronic records (electronic format), in consequence all signed electronically, several superior benefits can be gained. A kind of QP/QA cockpit view on all relevant data from all data sources might be a great vision. Moreover, on such a view data structures and results down to any raw data, audit trail data, master data, recorded data, or calculations can be fully provided. Would this just be a nice tool or gadget? Would it be nice to have or really something for GMP compliance?

First, it would be nice and comfortable when senior management, quality units, production heads, and others could have one single screen in front with all quality relevant data on it, starting with all materials including packaging materials used, overview or review of supply chain traceability of active substances, critical in-process controls and finished product/testing results, all significant deviations or nonconformances and investigations, changes to products/processes/systems, Marketing Authorization variations and dossiers, results of monitoring, qualification status of systems and personnel, contractual arrangements, and quality agreements. In addition, if necessary, such data is shown first in an executive summary or conclusion style, and more details can be request by just one button click instead of leaving the room for other departments or units.

In principle, GMP requires such a setup already. Projects like Electronic Batch Recording (EBR), Track & Trace, Document Management Systems, paperless labs, and many more are already running or have been implemented to reach such a centralized solution platform. The backgrounds are also regulatory requirements or expectations toward "real time release testing" (RTRT), described in the EMA Guideline on Real Time Release Testing from 2012.

It is based on a Quality by Design (QbD) approach, in contrast to the so-called traditional product development and process validation approach. Briefly, QbD is based on tripartite harmonized ICH Guidelines, and the EMA and US FDA have issued a similar Guidance Document for process validation and verification. The interesting parts here are in extracts of the so-called Design Space and Control Strategy. Whereas in a traditional approach instructions (refer to document type instructions/directions) are pretty much static and fixed, a Design Space is the multidimensional combination and interaction of input variables and process parameters in order to provide more operational flexibility. A control strategy is a planned set of controls, derived from current product and process understanding (knowledge management). Computerized systems realize such a Control Strategy, as for example by in-process control systems (e.g., process analytical tools [PAT]) or even active feedback control systems.

In EU GMP Chapter 4, there is a very interesting footnote (1) to the Certificate of Analysis: "Alternatively the certification may be based, in-whole or in-part, on the assessment of real time data (summaries and exception reports) from batch related process analytical technology (PAT), parameters or metrics as per the approved marketing authorization dossier."

Sometimes revolutions may start in a footnote section.

Data Rich–Information Poor (DRIP)

Quality by Design, Real Time Releases, audit trails, data warehouse—a lot of interesting topics and investments are required for such concepts. Is it worth it to implement such a concept in terms of a return of investment, improvement of efficiency, and cost savings? A modern Quality System and validation approach must focus on such elements in addition to product quality and patient safety. Can such DRIP systems be found in the GMP-regulated industries and, if so, how can they be avoided?

EU GMP Chapter 4 in combination with EU GMP Annex 11 goes directly into areas of data management, data mining and profiling, and data mapping with electronic records. The *Principles* section of Annex 11 says, "The application should be validated; IT infrastructure should be qualified." It might be very interesting to note that the EMA has not defined that "computerized systems should be validated"; instead of the term "computerized system," they use the term "application." The term "computerized system" has historical reasons from the 1980s, and the term "application" should also reflect the current status that "computers" are no longer run as stand-alone solutions and connected horizontally and vertically to each other.

One of the biggest disadvantages of a hybrid system approach and paper printouts are that any data or information on paper are dead assets. Regulatory requirements for trending and analyzing data or outcomes, irrespective if order/batch related or company wide/periods based, cannot be performed easily or at least efficiently on paper.

Such analyzed data is the basis for process understanding and knowledge. Knowledge Management is defined according to ICH Q10 as a systematic approach to acquiring, analyzing, storing, and disseminating information related to products, processes, and components. Knowledge and Risk Management enable Quality Decisions. However, it is not only about quality decisions, it is also in general about other strategic business decisions. Moreover, how or on which basis are decisions made today—on gut instinct or reliable information and data?

GMP Datability

A new coinage word is "Datability"—created out of the words Data and Ability, Sustainability, Responsibility. This implies the ability to use data in order to generate knowledge and understanding as a basis for "good decisions." The industry is performing projects like "Industry 4.0" (equivalent to "Advanced Manufacturing" in the United States), which includes a totally integrated approach of all systems. The basis of this must be a harmonized and well-managed IT infrastructure and landscape. EU GMP Annex 11 is therefore requiring that the IT infrastructure be qualified and, in such a way, it should be interpreted.

Having data that are reliable, consistent, and well linked is one of the biggest challenges facing regulated companies. The ability to manage and integrate data generated at all product and process stages, from research to commercial manufacturing, is a fundamental requirement to allow companies to derive maximum benefit. Effective horizontal and vertical data integration establishes the data source for all pieces of information to gain knowledge.

Implementing data integration requires a number of capabilities and methods, including GMP, product and process knowledge, technical knowledge, IT project management, and validation. Relevant data types and objects need to be prioritized, and data-warehousing capabilities might be required and subsequently implemented. Pharmaceutical companies have or will need to understand that 50% of their output is the finished product—the other 50% of the output are the data sets assigned to the finished products. Datability will be a contributing factor for the success of the pharmaceutical operation.

Validation and Data Integrity

EU GMP Annex 11 and Chapter 4–Documentation must be read and understood. In addition, other GMP aspects should be considered. How is computer system validation affected by the new revisions of Annex 11 and Chapter 4?

Traditionally, computer system validation is purely based on a system-based approach with the steps of DQ, IQ, OQ, PQ, and testing being functional oriented. Some people would say that their current project is to validate an ERP or any other system. However, in real terms, validation should focus on data, process flows, and data integrity. This starts in an early phase of the overall process design followed by defining the requirements to the system.

Figure 25.1 shows a modified and enhanced V-model, which is not system based; instead, it contains a data flow according to EU GMP Chapter 4 toward the final quality decision.

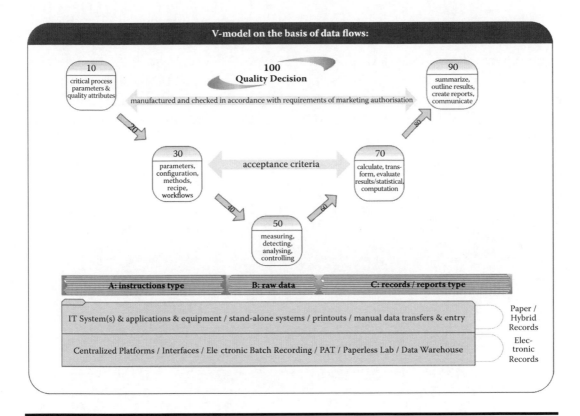

Figure 25.1 V-model—data flow.

The V-model shows the process flow from Step 10 to 100:

■ Step 10: The critical process parameters and quality attributes must be identified. These are the critical data sets as an input for the quality decision (Step 100). Step 90 is the verification and review of this data.

■ Steps 20, 40, 60, and 80 are the steps where data is transferred, manually or by automated interfaces (preferred).

■ Sections A, B, and C are showing according to EU GMP Chapter 4 the instructions type, raw data, and records/reports type areas.

■ Step 30 can be defined as the Control Strategy or process input elements

■ In Step 50, raw data is created. In Step 70, processes according to the directions of Step 30 are described.

■ The corresponding quality decision is made in Step 100 on the basis of Step 90.

The basic principles and characteristics of paper/hybrid and electronic records are also noted.

If based on this model the data flow is considered for validation, which most likely goes over several systems, data integrity and information management would be included. EU GMP Annex 11 requires such "data integrity controls" and Chapter 4 states: "Suitable controls should be implemented to ensure the accuracy, integrity, availability and legibility of documents." Compared with the traditional validation model, this V-model on a data-flow basis might bring several advantages with it.

Chapter 26

Annex 11 and Electronic Records Integrity

Introduction*

Data may be recorded by electronic data processing systems or by photographic or other reliable means. There is no requirement in the EU GMPs to maintain electronic copies of records in preference to other media such as microfiche or paper. If the regulated user decides to maintain regulated records in electronic format, this chapter provides how Annex 11 expects such activity be performed and controlled.

Data Integrity

The property that data has not been altered in an unauthorized manner. Data integrity covers data in storage, during processing, and while in transit.

NIST SP 800-33

---

* This chapter is an update of a paper published on May 20, 2014, by the *Journal of GXP Compliance*, 1(2), http://www.ivtnetwork.com/article/eu-annex-11-and-integrity-erecs.

The integrity of a record refers to the record being unaltered (NIST SP 800-33). It is necessary that a record be protected against alteration without appropriate permission. Records management policies and procedures should specify what, if any, additions or annotations may be made to a record after it is created, under what circumstances additions or annotations may be authorized, and who is authorized to make them. Any authorized annotation or addition to a record made after it is complete should be explicitly indicated as annotations or additions. Another aspect of integrity of a record is the structural integrity of it. The structure of a record, that is, its physical and logical format and the relationships between the data elements comprising the record, should remain physically or logically intact. Failure to maintain the record's structural integrity may impair its reliability and authenticity.

It is a requisite of trustworthy systems to achieve records integrity. Trustworthy computer systems consist of computer infrastructure, application(s) and procedures that are designed to prevent intrusion and misuse, and adhere to generally accepted security principles.

The technological and procedural safety controls implemented to a computer system are reflected by the confidentiality, integrity and availability of the system. The integrity of the trustworthy computer system includes the integrity of the electronic records* (e-recs).

In manufacturing control systems, data integrity supports process integrity for making regulated products of specified safety and quality. In clinical database systems, data integrity supports decisions on consumer safety and product efficacy. In laboratory systems supporting GMP operations, both data capture and database management systems are used for product analysis studies. The integrity of electronic data is an essential quality component in manufacturing.

When a regulatory agency or competent authority inspector has to assess the intended use of a particular system,[†] the inspector considers the potential risks, from the computer system to product/material quality or data integrity, as identified and documented by the regulated user.

E-recs must be secure and protected from unauthorized access and tampering. Procedures should be in place to ensure data integrity of e-recs.

---

* Records: Provide evidence of various actions taken to demonstrate compliance with instructions—for example, activities; events; investigations; and, in the case of manufactured batches, a history of each batch of product, including its distribution. Records include the raw data, which is used to generate other records. For electronic records, regulated users should define which data are to be used as raw data. At least, all data on which quality decisions are based should be defined as raw data (Eudralex Vol 4 Ch 4).

† PIC/S Guide PI 011-3, Good Practices for Computerised Systems in Regulated "GXP" Environments, Section 4.12, September 2007.

The e-recs can be easily changed with no cross-outs or other indications of the change. On commercial databases, procedures can be incorporated into functions to automatically maintain an audit trail of changed e-recs. This audit trail should maintain original e-recs and their source and any changed e-recs, along with the date and identity of the initiator. Alternatively, access to software and e-recs files can be restricted with physical and logical methods to authorized individuals and the use of manual methods to create and maintain audit trails.

The second edition of Annex 11 provides criteria for the effective implementation, control, and use of computer systems performing functions established in Directive 2003/94/EC* and Directive 91/412/EEC.†

EU Annex 11 is not a legal requirement; it is a guideline in the context of the EU GMPs. However, Annex 11 is mandatory on each EU national level because the member states have to endorse the EU GMP Guideline within the scope of the national healthcare legislation.

The precise implementation of Annex 11 ensures that the computer systems can be used in the manufacture of medicinal products without any adverse impact on quality, efficacy, or patient safety, including electronic records integrity.

This chapter discusses the controls proposed by Annex 11 in support of the integrity of electronic records.

Data Integrity

Since 2004, the worldwide inspection trends had been on data integrity. By 2007, data integrity issues gained prominence in the United States. The US FDA was worried about oversight by the regulated user to the manipulation of the operators of laboratory automated systems. By 2007, the US FDA considered data integrity allegations the most serious and damaging allegations to be made against regulated users because of the complete trust that the US FDA had to have in the records that were provided to inspectors.‡

---

* European Union Directive 2003/94/EC, European Commission Directive Laying Down the Principles and Guidelines of Good Manufacturing Practice for Medicinal Products for Human Use and Investigational Medicinal Products for Human Use, 2003.
† European Union Directive 91/412/EEC, European Commission Directive Laying Down the Principles and Guidelines of Good Manufacturing Practice for Veterinary Medicinal Products, 1991.
‡ The Golden Sheet, "Data Integrity Issues Highlighted In FY 2007 Warning Letters," June 2008.

As an example, around 2007, three major cases on data integrity in the United States were Able Laboratories (2006), Leiner Healthcare Products (2007), and Actavis Totowa (2007).

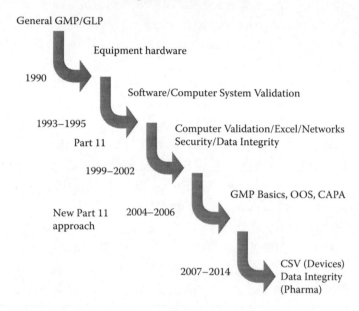

The Actavis Totowa case was related to data integrity in e-recs. The US FDA found many occurrences where data in computer systems were inconsistent with notebook data. The FDA also saw no evidence that the manufacturer checked data files for accuracy.

The latest data integrity issues by the regulated users (refer to Table 26.1) uncovered by the regulatory agencies and competent authorities have resuscitated the dialog among the industry on this subject.

This attention to e-recs integrity may be related with the better understanding by the regulatory agencies, competent authorities, and the regulated user around the US FDA 21 CFR Part 11, Electronic Records: Electronic Signatures.[*]

Table 26.1 depicts the recent cases on computer-related data integrity documented by regulatory agencies or competent authorities after the associated inspections.

The data integrity– or data reliability–related deficiencies found in the recent cases include insufficient controls on security, inconsistencies between e-recs and paper-based records, computer users in the laboratory

---

[*] 62 FR 13464, Mar. 20, 1997.

Table 26.1 2013–2014 Cases of Data Integrity

Company Name	Date	Action	Regulation	Note
Hospira	Mar 2013	483	211.180(d)	Data integrity. The raw data generated from the semi-automated tester used to measure the thickness of perimeter seals on bags used as container closure systems for injectable drugs can be overwritten with new data without explanation and the original data is erased from the computer's memory.
Puget Sound Blood Center and Program	Apr 2013	Warning Letter (WL)	211.68(b)	Lack of I/O verification (data accuracy).
RPG Life Sciences Limited	May 2013	WL	211.68(b)	The computer system being used for HPLC did not have adequate controls to prevent unrecorded changes to data.
Fresenius Kabi AG	Jul 2013	WL	API	Unacceptable practices in the management of electronic data.
Aarti Drug Limited	Jul 2013	WL	API	Failure to implement access controls and audit trails for laboratory computer systems.
Wockhardt Limited	Jul 2013	Statement of noncompliance with GMPs	2003/94/EC (EU GMPs)	Critical deficiency: Issues were identified that compromised the integrity of analytical data produced by the QC department. Evidence was seen of data falsification. A significant number of product stability data results reported in the Product Quality Reviews had been fabricated. Neither hard copy nor electronic records were available. In addition, issues were seen with HPLC electronic data indicating unauthorized manipulation of data and incidents of unreported trial runs prior to reported analytical runs. (MHRA)

(continued)

Table 26.1 2013–2014 Cases of Data Integrity (continued)

Company Name	Date	Action	Regulation	Note
Wockhardt Limited	Jul 2013	WL	211.194(a)	Failure to ensure that laboratory records included complete data derived from all tests necessary to ensure compliance with established specifications and standards.
Posh Chemicals Pvt Ltd.	Aug 2013	WL	API	Failure to protect computerized data from unauthorized access or changes.
Agila Specialist Private Limited	Sep 2013	WL	211.68(b)	The computer system being used for HPLC did not have adequate controls to prevent unrecorded changes to data.
Smruthi Organics Ltd.	Oct 2013	Statement of noncompliance with GMPs	Article 47 of 2001/83/EEC	The agency observed manipulation and falsification of documents and data in different departments. There was no raw data available in the Quality Control laboratory for the verification of compendial analytical methods (French Health Products Safety Agency).
Ind-Swift Limited	Oct 2013	Statement of noncompliance with GMPs	Article 47 of 2001/83/EEC	It was not possible to confirm the validity of stability testing data. Several falsified and inaccurate results had been reported in long-term stability and batch testing. Discrepancies between electronic data and those results formally reported were identified. Established processes to verify data accuracy and integrity had failed and there had been no formal investigation raised by the company. The company provided commitments to address the data integrity concerns and initiated a wider review of quality critical data. Additional discrepancies were identified in process validation and release data. During ongoing

				communications with the licensing authority regarding the data review, the company failed to disclose data integrity issues for all products. No satisfactory explanation was given for this discrepancy (MHRA).
Zeta Analytical Ltd.	Nov 2013	Statement of noncompliance with GMPs	European Union's GMP guideline	The computer system being used for HPLC did not have adequate controls to prevent unrecorded changes to data (MHRA).
Wockhardt Limited	Nov 2013	Statement of noncompliance with GMPs	2003/94/EC (EU GMPs)	The deficiency related to data integrity, deleted electronic files with no explanation. (MHRA)
Wockhardt Limited	Dec 2013	WL	211.68(b)	The computer system being used for HPLC did not have adequate controls to prevent unrecorded changes to data.
Seikagaku Corporation	Dec 2013	Statement of noncompliance with GMPs	2003/94/EC (EU GMPs)	The critical deficiency concerns systematic rewriting/manipulation of documents, including QC raw data. The company has not been able to provide acceptable investigations and explanations to the differences seen in official and unofficial versions of the same documents (Competent Authority of Sweden).
Smruthi Organics Ltd.	Jan 2014	Statement of noncompliance with GMPs	Article 47 of 2001/83/EEC	There was no raw data available in the Quality Control laboratory for the verification of compendial analytical methods. (http://www.pharmamedtechbi.com/publications/the-gold-sheet/48/2/eu-gmp-noncompliance-reports-in-brief, Health Products Safety Agency)

(continued)

Table 26.1   2013–2014 Cases of Data Integrity (continued)

Company Name	Date	Action	Regulation	Note
Ranbaxy Laboratories, Inc.	Jan 2014	483	211.68(b)	The computer system being used for HPLC did not have adequate controls to prevent unrecorded changes to data.
Punjab Chemicals and Crop Corporation Limited	Jan 2014	Statement of noncompliance with GMPs	Article 47 of 2001/83/EEC	One individual training file of an employee has been observed to be recently rewritten; the batch manufacturing record was lacking details with regard to manufacturing steps and in-process controls; the sample retention logbook for Trimethoprim had falsified entries (French Health Products Safety Agency).
USV Limited	Feb 2014	WL	211.68(b)	The computer system being used for quality control laboratory did not have adequate controls to prevent unrecorded changes to data.
Canton Laboratories Private Limited	Feb 2014	WL	API	The computer system being used for atomic absorption spectrophotometer did not have adequate controls to prevent unrecorded changes to data.
SOMET	Mar 2014	Statement of noncompliance with GMPs	Article 47 of 2001/83/EEC Article 51 of 2001/82/EC	Complete records of raw data generated during cleanliness tests by thin layer chromatography are missing (French Health Products Safety Agency).
Smruthi Organics Ltd.	Mar 2014	WL	API	Failure to maintain complete and accurate laboratory test data generated in the course of establishing compliance of your APIs to established specifications and standards.

		Statement of noncompliance with GMPs	2003/94/EC (EU GMPs) Article 47 of 2001/83/EEC	
Wockhardt Limited	Mar 2014			A critical deficiency was cited about data integrity of GMP records; entries were seen to be made when personnel were not present on site and documentation was seen that was not completed contemporaneously despite appearing to be completed in this manner (Competent Authority of United Kingdom).
Steris Corporation	May 2014	WL	820.70(i)	The application is set up to automatically discard any dosimeter absorbance readings outside the set operating range of (b)(4) to (b)(4) absorbance units.
Sun Pharmaceutical Industries Limited	May 7, 2014	WL	211.68(b)	Delete raw data files on computers used for your GC instruments in your quality control laboratory. No computer systems security controls.
Wockhardt's Illinois	May 30, 2014	483	211.68(b)	A general log-in on one computer allows data stored on the hard drives of these instruments to be changed or deleted by any user.
Micro Labs Ltd.	May 2014	Notice of Concern (WHO)	WHO references 15.9, 17.3d, 15.1	HPLCs did not have audit trails enabled, some audit trails missing when peaks were manually integrated, no SOP to describe when manual integration is acceptable. Some instruments had date and time functions unlocked and were not linked to a server, so time stamps could be manipulated. One HPLC had a shared password so actions were not attributable to an individual. In some cases, trial injections were made but were not part of the test record.

(continued)

Table 26.1 2013–2014 Cases of Data Integrity (continued)

Company Name	Date	Action	Regulation	Note
Apotex, Inc.	June 16, 2014	WL	API	General lack of reliability and accuracy of data generated by your firm's laboratory, which is a serious CGMP deficiency that raises concerns about the integrity of all data generated by your firm.
Trifarma S.p.A.	July 7, 2014	WL	API	The firm deleted all electronic raw data supporting the company's high-performance liquid chromatography (HPLC) testing. The computer system grants all laboratory personnel full privileges to delete or alter raw data on the laboratory systems. At the time of the inspection, the company's HPLC and gas chromatograph software had no audit trails to show when raw data was changed and who changed it.
Impax	Jul 2014	483	211.68(b)	The plant has two spectrophotometers that don't have adequate controls to ensure analysts can't rewrite or delete analytical data. The systems are used in testing raw materials, stability and release.[a]
Renown Pharmaceuticals Pvt. Ltd.	Aug 2014	Statement of noncompliance GMPs.	2003/94/EC (EU GMPs)	Record integrity and veracity: some records were fabricated or altered. Lack of mechanisms to ensure integrity of analytical data. (Spanish Agency of Medicines and Medical Devices)
Hebei Dongfeng Pharmaceutical Co., Ltd.	Aug 2014	Statement of noncompliance with GMPs.	Article 47 of 2001/83/EEC	Data recording and integrity in the QC laboratory. (Competent authority of Romania)

Fujian South Pharmaceutical	Sep 2014	Statement of noncompliance to GMPs.	Art. 111(7) of Directive 2001/83/EC	The implementation of sound computerized systems, including data integrity issues. (Italian Medicines Agency)
Taishan City Chemical Pharmaceutical Co. Ltd.	Sep 2014	EU Statement of Noncompliance	GMPs Article 47 of Directive 2001/83/EC	Insufficient security of electronic raw data in the Quality Control laboratory (No limitation of access levels, no restriction on the deletion of data, no audit trail, inadequate traceability and archiving practices) (French Health Products Safety Agency)[b]
Cadila Pharmaceuticals Limited	Oct 2014	WL	API	Failure to prevent unauthorized access or changes to data and to provide adequate controls to prevent omission of data.[c]
Sharp Global Limited	Oct 2014	WL	API	Printing batch records from personal computers over which the company lacked adequate controls. Gas chromatographs didn't prevent the deletion or altering of raw data files, and lacked audit trails that record any changes to data. Sharp management told investigators that the company's practice was to delete raw data files once the chromatograms were printed.[d]

(continued)

Table 26.1 2013–2014 Cases of Data Integrity (continued)

Company Name	Date	Action	Regulation	Note
Zhejiang Apeloa Kangyu Bio-Pharmaceutical Co. Ltd.	Oct 2014	The EU Statement of Noncompliance	GMPs Art. 80(7) of Directive 2001/82/EC	The company failed to establish a procedure to identify and validate GMP-relevant computerized systems in general. Two batch analysis reports for Colistin Sulfate proved to be manipulated. HPLC chromatograms had been copied from previous batches and renamed with different batch and file names. Several electronically stored HPLC runs had not been entered into the equipment logbooks. The nature of these data could not be clarified. Neither the individual workstation nor the central server had been adequately protected against uncontrolled deletion or change of data. The transfer of data between workstations and server showed to be incomplete. No audit trail and no consistency checks had been implemented to prevent misuse of data.

[a] *Source:* Quality Management Network Vol. 6, No. 33 (August 15, 2014).

[b] *Source:* https://www.linkedin.com/groups/Data-Integrity-Issue-TAISHAN-CITY-3845497.S.5939136115691773952?trk=groups_most_recent-0-b-ttl&goback=%2Egmr_3845497

[c] *Source:* Quality Management Network Vol. 6, No. 46 (November 14, 2014).

[d] *Source:* Quality Management Network Vol. 6, No. 46 (November 14, 2014).

able to delete data from analyses, audit trail function disabled, fabricating training data, lack of records for the acquisition or modification of laboratory data, personnel shared login IDs for systems, no procedure for the backup and protection of data on the stand-alone workstations, analysts shared the username and password for the Windows operating system, no computer lock mechanism had been configured to prevent unauthorized access to the operating systems, and so on.

The principles set forth in Annex 11 will not correct the behavior of the regulated users who deliberately employ unreliable or unlawful behavior. This is not related to training or understanding a particular technical or quality concept but is related mainly to honesty and ethical issues. Further, what is more disturbing is that senior management and company owners appear to support such practices covertly or overtly and in many instances encourage them.[*]

In December 2013, the Medicine and Healthcare Products Regulatory Agency (MHRA, UK's medicines and medical devices regulatory agency) declared that as of 2014, pharmaceutical manufacturers, importers, and contract laboratories were expected to verify data integrity in the context of self-inspections.

The US FDA intends to step up its scrutiny of companies' data integrity protections during manufacturing inspections, after 12 of 13 warning letters issued during the first six months of 2014 contained issues on data integrity.[†]

Annex 11 E-recs Integrity Basis

E-recs integrity controls preserve and ensure the accuracy and consistency of e-recs over their entire life cycle. E-recs integrity is a critical characteristic to the design, implementation, and usage of any system that stores, processes, or retrieves GMP-related records (a.k.a. regulated records in this chapter) in electronic format.

The Commission Directive 2003/94/EC, setting out the legal requirements for EU GMP, establishes the basic principles of e-recs integrity in its Chapter II, Article 9(2):

> The electronically stored data shall be protected, by methods such as duplication or back-up and transfer on to another storage system, against loss or damage of data, and audit trails shall be maintained.

---

[*] U. Shetty, "Can Data from Indian Companies be Trusted?" Drug Regulations, http://www.drug regulations.org/, July 2013.
[†] *Quality Management Network,* Vol. 6 No. 29, July 2014.

Table 26.2 Annex 11 Clauses and E-rec Life Cycle

Analysis and Design	E-recs Creation, Access, Use, and Reuse	E-recs Archiving	E-recs Destruction
11-1 Note: Based on Annex 11-1, the implementation to the Annex 11 items listed under "Access, Use and Reuse" are designed Project Phase.	11-4.8; 11-5; 11-6; 11-7; 11-8; 11-9; 11-11; 11-12; 11-16	11-17	Discard and purge e-recs according to an approved procedure.

Similar requirements can be found in 91/412/EEC.[*]

These two directives are implemented via Annex 11. As depicted in Table 26.2, Annex 11 covers the preservation of the content, context, and structure of the electronic records implementing the following controls on e-recs, e-recs storage, audit trails, periodic review, and security.

Each of the Annex 11 clauses is implemented during the applicable SLC phase. Refer to Table 26.3 toward the end of the chapter.

Annex 11 E-recs Integrity Approach

To establish the integrity of the e-recs, they must be trustworthy.

In the context of the Good Clinical Practice (GCP),[†] to consider trustworthy the electronic source data[‡] and the e-recs that hold those source data, a number of attributes must be achieved. These include that the data and records are

---

[*] 91/412/EEC Laying Down the Principles and Guidelines of Good Manufacturing Practice for Veterinary Medicinal Products, July 1991.

[†] EMA/INS/GCP/454280/2010, GCP Inspectors Working Group (GCP IWG), "Reflection Paper on Expectations for Electronic Source Data and Data Transcribed to Electronic Data Collection Tools in Clinical Trials," August 2010.

[‡] Electronic source data: Data initially recorded in electronic format or certified copies of original records (EMA/INS/GCP/454280/2010 GCP Inspectors Working Group ([GCP IWG]), "Reflection Paper on Expectations for Electronic Source Data and Data Transcribed to Electronic Data Collection Tools in Clinical Trials"). Certified copy: A copy (paper or electronic) of original information that has been verified, as indicated by a dated signature, as an exact copy, having all the same attributes and information as the original (Guidance for Industry–Electronic Source Data in Clinical Investigations, September 2013).

- Accurate
- Attributable
- Available when needed
- Complete
- Consistent
- Contemporaneous
- Enduring
- Legible
- Original

Centered on the US National Archives and Records Administration (NARA) record management viewpoint, all the above trustworthy attributes to the e-recs can be summarized as reliability, authenticity, integrity, and usability.

- Reliability—A reliable record is one whose contents can be trusted as a complete and accurate representation of the transactions, activities, or facts to which they attest and can be depended on in the course of subsequent transactions or activities (NARA).
- Authenticity—A record proves it is authentic or genuine based on its mode (i.e., method by which a record is communicated over space or time), form (i.e., format or media that a record has when it is received), state of transmission (i.e., the primitiveness, completeness, and effectiveness of a record when it is initially set aside after being made or received), and manner of preservation and custody (DOD 5015.2-STD).
- Integrity—Data that has retained its integrity has not been modified or tampered with.
- Usability—In the context of e-recs, usability is the extent to which the e-recs can be used by specified users to achieve specified goals with effectiveness, efficiency, and satisfaction in a specified context of use (ISO 9241).

These attributes allow those individuals who depend on the e-recs to correctly fulfill their job function.

To ensure authentic, reliable, complete, and usable records, a record-keeping system must preserve the following:

- Content—the information within the records
- Context—the circumstances under which the records were created or received (who, when, how, and why)
- Structure—the relationship between the parts of the record

If these three factors are not properly controlled, the information that the e-recs must convey might not be complete, accurate, or usable.

Regulatory Guidance

"A means of ensuring data protection should be established for all computerised systems."

Health Canada GMP Guidelines for API (GUI-0104) Dec 2013 and ICH Q7 Aug 2001

The processing and integrity of the data initially recorded in electronic format (electronic source data) to the final output (e-recs) are considered to be critical for every computer system. Added criticality can be characterized to computer systems performing decisions on product quality.

The technical and procedural controls of a computer system should address the e-recs integrity issues, from the source data, e-recs throughout the record retention period, and destruction of the record. Annex 11 sees the risk associated with e-recs as a risk-based continuum.

The validation of a computer system must address the implementation and maintenance of the controls to enable integrity, including data entered manually, automatically acquired, and data processing.

Technical and procedural controls are required to maintain the accuracy, integrity, and reliability of e-recs. Documentary evidence is needed to demonstrate these controls are fit for purpose:

- Written specification and design that describes what the system is intended to do and how it is intended to do it.
- Written test plan based on the specification and design, including both structural and functional analyses.
- Test results and an evaluation of how these results demonstrate that the predetermined specification, design, and controls have been met and periodic verifications and evaluations of the implementation of the controls to assess business and regulatory compliance.

Understanding the e-recs life-cycle concept can help one understand the controls applicable to ensure authenticity and trustworthiness of the records. Creation; access, use, and reuse; and, finally, destruction of e-recs can be considered as the phases of the e-recs life cycle.* Refer to Table 26.2.

Table 26.3 contains a set of controls that should be in place to protect the e-recs. These controls are compiled based on the Annex 11 computer SLC phase.†

The above correlation establishes the applicable controls relative to the computer system life cycle phase. Note that a risk evaluation and mitigation are processes that must be applied during the operational phase via the regular periodic reviews (11-11) and as part of investigation of incidents.

Note that the regulatory requirements about the integrity of e-recs cover paper-based records as well. For each control described previously, there is an equivalent control in the paper world.

One of the most neglected areas in e-recs integrity is the preservation of e-recs as part of the planning to retire the computer system generating e-recs.

The e-recs preservation plan must include one of the following options:

■ Make sure that a new system will be able to retrieve e-recs from previous systems.
■ Preserve previous applications.
■ Archive hard copies (when allowed).
■ Complete the system documentation and validation dossier.

After executing the e-recs preservation plan, ensure that the Quality Assurance (QA) unit of the regulated user performs an audit on the preservation documentation. The audit will verify the traceability between planning and implementation and will assess the successful execution of the preservation plan.‡

Conclusion

Since 2004, the worldwide inspection trends have been on data integrity.

---

* ISPE/PDA, Good Practice and Compliance for Electronic Records and Signatures. Part 1. "Good Electronic Records Management (GERM)," July 2002.
† Life cycle: All phases in the life of the system from initial requirements until retirement including design, specification, programming, testing, installation, operation, and maintenance (EU Annex 11).
‡ CEFIC, "Computer Validation Guide," API Committee of CEFIC, December 2002.

Table 26.3 Controls Based on SLC Phase

Computer SLC Phase	Records Life Cycle[a]	E-recs Controls
General Phase– Requirements	Analysis	1. Identify the applicable critical records. Critical records are identified in the course of the risk analysis (Annex 11-1).
		2. Identify data and e-recs integrity–related controls based on a risk assessment. Manage the controls to mitigate the risks through the SLC (11-1).
		3. If data are transferred to another data format, identify the new format (11-4.8 and 11-8.1) and control requirements (11-5).
		4. Identify interfaces (11-5) and the data to be entered manually (11-6).
		5. Based on risk assessment, assess the need of audit trails (12.4) and controls to prevent unauthorized access to the application and the operating systems (11-7.1, 11-12, and 21 CFR 11.10(g)).
		6. The requirements document must include requirements uncovered during the assessments of the risks.
		7. Design the reports (11-8.1), accuracy checks (11-6), operational system checks (21 CFR Part 11.10(f)), authority checks (21 CFR Part 11.10(g)), and device checks (21 CFR Part 11.10(h)).
Project Phase– Specification, Design, Programming, Testing, Installation	Analysis	1. As part of the qualification of the application and associated controls, test the backup and restoration procedures and verify the output of the backup (11-7.2). Each backup set should be checked to ensure that it is error free.
		2. Verify audit trail capabilities, as applicable (11-7.1).
		3. Verify accuracy of reports and audit trail reports (11-8).
		4. As applicable and based on the operational sequencing, test accuracy of e-recs (11-7.1).

		5. If e-recs are transferred to another format (refer to Chapter 8), the qualification must include checks that the new format or meaning is not altered during the migration process (11-4.8).
		6. IT infrastructure must be qualified to ensure security and e-recs integrity (Principle b).
Operational and Maintenance Phases	Creation, Access, Use and Reuse, Archiving, Transfer, Archiving, or Destruction	1. A means of ensuring e-recs protection must be established for all computer systems (Health Canada GMP Guidelines for API [GUI-0104] Dec 2013, ICH Q7 Aug 2001, EU Annex 11-4.8, 11-5, 11-6, 11-7, 11-8.1, 11-12).
		2. Written procedures must be available for the operation and maintenance of computer systems.[b] Management of records, performance monitoring (11-12), change control program (11-10) and e-recs security (11-12), calibration and maintenance (11-10), personnel training (11-2), emergency recovery (11-16), management of incidents (11-17), e-recs entry (11-6) and modifications (WHO 4.2), and periodic re-evaluation (11-11) are some of the procedures impacting e-recs integrity.
		3. The procedures and records pertaining to the security of the system and security of the e-recs are very important and must be based on the IT policies of the regulated user and in conformance with the relevant regulatory requirements (11-12.1).
		4. There should be written procedures for recovery of the system following a breakdown; these procedures should include documentation and record requirements to ensure retrieval and maintenance of GXP information (11-16).
		5. E-recs must be secured by both physical and electronic means against damage, including unauthorized access and changes to e-recs (11-12). As part of the physical security, it must be considered security to devices used to store programs, such as tapes, disks, and magnetic strip cards. Access to these devices should be controlled.

(continued)

Table 26.3   Controls Based on SLC Phase (continued)

Computer SLC Phase	Records Life Cycle[a]	E-recs Controls
		6. Periodic (or continuous) reviews must be performed after the initial validation (11-11). As part of a periodic review, verify stored backup and archived e-recs for accessibility, readability, and accuracy; verify the output of the backup; accuracy of audit trail. As applicable, verify accurate and reliable e-recs transfer (WHO 3.2).
		7. Access to e-recs should be ensured throughout the retention period (11-7.1).
		8. The electronically stored e-recs should be checked regularly for availability and integrity (11-7.1).
		9. Following changes to the system, change control should ensure the availability and integrity of the e-recs on the backup copies by restoring the e-recs on a trial basis (11-10 and 11-7.2).
		10. E-rec errors, complete loss in data, and loss of data integrity must be reported and investigated. Corrective actions must be taken in accordance to the investigation (11-13). The GMP regulators expect any resulting recommendations to be implemented as soon as reasonably practical.
		11. When applicable, there must be controls to prevent system turn-off and e-recs not captured (11-5).
		12. For critical records entered or e-recs amended (WHO 4.2) manually, there should be an additional check on the accuracy of the data and entered only by persons authorized to do so (11-6).

		13. Where an e-rec is deleted prior to meeting its approved retention, an audit trail of the deletion is required until the end of the approved retention period (11-7.1). 14. When outside agencies are used to provide a computer service, there should be a formal agreement including a clear statement of the responsibilities of that outside agency (11-3.1).
Retirement Phase	E-rec Destruction	1. In the context of the computer system retirement: • If the e-recs are transferred to another e-recs format or system, validation should include checks that e-recs are not altered in value or meaning during this migration process (11-4.8). • If the e-recs are transferred to another system, the ability to retrieve the e-recs should be ensured and tested (11-7).

a ISPE/PDA, Good Practice and Compliance for Electronic Records and Signatures. Part 1. Good Electronic Records Management (GERM), July 2002.

b O. López, "Maintaining the Validated State in Computer Systems," *Journal of GXP Compliance*, 17(2), August 2013 (http://www.ivtnetwork.com/article/maintaining-validated-state-computer-systems).

To ensure integrity of the GMP records, traceability controls must be applied during their entire life cycle, from their initial creation to their eventual disposal. In addition, the record-keeping functions within the computer system must preserve the content, context, and structure of the electronic records.

All necessary controls must be taken to ensure the protection of data. These controls must ensure that safeguards against unauthorized data additions, deletions, or modifications, and transfer of information are in place to resolve record discrepancies and to prevent unauthorized disclosure of such information.

The controls to preserve the content, context, and structure of electronic records are comprehensively contained in Annex 11.

These controls must be part of the design and enforced during the operations of computer systems. During periodic reviews, the system and the risks associated with the computer system are reviewed, and the controls may be re-evaluated. As risk and requirements, data integrity must be embedded into the SLC and managed accordingly during the SLC.

The implementation of robust controls may correct the behavior of the regulated users who deliberately employ unreliable or unlawful behavior.

References

CEFIC, *Computer Validation Guide*, API Committee of CEFIC, December 2002.

EMA/INS/GCP/454280/2010, GCP Inspectors Working Group (GCP IWG), "Reflection Paper on Expectations for Electronic Source Data and Data Transcribed to Electronic Data Collection Tools in Clinical Trials," August 2010.

EudraLex, The Rules Governing Medicinal Products in the European Union, Volume 4, "Good Manufacturing Practice, Medicinal Products for Human and Veterinary Use, Chapter 4: Documentation," June 2011.

European Commission (EC), "General Data Protection Regulation (GDPR)," January 2012 (Proposed regulation to replace EU Data Protection Directive 95/46/EC).

European Union Agency for Fundamental Rights, "Handbook on European data protection law," fra.europa.eu, December 2013.

GAMP/ISPE, "Risk Assessment for Use of Automated Systems Supporting Manufacturing Process—Risk to Record," Pharmaceutical Engineering, Nov/Dec 2002.

IDA Programme of the European Commission, "Model Requirements for the Management of Electronic Records," http://www.cornwell.co.uk/moreq.html, www.cornwell.co.uk/moreq.html, October 2002.

ISPE/PDA, "Good Practice and Compliance for Electronic Records and Signatures. Part 1 Good Electronic Records Management (GERM)," July 2002.

López, O., "A Computer Data Integrity Compliance Model," *Pharmaceutical Engineering,* Vol. 35, No. 2, March/April 2015.

McDowall, R.D., "Ensuring Data Integrity in a Regulated Environment," *Scientific Computing*, March/April 2011.

Schmitt, S., "Data Integrity," *Pharmaceutical Technology,* Vol. 38, No. 7, July 2014.

Wechsler, J., "Data Integrity Key to GMP Compliance," BioPharm International.com, September 2014. http://www.biopharminternational.com/data-integrity-key-gmp-compliance

WHO, Technical Report Series No. 937, Annex 4. Appendix 5, "Validation of Computerised Systems," 2006.

Wingate, G., *Validating Automated Manufacturing and Laboratory Applications: Putting Principles into Practice*, Taylor & Francis, Boca Raton, FL, 1997.

Chapter 27

Annex 11 and 21 CFR Part 11
Comparisons for International Compliance*

Introduction

The two essential resources available to regulated life-science profession-als regarding the validation of computer systems are the Food and Drug Administration's (FDA) rule on Electronic Records/Signatures[†] (21 CFR Part 11, aka Part 11) and the European Medicines Agency's (EMA[‡]) Guidelines to Good Manufacturing Practice (GMPs)–Annex 11, Computerised Systems (aka EU Annex 11).

Part 11 establishes the requirements for the technical and procedural con-trols that must be met by the regulated user[§] if the regulated user chooses to maintain critical data electronically. Part 11 applies to critical data in electronic form that are created, modified, maintained, archived, retrieved, or transmitted under any records requirements set forth in the FDA predicate regulations.

---

[*] This chapter was originally published in the *Master Control Newsletter*. O. López, "Annex 11 and 21 CFR Part 11: Comparisons for International Compliance," *Master Control Newsletter*, Jan 31, 2012, http://www.mastercontrol.com/newsletter/annex-11-21-cfr-part-11-comparison.html.

[†] FDA, 21 CFR Part 11, "Electronic Records; Electronic Signatures; Final Rule," *Federal Register*, 62(54), 13429, March 20, 1997.

[‡] The European Medicines Agency is an agency of the European Union. The Agency is responsible for the scientific evaluation of medicines developed by pharmaceutical companies for use in the European Union.

[§] Regulated user: The regulated Good Practice entity, which is responsible for the operation of a computerized system and the applications, files, and data held thereon (PIC/S PI 011-3).

Part 11 came into effect in March 1997. It is strictly applicable in the United States to all FDA program areas. Part 11 is also applicable to manufacturers outside the United States and its territories who wish to gain FDA market approval.

For the purpose of this analysis, it is required to consider the Part 11 Guideline (2003). This guideline is the one used by the FDA for interpretation and to enforce the Part 11 requirements established in the Part 11 regulation. (See Analysis of Part 11.[*])

European Union (EU) Annex 11 covers the interpretation of the principles and guidelines pertinent to computer systems of GMP-regulated activities. The first edition of EU Annex 11 dates back to 1992. The current version was published in January 2011. EU Annex 11 is strictly applicable to the EU, although US manufacturers who wish EU market approval need to take it into account as an applicable requirement. It applies to GMP for medicinal products for human use, investigational medicinal products for human use, and veterinary medicinal products. (See Analysis of EU Annex 11.[†])

This chapter discusses how the updated Annex 11 compares with Part 11. Refer to Appendix 5 for a matrix containing a comprehensive comparison of Annex 11, Part 11 and other regulations/guidelines.

Comparing the 11s

There are two primary common areas between the EU's EMEA Annex 11 and the FDA's Part 11. The first common area is the electronic signatures (e-sigs) elements within these documents. The second common area is the elements covered in Part 11.10, *Controls for Closed Systems.*

Electronic Signatures

Speaking strictly about e-sigs, Part 11 goes beyond Annex 11. Back in the early 1990s, the main reason for initiating Part 11 was to approve online electronic batch records.[‡]

---

[*] http://www.askaboutvalidation.com/wp-content/uploads/2012/07/An-Easy-to-Understand-Guide-to-Annex-11.pdf

[†] http://www.askaboutvalidation.com/wp-content/uploads/2012/07/An-Easy-to-Understand-Guide-to-Annex-11.pdf

[‡] http://www.mastercontrol.com/batch_records/electronic_batch_records.html?lne=lkey

E-sigs in the EU Annex 11 are covered under 11-14. The use of e-sigs to sign electronic records (e-recs) is permitted. It is expected that e-sigs will:

- have the same impact as handwritten signatures within the boundaries of the company (11.100(a) and (b) 11.200(a)(2));
- be permanently linked to their respective record(s) (11.70); and
- include the time and date of signature (11.50(a)(2)).

The direct EU Annex 11 corresponding e-sigs guideline associated with Part 11 regulation can be found in parentheses above.

In addition, Part 11 includes the following e-sig requirements not covered in the EU Annex 11.

11.50(a)(1) and (3); 11.50(b)

Section 11.50 requires signature manifestations to contain information associated with the signing of e-recs. This information must include the printed name of the signer and the meaning (such as review, approval, responsibility, and authorship) associated with the signature. In addition, this information is subject to the same controls as e-recs and must be included in any human readable forms of the e-rec (such as electronic display or printout).

11.100(c)(1) and (2)

Under the general requirements for e-sigs, at Section 11.100, before an organization establishes, assigns, certifies, or otherwise sanctions an individual's e-sig, the organization shall verify the identity of the individual.

11.200(a)(1)(i) and (ii); 11.200(a)(3); 11.200(b)

Section 11.200 provides that e-sigs not based on biometrics must employ at least two distinct identification components such as an identification code and password. In addition, when an individual executes a series of signings during a single period of controlled system access, the first signing must be executed using all e-sig components, and the subsequent signings must be executed using at least one component designed to be used only by that individual. When an individual executes one or more signings not performed during a single period of controlled system access, each signing must be executed using all the e-sig components.

E-sigs not based on biometrics are also required to be administered and executed to ensure that attempted use of an individual's e-sig by anyone else requires the collaboration of two or more individuals. This would make it more difficult for anyone to forge an e-sig. E-sigs based on biometrics must be designed to ensure that such signatures cannot be used by anyone other than the genuine owners.

11.300

Under Section 11.300, e-sigs based on use of identification codes in combination with passwords must employ controls to ensure security and integrity. The controls must include the following provisions: (1) The uniqueness of each combined identification code and password must be maintained in such a way that no two individuals have the same combination of identification code and password; (2) persons using identification codes or passwords must ensure that they are periodically recalled or revised; (3) loss-management procedures must be followed to de-authorize lost, stolen, missing, or otherwise potentially compromised tokens, cards, and other devices that bear or generate identification codes or password information; (4) transaction safeguards must be used to prevent unauthorized use of passwords or identification codes and to detect and report any attempt to misuse such codes; (5) devices that bear or generate identification codes or password information, such as tokens or cards, must be tested initially and periodically to ensure that they function properly and have not been altered in an unauthorized manner.

The above Part 11 e-sig descriptions were directly obtained from the Part 11 regulation preamble.[*]

Controls for Closed Systems

Section 11.10 describes the controls that must be designed by the regulated user to ensure the integrity of the computer system operations and the data stored in the computer system. In the context of Annex 11, the data integrity is discussed in Chapters 12 and 26 Annex 11 and Electronic Records Integrity.

---

[*] Preamble: Analysis preceding a proposed or final rule that clarifies the intention of the rule making and any ambiguities regarding the rule. Responses to comments made on a proposed rule are published in the preamble preceding the final rule. Preambles are published only in the FR and do not have a binding effect.

On the controls framework, the Part 11 regulation considers computer systems in two groupings: closed and open. Closed and open systems are defined in Part 11.3. The system owner controls the access in closed systems. An open system is an environment in which the system owner does not control system access. Annex 11 does not make this distinction. Implicitly, Annex 11 covers these security-related controls in 11-12.

Speaking strictly about the integrity of system operations and data stored in the system, Annex 11 goes beyond Part 11 (refer to Chapter 26). Annex 11 sees the risk associated with e-recs/e-sigs as a risk-based continuum rather than a question of open/closed systems.

The requirements covered by Part 11 about the controls for closed systems are validation, copy and protection of e-recs, audit trails, system documentation, computer system access, and experience of people developing/maintaining/using the computer system.

Validation (11.10(a))

Validation is the

> formal assessment and reporting of quality and performance measures for all the lifecycle stages of software and system development, its implementation, qualification and acceptance, operation, modification, re-qualification, maintenance and retirement. This should enable both the regulated user, and competent authority to have a high level of confidence in the integrity of both the processes executed within the controlling computer system(s) and in those processes controlled by and/or linked to the computer system(s), within the prescribed operating environment(s).

The FDA has maintained the requirement for validation because the agency believes that it is necessary that software be validated to the extent possible to adequately ensure performance.

The correct validation implementation program on computer systems "ensures accuracy, reliability, consistent intended performance, and the ability to discern invalid or altered records."

In the EU Annex 11, validation of computer systems is an element of the project phase and takes center stage. The validation phase has been extensively expanded in the updated Annex 11 to cover the complete computer system life cycle. One of the main principles of this Annex states: *"The application should be validated; IT infrastructure should be qualified."*

A significant and essential activity at the beginning of a computer system's life cycle is to establish the intended use and proper performance of computer systems. The intended use is one of the factors to account for to determine the granular level of the computer system's validation.[*]

The phrase "proper performance" relates to the general principle of validation. Planned and expected performance is based on predetermined design specifications, consequently, "intended use."

All computer systems automating any regulated function must be validated for its intended use. This requirement applies to any computer system automating the design, testing, raw material or component acceptance, manufacturing, labeling, packaging, distribution, and complaint handling, or to automate any other aspect of the quality system.

In addition, computer systems creating, modifying, and maintaining e-recs and managing e-sigs are also subject to the validation requirements. Such computer systems must be validated to ensure accuracy, reliability, consistent intended performance, and the ability to discern invalid or altered records.

Software for the above applications may be developed in house or under contract. However, software is frequently purchased off the shelf for a particular intended use. All production or quality system software, even if purchased off the shelf, should have documented requirements that fully define its intended use, and information against which testing results and other evidence can be compared, to show that the software is validated for its intended use.

Appropriate installation and operational qualifications should demonstrate the suitability of computer hardware and software to perform assigned tasks.

The Ability to Generate Accurate, Complete Copies of Records (11.10(b))

According to this requirement, also contained in Annex 11-5 and 11-8 documentation, it must be possible to obtain clear, printed copies of electronically stored e-recs. When generating an electronic copy of an e-rec, any file conversions must be qualified.

---

[*] http://www.mastercontrol.com/validation/computer_systems_validation.html?lne=lkey

Protection of Records (11.10(c) and (d))

Computer systems e-recs must be controlled including records retention, backup, and security.

The data collected in a computer system should be secured by both physical and electronic means against damage. The access to data should be ensured throughout the retention period.

One of many activities supporting this requirement is backups. Backups must be performed on electronic copies of e-recs and stored separately from the primary e-recs. The objective of the backup is to guarantee the availability of the stored data and, in case of loss of data, to reconstruct all GMP-relevant documentation.

According to 11-7.2 and similarly to an electronic file, the integrity and accuracy of backup data and the ability to restore the data should be verified during validation and periodically (Annex 11-7.1). The frequency and extent of backup should be based on the effort involved to recreate the data. This should be defined in the backup procedure.

Measures must be taken, however, to ensure that backup data are exact and complete and that they are secure from alteration, inadvertent erasure, and loss.

Security is an issue covered in all regulations. The basic principle in Annex 11 is that computer systems must have adequate controls to prevent unauthorized access or changes to data, inadvertent erasures, or loss (Annex 11-7.1).

Use of Computer-Generated, Time-Stamped Audit Trails (11.10(e), (k)(2) and Associated Requirements in 11.30)

One of the first references on the use of audit trails in FDA guidelines is from the 1978 cGMP preamble. The comment in paragraph 186 states: *"If a computer system has the capability, however, to verify its output, such as with audit trails, this could be considered as a check for accuracy."*

As in Annex 11-9, the system-generated audit trail[*] referenced in 11.10(e) or other physical, logical, or procedural security measures must be in place *to ensure the trustworthiness and reliability of the records. The appropriate*

---

[*] An electronic means of auditing the interactions with records within an electronic system so that any access to the system can be documented as it occurs for identifying unauthorized actions in relation to the records, for example, modification, deletion, or addition (DOD 5015.2-STD).

measures should be based on a risk assessment. For change or deletion of cGMP-relevant data, the reason should be documented.

This is one requirement where, since 2003, the FDA has exercised enforcement discretion. Regulated firms must still comply with all applicable predicate rule requirements related to documentation of date, time, or sequencing of events, as well as any requirements for ensuring that changes to records do not obscure previous entries.

Audit trails are appropriate when the regulated user is expected to create, modify, or delete regulated records during normal operation.

Use of Appropriate Controls over Systems Documentation

Computer system documentation means records that relate to system operation and maintenance, from high-level design documents to end-user manuals. All regulatory provisions applicable to software are also applicable to its documentation.

Computer system documents are generated/updated during the implementation/maintenance project, correspondingly. These documents may be either printed material or e-recs, such as computer files, storage media, or film. Storing a large number of documents increases the cost of document management[*] because of the increasing difficulty of keeping the documents consistent with the computer system. Computer system documents must be available if needed for review. Obsolete information must be archived or destroyed in accordance with a written record retention plan.

Even Annex 11 provides guidance on documentation; there is no explicit guidance on controls over computer systems documentation. The applicable controls on documentation can be found in the new version of Chapter 4 ("Documentation") of the EU Guideline to GMP. Chapter 4 can be used as a guidance to implement 11.10(k).

System Access Limited to Authorized Individuals (11.10(d), (g) and (h))

Security is a key issue in computer systems, including the use of authority checks (21 CFR 11.10(g)) to ensure that only authorized individuals can use the system and alter records.

---

[*] http://www.mastercontrol.com/document_management_software/management/index.html?lne=lkey

Part 11 security requirements listed in 11.10(d), (g), and (h), are covered in Annex 11-7.1 and 11-12. In addition, Annex 11-4.3 calls for *"An up-to-date listing of all relevant* systems *and their GMP functionality (inventory) should be available . . . and security measures should be available."*

A determination that persons who develop, maintain, or use e-recs and signature systems have the education, training, and experience to perform their assigned tasks.

Annex 11-2 covers this Part 11 requirement.

Conclusion

The revised Annex 11 lists in a comprehensive manner 11.10 requirements.

In the context of the content of Part 11 and Annex 11, the main difference between the two is that Part 11 is a regulation. The nature of a regulation restricts the granularity of the guidance that a regulator may provide. The regulated user will get less guidance in Part 11 than in Annex 11. The guidance by the regulator on Part 11 can be found in the preamble of this regulation and in the 2003 guidance document.

Annex 11 has a much broader scope than Part 11. Speaking strictly about e-recs and e-sigs, Part 11 goes beyond Annex 11, but Annex 11 works well with 21 CFR Part 11. Annex 11 can be used in different regulated environments, such as the United States, as a regulatory guideline to comply with the regulatory requirements applicable to computer systems supporting GXP applications.

The narrow scope of Part 11 started the awareness of regulated industry on e-recs and e-sigs. The updated EU Annex 11 has improved the standard for regulated users and systems. EU Annex 11 gives the specific guidance in areas that are not covered in Part 11 regulations.[*]

References

Appel, K., "How Far Does Annex 11 Go Beyond Part 11?" Pharmaceutical Processing, September 2011.

EudraLex, "The Rules Governing Medicinal Products in the European Union Volume 4, Good Manufacturing Practice, Medicinal Products for Human and Veterinary Use, Chapter 4: Documentation," Section 4.32, June 2011.

---

[*] http://www.mastercontrol.com/21_cfr_regulations/21_cfr_part_11/

EudraLex, Volume 4, "EU Guidelines to Good Manufacturing Practice, Medicinal Products for Human and Veterinary Use, Annex 11–Computerised Systems," June 2011.

PI 011-3. "Good Practices for Computerised Systems in Regulated 'GXP' Environments," Pharmaceutical Inspection Cooperation Scheme (PIC/S), September 2007.

US FDA, 21 CFR Part 11, "Electronic Records; Electronic Signatures; Final Rule." *Federal Register* 62(54), 13429, March 20, 1997.

US FDA, "Guidance for Industry, Electronic Records; Electronic Signatures—Scope and Application," August 2003.

Appendix A:
EMA Annex 11, Rev 1992

Principle

The introduction of computerized systems into systems of manufacturing, including storage, distribution, and quality control, does not alter the need to observe the relevant principles given elsewhere in the Guide. Where a computerized system replaces a manual operation, there should be no resultant decrease in product quality or quality assurance. Consideration should be given to the risk of losing aspects of the previous system, which could result from reducing the involvement of operators.

Personnel

1. It is essential that there is the closest cooperation between key personnel and those involved with computer systems. Persons in responsible positions should have the appropriate training for the management and use of systems within their field of responsibility, which utilizes computers. This should include ensuring that appropriate expertise is available and used to provide advice on aspects of design, validation, installation, and operation of computerized systems.

Validation

2. The extent of validation necessary will depend on a number of factors, including the use to which the system is to be put, whether the validation is to be prospective or retrospective, and whether novel elements are incorporated. Validation should be considered part of the complete life cycle of a computer system. This cycle includes the stages of planning, specification, programming, testing, commissioning, documentation, operation, monitoring, and modifying.

System

3. Attention should be paid to the siting of equipment in suitable conditions where extraneous factors cannot interfere with the system.
4. A written detailed description of the system should be produced (including diagrams as appropriate) and kept up to date. It should describe the principles, objectives, security measures, and scope of the system and the main features of the way in which the computer is used and how it interacts with other systems and procedures.
5. The software is a critical component of a computerized system. The user of such software should take all reasonable steps to ensure that it has been produced in accordance with a system of Quality Assurance.
6. The system should include, where appropriate, built-in checks of the correct entry and processing of data.
7. Before a system using a computer is brought into use, it should be thoroughly tested and confirmed as being capable of achieving the desired results. If a manual system is being replaced, the two should be run in parallel for a time as a part of this testing and validation.
8. Data should be entered or amended only by persons authorized to do so. Suitable methods of deterring unauthorized entry of data include the use of keys, pass cards, personal codes, and restricted access to computer terminals. There should be a defined procedure for the issue, cancellation, and alteration of authorization to enter and amend data, including the changing of personal passwords. Consideration should be given to systems allowing for recording of attempts to access by unauthorized persons.
9. When critical data are being entered manually (e.g., the weight and batch number of an ingredient during dispensing), there should be an

additional check on the accuracy of the record that is made. This check may be done by a second operator or by validated electronic means.

10. The system should record the identity of operators entering or confirming critical data. Authority to amend entered data should be restricted to nominated persons. Any alteration to an entry of critical data should be authorized and recorded with the reason for the change. Consideration should be given to building into the system the creation of a complete record of all entries and amendments (an "audit trail").

11. Alterations to a system or to a computer program should be made only in accordance with a defined procedure, which should include provision for validating, checking, approving, and implementing the change. Such an alteration should be implemented only with the agreement of the person responsible for the part of the system concerned, and the alteration should be recorded. Every significant modification should be validated.

12. For quality auditing purposes, it should be possible to obtain clear printed copies of electronically stored data.

13. Data should be secured by physical or electronic means against willful or accidental damage, in accordance with item 4.9 of the Guide. Stored data should be checked for accessibility, durability, and accuracy. If changes are proposed to the computer equipment or its programs, the above-mentioned checks should be performed at a frequency appropriate to the storage medium being used.

14. Data should be protected by backing-up at regular intervals. Backup data should be stored as long as necessary at a separate and secure location.

15. There should be available adequate alternative arrangements for systems that need to be operated in the event of a breakdown. The time required to bring the alternative arrangements into use should be related to the possible urgency of the need to use them. For example, information required to effect a recall must be available at short notice.

16. The procedures to be followed if the system fails or breaks down should be defined and validated. Any failures and remedial action taken should be recorded.

17. A procedure should be established to record and analyze errors and to enable corrective action to be taken.

18. When outside agencies are used to provide a computer service, there should be a formal agreement including a clear statement of the responsibilities of that outside agency (see Chapter 7).

19. When the release of batches for sale or supply is carried out using a computerized system, the system should allow only a Qualified Person to release the batches, and it should clearly identify and record the person releasing the batches.

Appendix B:
EMA Annex 11, Rev 2011

European Commission
Health and Consumers Directorate-General
Public Health and Risk Assessment
Pharmaceuticals

Brussels
SANCO/C8/AM/sl/ares(2010)1064599

EudraLex
The Rules Governing Medicinal Products in the European Union

Volume 4
Good Manufacturing Practice
Medicinal Products for Human and Veterinary Use
Annex 11: Computerised Systems

Legal basis for publishing the detailed guidelines: Article 47 of Directive 2001/83/EC on the Community code relating to medicinal products for human use and Article 51 of Directive 2001/82/EC on the Community code relating to veterinary medicinal products. This document provides guidance for the interpretation of the principles and guidelines of good manufacturing practice (GMP) for medicinal products as laid down in Directive 2003/94/EC for medicinal products for human use and Directive 91/412/EEC for veterinary use.

Status of the document: revision 1

Reasons for changes: The Annex has been revised in response to the increased use of computerized systems and the increased complexity of these systems. Consequential amendments are also proposed for Chapter 4 of the GMP Guide.

Deadline for coming into operation: 30 June 2011
Commission Européenne, B-1049 Bruxelles/Europese Commissie,
B-1049 Brussel – Belgium
Telephone: (32-2) 299 11 11

Principle

■ This annex applies to all forms of computerized systems used as part of GMP-regulated activities. A computerized system is a set of software and hardware components which together fulfill certain functionalities.

■ The application should be validated; IT infrastructure should be qualified.

■ Where a computerized system replaces a manual operation, there should be no resultant decrease in product quality, process control, or quality assurance. There should be no increase in the overall risk of the process.

General

1. Risk Management

Risk management should be applied throughout the life cycle of the computerized system taking into account patient safety, data integrity, and product quality. As part of a risk management system, decisions on the extent of validation and data integrity controls should be based on a justified and documented risk assessment of the computerized system.

2. Personnel

There should be close cooperation between all relevant personnel such as Process Owner, System Owner, Qualified Persons, and IT. All personnel should have appropriate qualifications, level of access, and defined responsibilities to carry out their assigned duties.

3. Suppliers and Service Providers

3.1 When third parties (e.g., suppliers, service providers) are used, for example, to provide, install, configure, integrate, validate, maintain (e.g., via remote access), modify, or retain a computerized system or related service or for data processing, formal agreements must exist between the manufacturer and any third parties, and these agreements should include clear statements of the responsibilities of the third party. IT-departments should be considered analogous.

3.2 The competence and reliability of a supplier are key factors when selecting a product or service provider. The need for an audit should be based on a risk assessment.

3.3 Documentation supplied with commercial off-the-shelf products should be reviewed by regulated users to check that user requirements are fulfilled.

3.4 Quality system and audit information relating to suppliers or developers of software and implemented systems should be made available to inspectors on request.

Project Phase

4. Validation

4.1 The validation documentation and reports should cover the relevant steps of the life cycle. Manufacturers should be able to justify their standards, protocols, acceptance criteria, procedures, and records based on their risk assessment.

4.2 Validation documentation should include change control records (if applicable) and reports on any deviations observed during the validation process.

4.3 An up-to-date listing of all relevant systems and their GMP functionality (inventory) should be available.

For critical systems, an up to date system description detailing the physical and logical arrangements, data flows, and interfaces with other systems or processes, any hardware and software pre-requisites, and security measures should be available.

4.4 User Requirements Specifications should describe the required functions of the computerized system and be based on documented risk assessment and GMP impact. User requirements should be traceable throughout the life cycle.

4.5 The regulated user should take all reasonable steps to ensure that the system has been developed in accordance with an appropriate quality management system. The supplier should be assessed appropriately.

4.6 For the validation of bespoke or customized computerized systems, there should be a process in place that ensures the formal assessment and reporting of quality and performance measures for all the life-cycle stages of the system.

4.7 Evidence of appropriate test methods and test scenarios should be demonstrated. Particularly, system (process) parameter limits, data limits, and error handling should be considered. Automated testing tools and test environments should have documented assessments for their adequacy.

4.8 If data are transferred to another data format or system, validation should include checks that data are not altered in value or meaning during this migration process.

Operational Phase

5. Data

Computerized systems exchanging data electronically with other systems should include appropriate built-in checks for the correct and secure entry and processing of data, in order to minimize the risks.

6. Accuracy Checks

For critical data entered manually, there should be an additional check on the accuracy of the data. This check may be done by a second operator or by validated electronic means. The criticality and the potential consequences of erroneous or incorrectly entered data to a system should be covered by risk management.

7. Data Storage

7.1 Data should be secured by both physical and electronic means against damage. Stored data should be checked for accessibility, readability, and accuracy. Access to data should be ensured throughout the retention period.

7.2 Regular back-ups of all relevant data should be done. Integrity and accuracy of back-up data and the ability to restore the data should be checked during validation and monitored periodically.

8. Printouts

8.1 It should be possible to obtain clear printed copies of electronically stored data.

8.2 For records supporting batch release, it should be possible to generate printouts indicating if any of the data has been changed since the original entry.

9. Audit Trails

Consideration should be given, based on a risk assessment, to building into the system the creation of a record of all GMP-relevant changes and deletions (a system generated "audit trail"). For change or deletion of GMP-relevant data, the reason should be documented. Audit trails need to be available and convertible to a generally intelligible form and regularly reviewed.

10. Change and Configuration Management

Any changes to a computerized system including system configurations should only be made in a controlled manner in accordance with a defined procedure.

11. Periodic Evaluation

Computerized systems should be periodically evaluated to confirm that they remain in a valid state and are compliant with GMP. Such evaluations should include, where appropriate, the current range of functionality, deviation records, incidents, problems, upgrade history, performance, reliability, security, and validation status reports.

12. Security

12.1 Physical or logical controls should be in place to restrict access to computerized systems to authorized persons. Suitable methods of preventing unauthorized entry to the system may include the use of keys, pass cards, personal codes with passwords, biometrics, and restricted access to computer equipment and data storage areas.

12.2 The extent of security controls depends on the criticality of the computerized system.

12.3 Creation, change, and cancellation of access authorizations should be recorded.

12.4 Management systems for data and for documents should be designed to record the identity of operators entering, changing, confirming, or deleting data including date and time.

13. Incident Management

All incidents, not only system failures and data errors, should be reported and assessed. The root cause of a critical incident should be identified and should form the basis of corrective and preventive actions.

14. Electronic Signature

Electronic records may be signed electronically. Electronic signatures are expected to:

a. have the same impact as hand-written signatures within the boundaries of the company,
b. be permanently linked to their respective record,
c. include the time and date that they were applied.

15. Batch Release

When a computerized system is used for recording certification and batch release, the system should allow only Qualified Persons to certify the release of the batches and it should clearly identify and record the person releasing or certifying the batches. This should be performed using an electronic signature.

16. Business Continuity

For the availability of computerized systems supporting critical processes, provisions should be made to ensure continuity of support for those processes in the event of a system breakdown (e.g., a manual or alternative system). The time required to bring the alternative arrangements into use should be based on risk and appropriate for a particular system and the business process it supports. These arrangements should be adequately documented and tested.

17. *Archiving*

Data may be archived. This data should be checked for accessibility, readability, and integrity. If relevant changes are to be made to the system (e.g., computer equipment or programs), then the ability to retrieve the data should be ensured and tested.

Glossary

Application: Software installed on a defined platform/hardware providing specific functionality.

Bespoke/customized computerized system: A computerized system individually designed to suit a specific business process.

Commercial off-the-shelf software: Software commercially available, whose fitness for use is demonstrated by a broad spectrum of users.

IT infrastructure: The hardware and software such as networking software and operation systems, which makes it possible for the application to function.

Life cycle: All phases in the life of the system from initial requirements until retirement including design, specification, programming, testing, installation, operation, and maintenance.

Process owner: The person responsible for the business process.

System owner: The person responsible for the availability and maintenance of a computerized system and for the security of the data residing on that system.

Third party: Party not directly managed by the holder of the manufacturing or import authorization.

Appendix C: Glossary of Terms

For additional terms, refer to the *Glossary of Computerized System and Software Development Terminology**; "A Globally Harmonized Glossary of Terms for Communicating Computer Validation Key Practices"†; and EudraLex, Volume 4 Good Manufacturing Practice (GMP) Guidelines–Glossary.‡

Abstraction: This is a basic principle of software engineering and enables understanding of the application and its design and the management of complexity.

Acceptance Criteria: The criteria that a system or component must satisfy to be accepted by a user, customer, or other authorized entity (IEEE).

Acceptance Test: Testing conducted to determine whether a system satisfies its acceptance criteria and to enable the customer to determine whether to accept the system (IEEE).

Access: The ability or opportunity to gain knowledge of stored information (DOD 5015.2-STD).

Accuracy: Refers to whether the data values stored for an object are the correct values. To be correct, a data value must be the right value and must be represented in a consistent and unambiguous form.

Acquirer: An organization that acquires or procures a system, software product, or software service from a supplier (ISO 12207:1995§).

---

* FDA, *Glossary of Computerized System and Software Development Terminology*, Division of Field Investigations, Office of Regional Operations, Office of Regulatory Affairs, Food and Drug Administration, August 1995.

† Herr, Robert R. and Wyrick, Michael L., "A Globally Harmonized Glossary of Terms for Communicating Computer Validation Key Practices," *PDA Journal of Pharmaceutical Science and Technology*, March/April 1999.

‡ http://ec.europa.eu/health/files/eudralex/vol-4/pdfs-en/glos4en200408_en.pdf

§ Note: The 1995 revision is not the most recent version.

Application: Software installed on a defined platform/hardware providing specific functionality (EU Annex 11).

Application Developer: See **Software Developer**.

Approver: In the context of configuration management, the approver is the person responsible for evaluating the recommendations of the reviewers of deliverable documentation and for rendering a decision on whether to proceed with a proposed change and initiating the implementation of a change request.

Audit: An independent examination of a software product, software process, or set of software processes to assess compliance with specifications, standards, contractual agreements, or other criteria (IEEE).

Audit Trail: An electronic means of auditing the interactions with records within an electronic system so that any access to the system can be documented as it occurs for identifying unauthorized actions in relation to the records, for example, modification, deletion, or addition (DOD 5015.2-STD).

Auditor: In the context of configuration management, the auditor is the person responsible for reviewing the steps taken during a development or change management process to ensure that the appropriate procedures have been followed.

Authentication: The process used to confirm the identity of a person or to prove the integrity of specific information. In the case of a message, authentication involves determining its source and ensuring that the message has not been modified or replaced in transit (ABA).

Authenticity: A condition that proves that a record is authentic or genuine based on its mode (i.e., method by which a record is communicated over space or time), form (i.e., format or media that a record has when it is received), state of transmission (i.e., the primitiveness, completeness, and effectiveness of a record when it is initially set aside after being made or received), and manner of preservation and custody (DOD 5015.2-STD).

Automated Systems: Include a broad range of systems including, but not limited to, automated manufacturing equipment, automated laboratory equipment, process control, manufacturing execution, clinical trials data management, and document management systems. The automated system consists of the hardware, software, and network components, together with the controlled functions and associated documentation. Automated systems are sometimes referred to as computerized systems (PICS CSV PI 011-3*).

Bespoke Computerized System: A computerized system individually designed to suit a specific business process (EU Annex 11).

Best Practices: Practices established by experience and common sense.

Biometrics: Methods of identifying a person's identity based on physical measurements of an individual's physical characteristics or repeatable actions. Some examples of biometrics include identifying a user based on a physical signature, fingerprints, and so on.

Calibration: A set of operations that establish, under specified conditions, the relationship between values of quantities indicated by a measuring instrument or measuring system, or values represented by a material measure or a reference material, and the corresponding values realized by standards (PICS CSV PI 011-3).

Certificate: Certificates are used to verify the identity of an individual, organization, web server, or hardware device. They are also used to ensure nonrepudiation in business transactions as well as enable confidentiality using public-key encryption.

Certification Authority: As part of a public key infrastructure, an authority in a network that issues and manages from a Certificate Server security credentials and public key for message encryption and decryption (NARA).

Change: Any variation or alteration in form, state, or quality. It includes additions, deletions, or modifications impacting the hardware or software components used that affect operational integrity, service level agreements, or the validated status of applications on the system.

Change Control: A formal system by which qualified representatives of appropriate disciplines review proposed or actual changes that might affect the validated status of facilities, systems, equipment, or processes. The intent is to determine the need for action that would ensure and document that the system is maintained in a validated state (EU Annex 15, Qualification and Validation).

Cipher: Series of transformations that converts plaintext to ciphertext using the cipher key.

Cipher Key: Secret cryptography key that is used by the key expansion routine to generate a set of round keys.

---

* Pharmaceutical Inspection Cooperation Scheme, "Good Practices for Computerised Systems in Regulated GXP Environments," September 2007.

Ciphertext: Data output from the cipher or input to the inverse cipher.

Clear Printed: Printouts in which, apart from the values themselves, the units and the respective context can also be seen in the printout.*

Code Audit: An independent review of source code by a person, team, or tool to verify compliance with software design documentation and programming standards. Correctness and efficiency may also be evaluated (IEEE).

Code of Federal Regulations: The codification of the general and permanent rules published in the Federal Register by the executive departments and agencies of the federal government.

Code Inspection: A manual (formal) testing (error detection) technique where the programmer reads source code, statement by statement, to a group who ask questions analyzing the program logic, analyzing the code with respect to a checklist of historically common programming errors, and analyzing its compliance with coding standards. This technique can also be applied to other software and configuration items (Myers/NBS).

Code Review: A meeting at which software code is presented to project personnel, managers, users, customers, or other interested parties for comment or approval (IEEE).

Code Walk-through: A manual testing (error detection) technique where program (source code) logic (structure) is traced manually (mentally) by a group with a small set of test cases, while the state of program variables is manually monitored, to analyze the programmer's logic and assumptions.†

Commercial off-the-Shelf Software: Software commercially available, whose fitness for use is demonstrated by a broad spectrum of users (EU Annex 11).

Commissioning: Refer to **Site Acceptance Test** (SAT).

Competence: Having the necessary experience and/or training to adequately perform the job.

Completeness: The property that all necessary parts of the entity in question are included. Completeness of a product is often used to express the fact that all requirements have been met by the product.

---

* "Q&As on Annex 11," *Journal for GMP and Regulatory Affairs*, Issue 8, April/May 2012

† FDA, *Glossary of Computerized System and Software Development Terminology*, Division of Field Investigations, Office of Regional Operations, Office of Regulatory Affairs, Food and Drug Administration, August 1995.

Complexity: In the context of this book, complexity means the degree to which a system or component has a design or implementation that is difficult to understand and verify.

Compliance: Compliance covers the adherence to application-related standards or conventions or regulations in laws and similar prescriptions. Fulfillment of regulatory requirements.

Compliant System: A system that meets applicable guidelines and predicate rule requirements.

Computer: (1) A functional unit that can perform substantial computations, including numerous arithmetic operations and logical operations without human intervention. (2) Hardware components and associated software design to perform specific functions.

Computer System: (1) A system including the input of data, electronic processing, and the output of information to be used for either reporting or automatic control (PICS CSV PI 011-3). (2) A functional unit, consisting of one or more computers and associated peripheral input and output devices, and associated software, that uses common storage for all or part of a program and also for all or part of the data necessary for the execution of the program; executes user-written or user-designated programs; performs user-designated data manipulation, including arithmetic operations and logic operations; and can execute programs that modify themselves during their execution. A computer system may be a stand-alone unit or may consist of several interconnected units (ANSI).

Computer Systems Validation: (1) The *formal assessment and reporting* of quality and performance measures for all the life-cycle stages of software and system development, its implementation, qualification and acceptance, operation, modification, requalification, maintenance, and retirement. This should enable both the regulated user and competent authority to have a high level of confidence in the integrity of both the processes executed within the controlling computer system and in those processes controlled by or linked to the computer system, within the prescribed operating environment (PICS CSV PI 011-3[*]). (2) Documented evidence that provides a high degree of guarantee that a computerized system analyzes, controls, and records

---

[*] PI 011-3. "Good Practices for Computerised Systems in Regulated 'GXP' Environments," Pharmaceutical Inspection Cooperation Scheme (PIC/S), September 2007.

data correctly and that data processing complies with predetermined specifications (WHO).

Computer Validation: Refer to **Computer Systems Validation.**[*]

Computerized Process: A process where some or all of the actions are controlled by a computer.

Computerized System: (1) A system controlled partially or totally by a computer. (2) See **Automated Systems**.

Concurrent Validation: In some cases, a drug product or medical device may be manufactured individually or on a one-time basis. The concept of prospective or retrospective validation as it relates to those situations may have limited applicability. The data obtained during the manufacturing and assembly process may be used in conjunction with product testing to demonstrate that the instant run yielded a finished product meeting all its specifications and quality characteristics (FDA).

Confidentiality: Keeping secret data from unauthorized eyes.

Configurable Software: Application software, sometimes general purpose, written for a variety of industries or users in a manner that permits users to modify the program to meet their individual needs (FDA).

Configuration Item: Entity within a configuration that satisfies an end use function and that can be uniquely identified at a given reference point. (ISO 9000-3)

Consistency: The property of logical coherency among constituent parts. Consistency may also be expressed as adherence to a given set of rules.

Control System: Included in this classification are Supervisory Control and Data Acquisition (SCADA) systems, Distributed Control Systems (DCS), Statistical Process Control (SPC) systems, Programmable Logic Controllers (PLCs), intelligent electronic devices, and computer systems that control manufacturing equipment or receive data directly from manufacturing equipment PLCs.

Correctness: The extent to which software is free from design and coding defects, that is, fault free. It is also the extent to which software meets its specified requirements and user objectives.

Critical: Describes a process step, process condition, test requirement, or other relevant parameter or item that must be controlled within predetermined criteria to ensure that the product/process meets its specification.

---

[*] PI 011-3. "Good Practices for Computerised Systems in Regulated 'GXP' Environments," Pharmaceutical Inspection Cooperation Scheme (PIC/S), September 2007.

Critical Data: In this book, critical data is interpreted as meaning data with high risk to product quality or patient safety.[*]

Critical Requirement: A requirement that, if not met, has an adverse impact on any of the following: patient safety, product quality, requirements satisfying health authority regulation, cGXP data integrity, or security.

Critical Systems: Systems that directly or indirectly influence patient safety, product quality, and data integrity.

Criticality: In the context of this book, criticality means the regulatory impact to a system or component. See **Critical Systems**.

Custom-Built Software: Also known as a Bespoke System, custom-built software is software produced for a customer, specifically to order, to meet a defined set of user requirements (GAMP).

Customized Computerized System: See **Bespoke Computerized System**.

Data: A basic unit of information that has a unique meaning and can be transmitted.

Data Integrity: The property that data has not been altered in an unauthorized manner. Data integrity covers data in storage, during processing, and while in transit (NIST SP 800-33).

Data Migration: Process of moving data from one computer system to another without converting the data.

Decommissioning: A planned, systematic process to disassemble and retire from service a facility system and equipment without altering the integrity (validation state) of any other facility, system, or equipment previously connected to the facility, system, or equipment being decommissioned. The decommissioning is done via inspection, testing, and documentation.

Decryption: The transformation of unintelligible data ("ciphertext") into original data ("clear text").

Deliverable: A tangible or intangible object produced because of project execution, as part of an obligation. In validation projects, deliverables are usually documents.

Design Qualification: The documented verification that the proposed design of the facilities, systems, and equipment is suitable for the intended purpose. Also known as Design Verification (EU Annex 15, Validation and Qualification).

---

[*] ISPE GAMP COP Annex 11–Interpretation, July/August 2011.

Developer: An organization that performs development activities (including requirements analysis, design, and testing through acceptance) during the software life-cycle process.

Development: Software life cycle process that contains the activities of requirements analysis, design, coding, integration, testing, installation and support for acceptance of software products. (ISO 9000-3)

Deviation: When a system does not act as expected.

Digital Certificate: A credential issued by a trusted authority. An entity can present a digital certificate to prove its identity or its right to access information. It links a public-key value to a set of information, which identifies the entity associated with the use of the corresponding private key. Certificates are authenticated, issued, and managed by a trusted third party called a CA.

Digital Signature Standard (DSS): A National Institute of Standards and Technology (NIST) standard for digital signatures that is used to authenticate both a message and the signer. DSS has a security level comparable to RSA (Rivest-Shamir-Adleman) cryptography, having 1,024-bit keys.

Disaster Recovery: The activities required to restore one or more computer systems to their valid state in response to a major hardware or software failure or destruction of facilities.

Discrepancy: Any problem or entry into the Problem Reporting System. Includes all bugs and may include design issues.

Documentation: (1) Manuals, written procedures or policies, records, or reports that provide information concerning the uses, maintenance, or validation of a process or system involving either hardware or software. This material may be presented from electronic media. Documents include, but are not limited to, Standard Operating Procedures (SOPs), Technical Operating Procedures (TOPs), manuals, logs, system development documents, test plans, scripts and results, plans, protocols, and reports. Refer to *Documentation* and *Documentation, level of* in the *Glossary of Computerized System and Software Development Terminology,* August 1995. (2) Any written or pictorial information describing, defining, specifying, reporting, or certifying activities, requirements, procedures, or results (ANSI N45.2.10-1973).

Emergency Change: A change to a validated system that is determined to be necessary to eliminate an error condition that prevents the use of the system and interrupts the business function.

Emulation: Refers to the process of mimicking, in software, a piece of hardware or software so that other processes think that the original equipment/function is still available in its original form. Emulation is essentially a way of preserving the functionality of and access to digital information that might otherwise be lost due to technological obsolescence.

Encryption: (1) The process of converting information into a code or cipher so that people will be unable to read it. A secret key, or password, is required to decrypt (decode) the information. (2) Transformation of confidential plaintext into ciphertext to protect it. An encryption algorithm combines plaintext with other values called keys, or ciphers, so the data becomes unintelligible (45 CFR 142.304).

End User: Personnel who use the validated system.

Entity: A software or hardware product that can be individually qualified or validated.

Establish: Establish is defined in this book as meaning to define, document, and implement.

Evaluation: A systematic determination of the extent to which an entity meets its specified criteria.

Expected Result: What a system should do when a particular action is performed.

Factory Acceptance Test: An acceptance test in the supplier's factory, usually involving the customer (IEEE).

FDA Guidance Documents: FDA guidance documents represent the FDA current thinking on a particular subject. These documents do not create or confer any rights for or on any person and do not operate to bind FDA or the public. An alternative approach may be used if such an approach satisfies the requirements of the applicable statutes, regulations, or both.

Federal Register: A daily issuance of the US government that provides a uniform system for making available to the public regulations and legal notices issued by federal agencies.

Field Devices: Hardware devices that are typically located in the field at or near the process and are needed to bring information to the computer or to implement a computer-driven control action. Devices include sensors, analytical instruments, transducers, and valves.

Final Rule: The regulation finalized for implementation, published in the FR (preamble and codified) and codified in the CFR.

Function: A set of specified, ordered actions that are part of a process.

Functional Testing: Application of test data derived from the specified functional requirements without regard to the final program structure.

GMP: Good Manufacturing Practice. All elements in the established practice that will collectively lead to final products or services that consistently meet appropriate specifications and compliance with national and international regulations.

GMP Controls: Set of controls that ensure consistently continued process performance and product quality.

GMP-Regulated Activities: The manufacturing related activities established in the basic legislation compiled in Volume 1 and Volume 5 of the publication *The Rules Governing Medicinal Products in the European Union,* US FDA 21 CFR Part 211, "Current Good Manufacturing Practice In Manufacturing, Processing, Packing or Holding of Drugs; General and Current Good Manufacturing Practice For Finished Pharmaceuticals" or any predicate rule applicable to medicinal products for the referenced country.

GXP: A global abbreviation intended to cover GMP, GCP, GLP, and other regulated applications in context. The underlying international life science requirements such as those set forth in the US FD&C Act, US PHS Act, FDA regulations, EU Directives, Japanese MHLW regulations, Australia TGA, or other applicable national legislation or regulations under which a company operates (GAMP Good Practice Guide, IT Infrastructure Control and Compliance, ISPE 2005).

GXP Computerized Systems: Computer systems that perform regulated operation that is required to be formally controlled under GXP international life science requirements.

Human Readable: An electronic record, data, or signature that can be displayed in a viewable form, for example, on paper or computer screen, and has meaning (words in a written language).

Hybrid Systems: Include combinations of paper records (or other nonelectronic media) and electronic records, paper records and electronic signatures, or handwritten signatures executed to electronic records.

Impact of Change: The impact of change is the effect of the change on the GXP computer system. The components by which the impact of change is evaluated may include, but not be limited to, business considerations, resource requirements and availability, application of appropriate regulatory agency requirements, and criticality of the system.

Infrastructure: The hardware and software, such as networking software and operation systems, which makes it possible for the application to function (EU Annex 11).

Inspection: (1) A manual testing technique in which program documents (specifications [requirements, design], source code, or user's manuals) are examined in a very formal and disciplined manner to discover any errors, violations of standards, or other problems. Checklists are typical vehicles used in accomplishing this process. (2) A visual examination of a software product to detect and identify software anomalies, including errors and deviations from standards and specifications. Inspections are peer examinations led by impartial facilitators who are trained in inspection techniques. Determination of remedial or investigative action for an anomaly is a mandatory element of a software inspection, although the solution should not be determined in the inspection meeting.

Installation Qualification: Establishing confidence that process equipment and ancillary systems are capable of consistently operating within established limits and tolerances (FDA).

Integration Testing: Orderly progression of testing in which software elements, hardware elements, or both are combined and tested until all intermodule communication links have been integrated.

Integrity: Data that has retained its integrity has not been modified or tampered with.

Intended Use: (1) Use of a product, process, or service in accordance with the specifications, instructions, and information provided by the manufacturer (ANSI/AAMI/ISO 14971). (2) Refer to the objective intent of the persons legally responsible for the labeling of devices. The intent is determined by such persons' expressions or may be shown by the circumstances surrounding the distribution of the article. This objective intent may, for example, be shown by labeling claims, advertising matter, or oral or written statements by such persons or their representatives. It may be shown by the circumstances that the article is, with the knowledge of such persons or their representatives, offered and used for a purpose for which it is neither labeled nor advertised. The intended uses of an article may change after it has been introduced into interstate commerce by its manufacturer; for example, if a packer, distributor, or seller intends an article for uses different from those intended by the person from whom he received the devices.[*]

Interface: A shared boundary. To interact or communicate with another system component (ANSI/IEEE).

IT Infrastructure: The hardware and software such as networking software and operation systems that makes it possible for the application to function (EU Annex 11).

Key Practices: Processes essential for computer validation that consist of tools, workflow, and people (PDA).

Legacy Systems: (1) Production computer systems that are operating on older computer hardware or are based on older software applications. In some cases, the vendor may no longer support the hardware or software. (2) These are regarded as systems that have been established and are in use for some considerable time. For a variety of reasons, they may be generally characterized by lack of adequate GMP compliance–related documentation and records pertaining to the development and commissioning stage of the system. Additionally, because of their age, there may be no records of a formal approach to validation of the system (PICS CSV PI 011-3[†]).

Life Cycle: All phases in the life of the system from initial requirements until retirement including design, specification, programming, testing, installation, operation, and maintenance (EU Annex 11).

Life Cycle (record): The life span of a record from its creation to its final disposition is considered its life cycle. There are four stages in a record life cycle: Creation, Maintenance, Retention Management, and Disposal.

Life-Cycle Model: A framework containing the processes, activities, and tasks involved in the development, operation, and maintenance of a software product, spanning the life of the system from the definition of its requirements to the termination of its use (ISO 9000-3).

Living Document: A document (or collection of documents) revised as needed throughout the life of a computer system. Only the most recent version is effective and supersedes prior versions.

Logically Secure and Controlled Environment: A computing environment, controlled by policies, procedures, and technology, that deters

---

[*] US FDA Draft Guidance for Industry and Food and Drug Administration Staff–Mobile Medical Applications, July 2011.

[†] PI 011-3. "Good Practices for Computerised Systems in Regulated 'GXP' Environments," Pharmaceutical Inspection Cooperation Scheme (PIC/S), September 2007.

direct or remote unauthorized access that could damage computer components, production applications, or data.

Maintainer: An organization that performs maintenance activities (ISO 12207:1995*).

Major Change: A change to a validated system that is determined by reviewers to require the execution of extensive validation activities.

Manufacture: All operations of receipt of materials, production, packaging, repackaging, labeling, relabeling, quality control, release, storage and distribution of medicinal products and the related controls.

May: This word, or the adjective "OPTIONAL," means that an item is truly optional. Statements using "may" for permissible actions.

Meta-data: Data describing stored data; that is, data describing the structure, data elements, interrelationships, and other characteristics of electronic records (DOD 5015.2-STD).

Migration: Periodic transfer of digital materials from one hardware/software configuration to another or from one generation of computer technology to a subsequent generation.

Minor Change: A change to a validated system that is determined by reviewers to require the execution of only targeted qualification and validation activities.

Model: An abstract representation of a given object.

Module Testing: Refer to *Testing, Unit* in the *Glossary of Computerized System and Software Development Terminology*, August 1995.

NEMA Enclosures: Hardware enclosures (usually cabinets) that provide different levels of mechanical and environmental protection to the devices installed within them.

Nonconformance: A departure from minimum requirements specified in a contract, specification, drawing, or other approved product description or service.

Noncustom-Purchased Software Package: A generally available, marketed software product that performs specific data collection, manipulation, output, or archiving functions. Refer to *Configurable, off-the-shelf software* in the *Glossary of Computerized System and Software Development Terminology*, August 1995.

Nonrepudiation: Strong and substantial evidence of the identity of the signer of a message and of message integrity, sufficient to prevent a

---

* Note: The 1995 revision is not the most recent version.

party from successfully denying the origin, submission, or delivery of the message and the integrity of its contents.

Objective Evidence: Qualitative or quantitative information, records, or statements of fact pertaining to the quality of an item or service or to the existence of a quality system element, which is based on observation, measurement, or test and which can be verified.

Ongoing Evaluation: A term used to describe the dynamic process employed after a system's initial validation that can assist in maintaining a computer system in a validated state.

Operating Environment: All outside influences that interface with the computer system (GAMP).

Operating System: Software that controls the execution of programs and that provides services such as resource allocation, scheduling, input/output control, and data management. Usually, operating systems are predominantly software, but partial or complete hardware implementations are possible (ISO).

Operational Testing: Refer to *Operational Qualification* in the *Glossary of Computerized System and Software Development Terminology*, August 1995.

Operator: An organization that operates the system (ISO 12207:1995*).

Packaged Software: Software provided and maintained by a vendor/supplier, which can provide general business functionality or system services. Refer to *Configurable, off-the-shelf software* in the *Glossary of Computerized System and Software Development Terminology*, August 1995.

Part 11 Records: Records that are required to be maintained under predicate rule requirements and that are maintained in electronic format in place of paper format, or records that are required to be maintained under predicate rules that are maintained in electronic format in addition to paper format and that are relied on to perform regulated activities. Part 11 records include records submitted to the FDA under predicate rules (even if such records are not specifically identified in Agency regulations) in electronic format (assuming the records have been identified in docket number 92S-0251 as the types of submissions the Agency accepts in electronic format) (FDA guidance: Part 11 Scope and Application).

---

* Note: The 1995 revision is not the most recent version.

Password: A character string used to authenticate an identity. Knowledge of the password that is associated with a user ID is considered proof of authorization to use the capabilities associated with that user ID (CSC-STD-002-85).

Periodic Review: A documented assessment of the documentation, procedures, records, and performance of a computer system to determine whether it is still in a validated state and what actions, if any, are necessary to restore its validated state (PDA).

Person: Refers to an individual or an organization with legal rights and duties.

Personal Identification Number: A PIN is an alphanumeric code or password used to authenticate the identity of an individual.

Physical Environment: The physical environment of a computer system that comprises the physical location and the environmental parameters in which the system physically functions.

Planned Change: An intentional change to a validated system for which an implementation and evaluation program is predetermined.

Policy: A directive that usually specifies what is to be accomplished.

Preamble: Analysis preceding a proposed or final rule that clarifies the intention of the rule making and any ambiguities regarding the rule. Responses to comments made on a proposed rule are published in the preamble preceding the final rule. Preambles are published only in the FR and do not have a binding effect.

Predicate Regulations: Federal Food, Drug, and Cosmetic Act; the Public Health Service Act; or any FDA Regulation, with the exception of 21 CFR Part 11. Predicate regulations address the research, production, and control of FDA-regulated articles.

Procedural Controls: (1) Written and approved procedures providing appropriate instructions for each aspect of the development, operation, maintenance, and security applicable to computer technologies. In the context of regulated operations, procedural controls should have QA/QC controls that are equivalent to the applicable predicate regulations. (2) A directive usually specifying how certain activities are to be accomplished (PMA CSVC).

Process: (1) A set of specified, ordered actions required to achieve a defined result. (2) A set of interrelated or interacting activities that transform input into outputs.[*]

---

[*] Murphy and Singh, *Statistical Process Control and Process Capabilities*, Encyclopedia of Pharmaceutical Technology, Informa Healthcare.

Process Owner: The person responsible for the business process (EU Annex 11).

Process System: The combination of the process equipment, support systems (such as utilities), and procedures used to execute a process.

Production Environment: The operational environment in which the system is being used for its intended purpose, that is, not in a test or development environment.

Production Verification (PV): Documented verification that the integrated system performs as intended in its production environment. PV is the execution of selected Performance Qualification (PQ) tests in the production environment using production data.

Project: A project is an activity that achieves specific objectives through a set of defining tasks and effective use of resources.

Project Management: Project management is the application of knowledge, skills, tools, and techniques to project activities to meet the project requirements (ANSI).

Prospective Validation: Validation conducted prior to the distribution of either a new product or a product made under a revised manufacturing process, where the revisions may affect the product's characteristics (FDA).

Qualification: (1) Action of proving that any equipment works correctly and actually leads to the expected results. The word *validation* is sometimes widened to incorporate the concept of qualification (EU PIC/S). (2) Qualification is the process of demonstrating whether a computer system and associated controlled process/operation, procedural controls, and documentation are capable of fulfilling specified requirements. (3) The process of demonstrating whether an entity is capable of fulfilling specified requirements (ISO 8402: 1994, 2.13.1).

Qualification Protocol: A prospective experimental plan stating how qualification will be conducted, including test parameters, product characteristics, production equipment, and decision points on what constitutes an acceptable test. When executed, a protocol is intended to produce documented evidence that a system or subsystem performs as required.

Qualification Reports: These are test reports that evaluate the conduct and results of the qualification carried out on a computer system.

Quality: The totality of features and characteristics of a product or service that bears on its ability to satisfy given needs.

Quality Assurance: All planned and systematic activities implemented within the quality system and demonstrated as needed to provide adequate confidence that an entity will fulfill requirements for quality.

Quality Management: All activities of the overall management function that determine the quality policy, objectives, and responsibilities and implement them by such means as quality planning, quality control, quality assurance, and quality improvement within the quality system.

Raw Data: In this book, raw data means all data on which quality decisions are based.

Record: Provides evidence of various actions taken to demonstrate compliance with instructions—for example, activities; events; investigations; and, in the case of manufactured batches, a history of each batch of product, including its distribution. Records include the raw data that is used to generate other records. For electronic records, regulated users should define which data are to be used as raw data. At least, all data on which quality decisions are based should be defined as raw data (EudraLex Vol. 4 Ch. 4). A record consists of information, regardless of medium, detailing the transaction of business. Records include all books, papers, maps, photographs, machine-readable materials, and other documentary materials, regardless of physical form or characteristics, made or received by an agency of the United States government under federal law or in connection with the transaction of public business and preserved or appropriate for preservation by that agency or its legitimate successor as evidence of the organization, functions, policies, decisions, procedures, operations, or other activities of the government or because of the value of data in the record (44 U.S.C. 3301, reference (bb)).

Record Owner: A person or organization who can determine the contents and use of the data collected, stored, processed, or disseminated by that party regardless of whether the data was acquired from another owner or collected directly from the provider.

Record Reliability: A reliable record is one whose contents can be trusted as a full and accurate representation of the transactions, activities, or facts to which they attest and can be depended on in the course of subsequent transactions or activities (NARA).

Record Retention Period: Length of time the electronic record is to be retained, as mandated by the requirement of the record type, based on regulations or documented policies.

Record Retention Schedule: A list of record types with the required storage conditions and defined retention periods. The time (retention) periods are established based on regulatory, legal, and tax compliance requirements as well as operational need and historical value.

Re-engineering: The process of examining and altering an existing system to reconstitute it in a new form. May include reverse engineering (analyzing a system and producing a representation at a higher level of abstraction, such as design from code), restructuring (transforming a system from one representation to another at the same level of abstraction), documentation (analyzing a system and producing user or support documentation), forward engineering (using software products derived from an existing system, together with new requirements, to produce a new system), retargeting (transforming a system to install it on a different target system), and translation (transforming source code from one language to another or from one version of a language to another) (DOD-STD-498).

Regression Testing: The process of testing changes to computer programs to make sure that the older programming still works with the new changes. Regression testing is a normal part of the program development process and, in larger companies, is done by code testing specialists. Test department coders develop code test scenarios and exercises that will test new units of code after they have been written. These test cases form what becomes the *test bucket*. Before a new version of a software product is released, the old test cases are run against the new version to make sure that all the old capabilities still work. The reason they might not work is that changing or adding new code to a program can easily introduce errors into code that is not intended to be changed.

Regulated Operations: Process/business operations carried out on a regulated agency product that is covered in a predicated rule.

Regulated User: The regulated good practice entity that is responsible for the operation of a computerized system and the applications, files, and data held thereon (PIC/S PI 011-3). See also **User** and **Operator**.

Regulatory Requirements: Any part of a law, ordinance, decree, or other regulation that applies to the regulated article.

Release: Particular version of a configuration item that is made available for a specific purpose. (ISO 9000-3)

Reliable Records: Records that are a full and accurate representation of the transactions, activities, or facts to which they attest and can be depended on in the course of subsequent transactions or activities.

Remediate: In the context of this book, the software, hardware, or procedural changes employed to bring a system into compliance with the applicable GXP rule.

Remediation Plan: A documented approach on bringing existing computer systems into compliance with the regulations.

Replacement: The implementation of a new compliant system after the retirement of an existing system.

Reports: Document the conduct of particular exercises, projects, or investigations, together with results, conclusions, and recommendations (Eudralex Vol 4 Ch 4).

Requalification: Repetition of the qualification process or a specific portion thereof.

Requirement: A condition or capability that must be met or possessed by a system or system component to satisfy a contract, standard, specification, or other formally imposed document. The set of all requirements forms the basis for subsequent development of the system or system component (ANSI/IEEE).

Retention Period: The duration for which records are retained. Retention periods are defined in a retention schedule document. Retention schedules are based on business, country-specific regulations, and legal requirements.

Retirement Phase: The period in the SLC in which plans are made and executed to decommission or remove a computer technology from operational use.

Retrospective Evaluation: Establishing documented evidence that a system does what it purports to do based on an analysis of historical information. The process of evaluating a computer system, which is currently in operation, against standard validation practices and procedures. The evaluation determines the reliability, accuracy, and completeness of a system.

Retrospective Validation: See **Retrospective Evaluation**.

Review: A process or meeting during which a software product is presented to project personnel, managers, users, customers, user representatives, or other interested parties for comment or approval (IEEE).

Revision: Different versions of the same document. Can also be used in reference to software, firmware, and hardware boards. Implies a fully tested, fully functional, and released unit/component/document.

Risk Assessment: A comprehensive evaluation of the risk and its associated impact.

Risk Management: The tasks and plans that help avoid risk and help minimize damage.

SAT: Inspection or dynamic testing of the systems or major system components to support the qualification of an equipment system conducted and documented at the manufacturing site.

Self-inspection: An audit carried out by people from within the organization to ensure compliance with GMP and regulatory requirements.

Service Providers: All parties who provide any services irrespective if they belong to an independent (external) enterprise, the same company group/structure, or an internal service unit.

Shall: Used to express a provision that is binding, per regulatory requirement. Statements that use "shall" can be traced to regulatory requirements and must be followed to comply with such requirements.

Should: Used to express a nonmandatory provision. Statements that use "should" are best practices, recommended activities, or options to perform activities to be considered in order to achieve quality project results. Other methods may be used if it can be demonstrated that they are equivalent.

Signature, Handwritten: The scripted name or legal mark of an individual handwritten by that individual and executed or adopted with the present intention to authenticate writing in a permanent form (21 CFR 11.3(8)).

Site Acceptance Test: An acceptance test at the customer's site, usually involving the customer (IEEE).

Software Developer: Person or organization who designs software and writes the programs. Software development includes the design of the user interface and the program architecture as well as programming the source code.[*]

Software Development Standards: Written policies or procedures that describe practices a programmer or software developer should follow in creating, debugging, and verifying software.

Software Item: Identifiable part of a software product. (ISO 9000-3)

---

[*] TechWeb Network, http://www.techweb.com/encyclopedia/

Software Product: Set of computer programs, procedures, and possibly associated documentation and data. (ISO 9000-3)

Source Code: The human readable version of the list of instructions (programs) that enable a computer to perform a task.

Specification: A document that specifies—in a complete, precise, verifiable manner—the requirements, design, behavior, or other characteristics of a system or component and often the procedures for determining whether these provisions have been satisfied (IEEE).

Standard Instrument Software: These are driven by non–user-programmable firmware. They are configurable (GAMP).

Standard Operation Procedures: See **Procedural Controls**.

Standard Software Packages: A complete and documented set of programs supplied to several users for a generic application or function (ISO/IEC 2382-20:1990).

Static Analysis: (1) Analysis of a program that is performed without executing the program (NBS). (2) The process of evaluating a system or component based on its form, structure, content, or documentation (IEEE).

Subject Matter Experts (SME): Individuals with specific expertise and responsibility in a particular area or field.[*]

Supplier: An organization that enters into a contract with the acquirer for the supply of a system, software product, or software service under the terms of the contract (ISO 12207:1995[†]).

System: (1) People, machines, and methods organized to accomplish a set of specific functions (ANSI). (2) A composite, at any level of complexity, of personnel, procedures, materials, tools, equipment, facilities, and software. The elements of this composite entity are used together in the intended operational or support environment to perform a given task or achieve a specific purpose, support, or mission requirement (DOD). (3) A group of related objects designed to perform or control a set of specified actions.

System Backup: The storage of data and programs on a separate media and stored separately from the originating system.

System Documentation: The collection of documents that describe the requirements, capabilities, limitations, design, operation, and

---

[*] ASTM, E 2500 – 07 Standard Guide for Specification, Design, and Verification of Pharmaceutical and Biopharmaceutical Manufacturing Systems and Equipment.

[†] Note: The 1995 revision is not the most recent version.

maintenance of an information processing system. See **Specification, Test Documentation, User's Guide** (ISO).

System Integrity: The quality that a system has when it performs its intended function in an unimpaired manner, free from unauthorized manipulation. (NIST SP 800-33)

System Life Cycle: The period of time that starts when the system product is recommended until the system is no longer available for use or retired.

System Owner: The person responsible for the availability and maintenance of a computerized system and for the security of the data residing on that system (EU Annex 11).

System Retirement: The removal of a system from operational usage. The system may be replaced by another system or may be removed without being replaced.

System Software: See **Operating System**.

System Specification: In this book, system specification corresponds to requirements, functional or design specifications. Refer to **Specification**.

System Test: Process of testing an integrated hardware and software system to verify that the system meets its specified requirements.

Technological Controls: Program enforcing compliance rules.

Templates: Guidelines that outline the basic information for a specific set of equipment (JETT).

Test Documentation: Documentation describing plans for, or results of, the testing of a system or component, Types include test case specification, test incident report, test log, test plan, test procedure, test report. (IEEE)

Test Nonconformance: A nonconformance occurs when the actual test result does not equal the expected result or an unexpected event (such as a loss of power) is encountered.

Test Report: Document that presents test results and other information relevant to a test (ISO/IEC Guide 2:2004).

Test Script: A detailed set of instructions for execution of the test. This typically includes the following:

- Specific identification of the test
- Prerequisites or dependencies
- Test objective
- Test steps or actions

- Requirements or instructions for capturing data (e.g., screen prints, report printing)
- Pass/fail criteria for the entire script
- Instructions to follow in the event that a nonconformance is encountered
- Test execution date
- Person executing the test
- Review date
- Person reviewing the test results

For each step of the test script, the item tested, the input to that step, and the expected result are indicated prior to execution of the test. The actual results obtained during the steps of the test are recorded on or attached to the test script. Test scripts and results may be managed through computer-based electronic tools. Refer to *Test case* in the *Glossary of Computerized System and Software Development Terminology*, August 1995.

Testing: Examining the behavior of a program by executing the program on sample data sets.

Third Party: Parties not directly managed by the holder of the manufacturing or import authorization.

Time Stamp: A record mathematically linking a piece of data to a time and date.

Traceability: (1) The degree to which a relationship can be established between two or more products of the development process, especially products having a predecessor–successor or master–subordinate relationship to one another; for example, the degree to which the requirements and design of a given software component match (IEEE).
(2) The degree to which each element in a software development product establishes its reason for existing; for example, the degree to which each element in a bubble chart references the requirement that it satisfies.

Traceability Analysis: The tracing of (1) software requirements specifications to system requirements in concept documentation, (2) software design descriptions to software requirements specifications and software requirements specifications to software design descriptions, (3) source code to corresponding design specifications and design specifications to source code. Analyze identified relationships for correctness, consistency, completeness, and accuracy (IEEE).

Traceability Matrix: A matrix that records the relationship between two or more products; for example, a matrix that records the relationship between the requirements and the design of a given software component (IEEE).

Training Plan: Documentation describing the training required for an individual based on his or her job title or description.

Training Record: Documentation (electronic or paper) of the training received by an individual that includes, but is not limited to, the individual's name or identifier, the type of training received, the date the training occurred, the trainer's name or identifier, and an indication of the effectiveness of the training (if applicable).

Transient Memory: Memory that must have a constant supply of power or the stored data will be lost.

Trust: In the network security context, trust refers to privacy (the data is not viewable by unauthorized people), integrity (the data stays in its true form), nonrepudiation (the publisher cannot say it did not send it), and authentication (the publisher—and recipient—are who they say they are).

Trustworthy Computer Systems: Trustworthy computer systems consist of computer infrastructure, applications, and procedures that
  • are reasonably suited to performing their intended functions
  • provide a reasonably reliable level of availability, reliability, and correct operation
  • are reasonably secure from intrusion and misuse
  • adhere to generally accepted security principles.

Trustworthy Records: Reliability, authenticity, integrity, and usability are the characteristics used to describe trustworthy records from a record management perspective. (NARA)

Unit: A separately testable element specified in the design of a computer software element. Synonymous with component or module (IEEE).

Unit Test: Test of a module for typographic, syntactic, and logical errors; for correct implementation of its design; and for satisfaction of its requirements.

Unplanned (Emergency) Change: An unanticipated necessary change to a validated system requiring rapid implementation.

Usable Records: Records that can be located, retrieved, presented, and interpreted.

User: The company or group responsible for the operation of a system (GAMP) (see also **Regulated User**). The GXP customer, or user organization, contracting a supplier to provide a product. In the context of this document, therefore, it is not intended to apply only to individuals who use the system and is synonymous with Customer (EU Annex 11).

User Backup/Alternative Procedures: Procedures that describe the steps to be taken for the continued recording and control of the raw data in the event of a computer system interruption or failure.

User ID: A sequence of characters that is recognized by the computer and uniquely identifies one person. User ID is the first form of identification. User ID is also known as a PIN or identification code.

User's Guide: Documentation that describes how to use a functional unit, and that may include description of the rights and responsibilities of the user, the owner, and the supplier of the unit. Syn: user manual, operator manual. (US FDA)

Validated: It is used to indicate a status to designate that a system or software complies with applicable GMP requirements.

Validation: Action of proving, in accordance with the principles of Good Manufacturing Practices, that any procedure, process, equipment, material, activity, or system actually leads to the expected results (see also **Qualification**) (EU PIC/S).

Validation Coordinator: A person or designee responsible for coordinating the validation activities for a specific project or task.

Validation Plan: A multidisciplinary strategy from which each phase of a validation process is planned, implemented, and documented to ensure that a facility, process, equipment, or system does what it is designed to do. May also be known as a system or software quality plan.

Validation Protocol: A written plan stating how validation will be conducted, including test parameters, product characteristics, production equipment, and decision points on what constitutes acceptable test results (FDA).

Validation Summary Report: Documents confirming that the entire project-planned activities have been completed. On acceptance of the Validation Summary Report, the user releases the system for use, possibly with a requirement that continuing monitoring should take place for a certain time (GAMP).

Verification: (1) The process of determining whether the products of a given phase of the SLC fulfill the requirements established during the previous phase. (2) A systematic approach to verify that manufacturing systems, acting singly or in combination, are fit for intended use, have been properly installed, and are operating correctly. This is an umbrella term that encompasses all types of approaches to ensuring systems are fit for use such as qualification, commissioning and qualification, verification, system validation, or other (ASTM 5200). (3) Confirmation by examination and provision of objective evidence that specified requirements have been fulfilled (FDA Medical Devices). (4) In design and development, verification concerns the process of examining the result of a given activity to determine conformity with the stated requirement for that activity.

Walk-through: A static analysis technique in which a designer or programmer leads members of the development team and other interested parties through a software product, and the participants ask questions and make comments about possible errors, violation of development standards, and other problems (IEEE).

Will: This word denotes a declaration of purpose or intent by one party, not a requirement.

Work Products: The intended result of activities or processes (PDA).

Worst Case: A set of conditions encompassing upper and lower processing limits and circumstances, including those within standard operating procedures, that pose the greatest chance of process or product failure when compared with ideal conditions. Such conditions do not necessarily induce product or process failure (FDA).

Written: In the context of electronic records, the term "written" means recorded, or documented on media, paper, electronic or other substrate.

Appendix D:
Abbreviations and Acronyms

ABA	American Bar Association
ADP	Automated Data Processing
AKA	Also Known As
ANDA	Abbreviated New Drug Application
ANSI	American National Standards Institute
API	Active Pharmaceutical Ingredient
ASEAN	Association of Southeast Asian Nations
ASTM	American Society for Testing and Materials
CA	Certification Authority
CAPA	Corrective and Preventive Actions
CEFIC	Conseil Européen des Fédérations de l'Industrie Chimique
CFDA	China Food & Drug Administration
CFR	Code of Federal Regulations
cGMP	current Good Manufacturing Practice
CPG	FDA Compliance Policy Guide
CRC	Cyclic Redundancy Check
CRO	Contract Research Organization
CSV	Computer Systems Validation
DCS	Distributed Control System
DES	Data Encryption Standard
DQ	Design Qualification
DRM	Device Master Record
DSA	Digital Signature Algorithm
DSHEA	Dietary Supplement Health and Education Act
EC	European Commission
EDMS	Electronic Document Management System

EEA	European Economic Area
EEC	European Economic Community
EFS	Encrypted File System
EMA	European Medicines Agency
EMEA	European Medicines Agency
ERP	Enterprise Resource Planning
EU	European Union
EVM	Earned Value Management
FAT	Factory Acceptance Test
FD&C Act	US Food, Drug, and Cosmetic Act
FDA	US Food and Drug Administration
FR	US Federal Register
FTP	File Transfer Protocol
GAMP	Good Automated Manufacturing Practice
GCP	Good Clinical Practice
GLP	Good Laboratory Practice
GMP	US Good Manufacturing Practice
GXP	A global abbreviation intended to cover GMP, GCP, GLP, and other regulated applications. In context, GXP can refer to one specific set of practices or to any combination of the three.
HMI	Human–Machine Interface
IaaS	Infrastructure as a Service
ICH	International Conference on Harmonisation of Technical Requirements for Registration of Pharmaceuticals for Human Use
ICS	Industrial Control System
IEC	International Electrotechnical Commission
IEEE	Institute of Electrical & Electronics Engineers
IIS	Internet Information Services
IMDRF	International Medical Device Regulators Forum
I/Os	Inputs and outputs
ISA	International Society of Automation
ISO	International Organization for Standardization
ISPE	International Society for Pharmaceutical Engineering
IT	Information Technology
ITIL	IT Infrastructure Library
KMS	Key Management Service
LAN	Local Area Network
LIMS	Laboratory Information Management System
MA	Marketing Authorization

MES	Manufacturing Execution System
MHRA	Medicines and Healthcare Products Regulatory Agency
MRA	Mutual Recognition Agreement
MTBF	Mean Time Between Failures
MTTR	Mean Time to Repair or Mean Time to Recovery
NARA	National Archives and Records Administration
NBS	National Bureau of Standards
NDA	New Drug Application
NEMA	National Electrical Manufacturers Association
NIST	National Institutes of Standards and Technology
NTP	Network Time Protocol
OECD	Organisation for Economic Co-operation and Development
OLA	Operational Level Agreement
OMCL	Official Medicines Control Laboratory
OSHA	US Occupational Safety & Health Administration
OTS	Off-the-shelf
P&ID	Process and Instrumentation Drawing
PaaS	Platform as a Service
PAT	Process Analytical Tools
PDA	Parenteral Drug Association
PIC/S	Pharmaceutical Inspection Cooperation Scheme http://www.picscheme.org/
PIN	Personal Identification Number
PKCS	Public-Key Cryptography Standards
PKI	Public Key Infrastructure
PLC	Programmable Logic Controller
PQS	Pharmaceutical Quality System
QA	Quality Assurance
QbD	Quality by Design
QC	Quality Control
QMS	Quality Management System
QP	Qualified Person
R&D	Research and Development
RFP	Request for Proposal
RTU	Remote Terminal Unit
SaaS	Software as a Service
SAP	Systems, Applications, and Products
SAS	The Statistical Analysis System licensed by the SAS Institute, Inc.
SAT	Site Acceptance Test

SCADA	Supervisory Control and Data Acquisition
SDLC	Software Development Life Cycle
SLA	Service Level Agreement
SLC	System Life Cycle
SME	Subject Matter Expert
SOP	Standard Operating Procedure
SPC	Statistical Process Control
SQA	Software Quality Assurance
SQE	Software Quality Engineer
SSA	US Social Security Administration
SSL	Secure Sockets Layer
SWEBOK	Software Engineering Body of Knowledge
TGA	Therapeutic Goods Administration
TLS	Transport Layer Security
UC	Underlying Contract
UK	United Kingdom
UPS	Uninterruptible Power Supply
US	United States
VPN	Virtual Private Network
WAN	Wide Area Network
WBS	Work Breakdown Structure
WHO	World Health Organization

Appendix E: Comparison between EU Annex 11 and US FDA– 211, 820, 11; Other Guidelines and Regulations

		References			
	Old Annex 11	211	820	11	Others/Guidelines
Principle					GAMP 5–Management Appendix M3
a. This annex applies to all forms of computerized systems used as part of GMP-regulated activities. A computerized system is a set of software and hardware components that together fulfill certain functionalities.		211.68[a]	820.70(i)	11.2(b)	EU Directives 2003/94/EC and 91/412/EEC PIC/S PI 011-3 ISO 13485 7.5.2 Article 1 draft Annex 2 CFDA GMP
b. The application should be validated; IT infrastructure should be qualified.	11-3	211.68	820.70(i) 820.30(g) 820.170	11.10(a)	Eudralex Volume IV, Glossary PIC/S PI 011-3 Q7A Good Manufacturing Practice Guidance for Active Pharmaceutical Ingredients WHO, Technical Report Series, No. 937, 2006, Annex 4, Appendix 5, Section 7.1 (Hardware) ISO 13485 7.2; 7.2.1; 7.2.2; 7.3.6; 7.5.2 Article 10 draft Annex 2 CFDA GMP GAMP GPG: IT Infrastructure Control and Compliance, 2005

c. Where a computerized system replaces a manual operation, there should be no resultant decrease in product quality, process control or quality assurance. There should be no increase in the overall risk of the process.	Principle			PIC/S PI 011-3 US FDA CPG 7348.810—Sponsors, CROs, and Monitors Brazilian GMPs Title VII Art 570 Thailandia CSV GMPs Article 2 draft Annex 2 CFDA GMP
General				
1. Risk Management Risk management should be applied throughout the life cycle of the computerized system, taking into account patient safety, data integrity, and product quality. As part of a risk management system, decisions on the extent of validation and data integrity controls should be based on a justified and documented risk assessment of the computerized system.		211.68(b)[b]	820.30(g)	812.66[c] ICH Q9 Quality Risk Management NIST, Risk Management Guide for Information Technology Systems, Special Publication 800-30 GHTF, Implementation of risk management principles and activities within a Quality Management System ISO 14971:2007, Medical devices—Application of risk management to medical devices GAMP Forum, Risk Assessment for Use of Automated Systems Supporting Manufacturing Process—Risk to Record, Pharmaceutical Engineering, Nov/Dec 2002

(continued)

References				
Old Annex 11	211	820	11	Others/Guidelines
				GAMP/ISPE, Risk Assessment for Use of Automated Systems Supporting Manufacturing Process—Functional Risk, Pharmaceutical Engineering, May/Jun 2003
				EU Annex 20
				US FDA Guidance for the Content of Pre Market Submission for Software Contained in Medical Devices, May 2005
				Pressman, Roger S., *Software Engineering—A Practitioner's Approach*, McGraw Hill
				GAMP 5, Management Appendices M3 and M4; Operational Appendices O2, O6, O8, O9
				Brazilian GMPs Title VII Art 572
				ISO 13485 7.3.6
				WHO, Technical Report Series, No. 281, 2013
				Health Canada API, C.02.05, Interpretation #12
				Articles 3. 6, 12 draft Annex 2 CFDA GMP

	11-1	Sub Part B	820.20(b) (1) and (2); 820.25	11.10(i)	EudraLex, The Rules Governing Medicinal Products in the European Union, Volume 4, EU Guidelines for Good Manufacturing Practices for Medicinal Products for Human and Veterinary Use, Part 1, Chapter 2—Personnel, February 2014
2. Personnel There should be close cooperation between all relevant personnel such as Process Owner, System Owner, Qualified Persons, and IT. All personnel should have appropriate qualifications, level of access, and defined responsibilities to carry out their assigned duties.					21 CFR 110(c)
					21 CFR 606.160(b)(5)(v)
					ICH E6 GCP 4.1; 4.2.3, 4.2.4; 5.4.1; 5.5.1; 5.6.1
					21 CFR Part 312.53(a) and.53(d)
					21 CFR 58.29
					WHO, Technical Report Series, No. 937, 2006, Annex 4, Section 13
					GAMP 5, Operational Appendix O12
					Brazilian GMPs Title VII Art 571
					ISO 13485 5.5; 5.5.1; 5.5.3; 6.2; 6.2.1; 6.2.2
					Japan CSV Guideline (Guideline on Management of Computerized Systems for Marketing Authorization Holder and Manufacturing of Drugs and Quasi-drugs, October 2010), Section 6.8
					Thailandia CSV GMPs, Clause 510
					Health Canada API, C.02.006

(continued)

| | References | | | | |
	Old Annex 11	211	820	11	Others/Guidelines
3. Suppliers and Service Providers 3.1 When third parties (e.g., suppliers, service providers) are used to provide, install, configure, integrate, validate, maintain (e.g., via remote access), modify, or retain a computerized system or related service or for data processing, formal agreements must exist between the manufacturer and any third parties, and these agreements should include clear statements of the responsibilities of the third party. IT departments should be considered analogous. 3.2 The competence and reliability of a supplier are key factors when selecting a product or service provider. The need for an audit should be based on a risk assessment.	11-18	Sub Part B 211.34	820.20(b) (1) and (2), 820.50		21 CFR 110(c) ICH Q7 Good Manufacturing Practice Guidance for Active Pharmaceutical Ingredients ICH Q10 Section 2.7 Management of Outsourced Activities and Purchased Materials WHO, Technical Report Series, No. 937, 2006, Annex 4, Appendix 5, Section 6.2 GAMP 5, Management Appendices M2 and M6 Brazilian GMPs Title VII Art 589 ISO 13485 5.5; 5.5.1; 5.5.3; 6.2; 6.2.1; 6.2.2; 7.4; 7.4.1 China GMPs, Section 7 Thailandia CSV GMPs, Clause 527 PDA, Technical Report No. 32 Auditing of Supplier Providing Computer Products and Services for Regulated Pharmaceutical Operations, PDA Journal of Pharmaceutical Science and Technology, Sep/Oct 2004, Release 2.0, Vol. 58, No. 5

	Annex 11	21 CFR 211	21 CFR 820	21 CFR 11	References
3.3 Documentation supplied with commercial off-the-shelf products should be reviewed by regulated users to check that user requirements are fulfilled.					CEFIC CSV Guide, Section 7.4.6
3.4 Quality system and audit information relating to suppliers or developers of software and implemented systems should be made available to inspectors on request.					Article 4 draft Annex 2 CFDA GMP
Project Phase					
4. Validation	11-2; 11-4; 11-5; 11-7; 11-9	211.68; 211.100(a), (b)	820.3(z), 803.17, 820.40, 820.170, 820.30(g), 820.70(g), 820.70(i)	11.10(a); 11.10(k); 11.10(h)	Article 9 Section 2, Commission Directives 2003/94/EC
4.1 The validation documentation and reports should cover the relevant steps of the life cycle. Manufacturers should be able to justify their standards, protocols, acceptance criteria, procedures, and records based on their risk assessment.					Medicines and Healthcare products Regulatory Agency (MHRA) (UK)
					IEEE
					PIC/S PI 011-3
					21 CFR 606.160(b)(5)(ii) and 606.100(b)(15)
					ICH Q7 Good Manufacturing Practice Guidance for Active Pharmaceutical Ingredients
4.2 Validation documentation should include change			820.70(i)		ICH Q9 Quality Risk Management

(continued)

	References				
	Old Annex 11	211	820	11	Others/Guidelines
control records (if applicable) and reports on any deviations observed during the validation process.					11-1
					ICH E6 GCP 5.5.3 (a) and (b)
4.3 An up-to-date listing of all relevant systems and their GMP functionality (inventory) should be available. For critical systems, an up-to-date system description detailing the physical and logical arrangements, data flows and interfaces with other systems or processes, any hardware and software prerequisites, and security measures should be available.					21 CFR 58.61; 63(a) and (c); 58.81(c) and (d); 58.33
					21 CFR 59.190
					Blood Establishment Computer System Validation in the User's Facility, April 2013
					US FDA General Principles of Software Validation
					WHO, Technical Report Series, No. 937, 2006, Annex 4, Appendix 5
					GAMP 5 Development Appendices: D1–D7; Management Appendices M1– M10; Operational Appendix O1
4.4 User Requirements Specifications should describe the required functions of the computerized system and be based on documented risk assessment and GMP impact. User requirements should be			820.30(c); 820.3(z) and (aa); 820.30(f) and (g)		21 CFR 1271.160(d)
					21 CFR 803.17; 21 CFR 803.18
					EU Annex 15
					Brazilian GMPs Title VII Art 573, 574, 575, 576, 578
					ISO 13485 2.3; 6.3; 7.2; 7.2.1; 7.2.2; 7.3.6; 7.5.1.2.2; 7.5.2

traceable throughout the life cycle.[d]			Japan CSV Guideline (Guideline on Management of Computerized Systems for Marketing Authorization Holder and Manufacturing of Drugs and Quasi-drugs, October 2010), Sections 4, 5, and 9
4.5 The regulated user should take all reasonable steps to ensure that the system has been developed in accordance with an appropriate quality management system. The supplier should be assessed appropriately.	820.30 820.50		China GMPs Article 109 Thailandia CSV GMPs, Clauses 511, 512, 513, 514, 516
4.6 For the validation of bespoke or customized computerized systems, there should be a process in place that ensures the formal assessment and reporting of quality and performance measures for all the life-cycle stages of the system.			Health Canada API, C.02.05 Interpretation #12; #13; #14; 17. C.02.015 Interpretation #3; #13.5
4.7 Evidence of appropriate test methods[e] and test scenarios should be demonstrated. Particularly,			Articles 5, 7, 8, 9, 11, 13 draft Annex 2 CFDA GMP

(continued)

	References				
	Old Annex 11	211	820	11	Others/Guidelines
system (process) parameter limits, data limits, and error handling should be considered. Automated testing tools and test environments should have documented assessments for their adequacy. 4.8 If data are transferred to another data format or system, validation should include checks that data are not altered in value and/or meaning during this migration process.					
Operational Phase					GAMP 5, Operational Appendix O12
5. Data Computerized systems exchanging data electronically with other systems should include appropriate built-in checks for the correct and secure entry and processing of data in order to minimize the risks.	11-6	211.68(b) 211.194(d)	806.1 820.25 820.70(a) 820.180 820.184	11.10(a); 11.10(b); 11.10(e); 11.10(f); 11.10(g); 11.10(h); 11.30	US FDA 425.400; 803.1; 803.10; 803.14; 806.10; 806.30; 58.15; 58.33; 58.35; 59.190 EudraLex, Volume 4 Good Manufacturing Practice (GMP) Guidelines, Part I–Basic Requirements for Medicinal Products, Chapter 4–Documentation GAMP 5–Operational Appendix O9

Description	EU Annex 11	211	820	11.10	References
					Brazilian GMPs Title VII Art 577 ISO 13485 4.2.4; 6.2; 6.2.1; 6.2.2; 7.5; 7.5.1; 7.5.1.1 Thailandia CSV GMPs, Clause 515
6. Accuracy Checks For critical data^f entered manually, there should be an additional check on the accuracy of the data. This check may be done by a second operator or by validated electronic means. The criticality and the potential consequences of erroneous or incorrectly entered data to a system should be covered by risk management.	11-9	211.68(c)	820.25 820.70	11.10(f)	The APV Guideline "Computerized Systems" based on Annex 11 of the EU-GMP Guideline EudraLex, Volume 4 Good Manufacturing Practice (GMP) Guidelines, Part I–Basic Requirements for Medicinal Products, Chapter 4–Documentation PIC/S PI 011-3 EU Annex 11-1 WHO, Technical Report Series, No. 937, 2006, Annex 4, Appendix 5, Section 4.5 Brazilian GMPs Title VII Art 577, 580 ISO 13485 6.2; 6.2.1; 6.2.2; 7.5 Thailandia CSV GMPs, Clause 518 Health Canada API, C.02.015 Interpretation #18 Article 15 draft Annex 2 CFDA GMP
7. Data Storage 7.1 Data should be secured	11-13 11-14	211.68(b)	803.1 820.20	11.10(c) 11.10(d)	812.38 Chapter II Article 9 Section 2,

(continued)

	References			
Old Annex 11	211	820	11	Others/Guidelines
by both physical and electronic means against damage. Stored data should be checked for accessibility, readability, and accuracy. Access to data should be ensured throughout the retention period. 7.2 Regular backups of all relevant data should be done. Integrity and accuracy of backup data and the ability to restore the data should be checked during validation and monitored periodically.		820.40 820.180 806.1	11.10(e) 11.10(g) 11.10(h) 11.30	Commission Directives 2003/94/EC PIC/S PI 011-3 EudraLex, Volume 4 Good Manufacturing Practice (GMP) Guidelines, Part I–Basic Requirements for Medicinal Products, Chapter 4–Documentation ICH E6 GCP 5.5.3(d) and (f) 21 CFR 58.33;.190(d);.35;.195 Specific records retention requirements are found in applicable predicate rule; for example, 21 CFR 211.180(c), (d), 108.25(g), 108.35(h), and 58.195 812.140(a) and (b) WHO, Technical Report Series, No. 937, 2006, Annex 4, Appendix 5, Sections 5 and 7.2.2 21 CFR 123.9(f) GAMP Appendix O9 and O11 Brazilian GMPs Title VII Art 585 ISO 13485 6.2; 6.2.1; 6.2.2; 7.5

	11-12	211.180(c)		11.10(b)	
8. Printouts 8.1 It should be possible to obtain clear printed copies of electronically stored e-recs. 8.2 For records supporting batch release, it should be possible to generate printouts indicating if any of the e-recs have been changed since the original entry.		43 FR 31508, July 21, 1978 803.1 803.10 803.14 806.30 820.40 820.180 806.1			Japan CSV Guideline (Guideline on Management of Computerized Systems for Marketing Authorization Holder and Manufacturing of Drugs and Quasi-drugs, October 2010), Section 6.3 Japan's Pharmaceutical and Food Safety Bureau "Using electromagnetic records and electronic signatures for application for approval or licensing of drugs," Section 3, April 2005 Thailandia CSV GMPs, Clause 517, 522, 523 Health Canada API, C.02.05, Interpretation #16 Article 19 draft Annex 2 CFDA GMP 812.150, 58.15 Directive 1999/93/EC of the European Parliament and of the Council of 13 December 1999 on a Community framework for electronic signatures PIC/S PI 011-3 FDA, Guidance for Industry Part 11, Electronic Records; Electronic Signatures—Scope and Application, August 2003

(continued)

	References				
	Old Annex 11	211	820	11	Others/Guidelines
					The APV Guideline, "Computerized Systems" based on Annex 11 of the EU-GMP Guideline US FDA CPG Sec. 130.400 Use of Microfiche and/or Microfilm for Method of Records Retention Brazilian GMPs Title VII Art 583 ISO 13485 4.2.3; 4.2.4 Thailandia CSV GMPs, Clause 521
9. Audit Trails Consideration should be given, based on a risk assessment, to building into the system the creation of a record of all GMP-relevant changes and deletions (a system-generated "audit trail"). For change or deletion of GMP-relevant data, the reason should be documented. Audit trails need to be available and convertible to a generally intelligible form and regularly reviewed.	11-10		803.18 820.40	11.10(e); 11.10(k)(2)	1978 US CGMP rev. Comment paragraph 186 FDA, Guidance for Industry Part 11, Electronic Records; Electronic Signatures—Scope and Application, August 2003 The APV Guideline "Computerized Systems" based on Annex 11 of the EU-GMP Guideline PIC/S PI 011-3 ICH Q7 Good Manufacturing Practice Guidance for Active Pharmaceutical Ingredients

Note: In addition to the system-generated audit trail, some implementation includes the documentation that allows reconstruction of the course of events. Implicitly, this approach does not require a computer system-generated audit trail.					ICH E6 GCP 4.9.3; 5.5.3(c); 5.5.4 21 CFR 58.130(d) Glossary of the Note for Guidance on Good Clinical Practice (CPMP/ICH/135/95) Brazilian GMPs Title VII Art 581 ISO 13485 4.2.3 Thailandia CSV GMPs, Clause 519 Health Canada API, C.02.05, Interpretation #15
10. Change and Configuration Management Any changes to a computerized system including system configurations should be made only in a controlled manner in accordance with a defined procedure.	11-11	211.68	820.30(i) 820.70(i) 820.40	11.10(d) 11.10(e)	PIC/S PI 011-3 The APV Guideline "Computerized Systems" based on Annex 11 of the EU-GMP Guideline WHO, Technical Report Series, No. 937, 2006, Annex 4, Section 12 Pressman, Roger S., *Software Engineering—A Practitioner's Approach,* McGraw Hill GAMP 5, Management Appendix M3; GAMP 5–Operational Appendices O6 and O7 Brazilian GMPs Title VII Art 582 ISO 13485 4.2.3; 7.3.7; 7.5.2;

(continued)

		References			
	Old Annex 11	211	820	11	Others/Guidelines
11. Periodic Evaluation Computerized systems should be periodically evaluated to confirm that they remain in a valid state and are compliant with GMP. Such evaluations should include, where appropriate, the current range of functionality, deviation records, incidents, problems, upgrade history, performance, reliability, security, and validation status reports.		211.68 211.180(e)	820.20(c)	11.10(k) 11.300(b) and (e)	US FDA CPG 7132a.07, Computerized Drug Processing; Input/Output Checking ICH Q7, 12.6 WHO, Technical Report Series, No. 937, 2006, Annex 4, Appendix 5, Section 1.5 GAMP 5, Management Appendix M3; GAMP 5–Operational Appendices O3 and O8 58.35; 58.190; 58.195 Annex 15 Clauses 23 and 45. ISO 13485 5.6; 5.6.1; 5.6.2; 5.6.3; 8.2.2; 8.5; 8.5.1 China GMPs Section 8
					Japan CSV Guideline (Guideline on Management of Computerized Systems for Marketing Authorization Holder and Manufacturing of Drugs and Quasi-drugs, October 2010), Section 6.6 China GMP, Articles 240–246 Thailandia CSV GMPs, Clause 520 Health Canada API, C.02.015 Interpretation #20 Article 17 draft Annex 2 CFDA GMP

12. Security	11-8	211.68(b)		11.10(c) 11.10(d) 11.10(e) 11.10(g) 11.300	PIC/S PI 011-3
12.1 Physical and/or logical controls should be in place to restrict access to computerized systems to authorized persons. Suitable methods of preventing unauthorized entry to the system may include the use of keys, pass cards, personal codes with passwords, biometrics, and restricted access to computer equipment and data storage areas.					ICH E6 GCP 4.1.5; 5.5.3(c), (d) and (e)
					21 CFR Part 58.51; 58.190(d)
					WHO, Technical Report Series, No. 937, 2006, Annex 4, Appendix 5, Section 4
					GAMP 5, Management Appendix M9; GAMP 5–Operational Appendix O11
					Brazilian GMPs Title VII Art 579
12.2 The extent of security controls depends on the criticality of the computerized system.					Japan CSV Guideline (Guideline on Management of Computerized Systems for Marketing Authorization Holder and Manufacturing of Drugs and Quasi-drugs, October 2010), Section 6.4
12.3 Creation, change, and cancellation of access authorizations should be recorded.					Thailandia CSV GMPs, Clause 517
					Health Canada API, C.02.05, Interpretation #15
12.4 Management systems for data and for documents should be designed to record the identity of operators entering, changing, confirming, or deleting data including date and time.					Articles 14, 16 draft Annex 2 CFDA GMP

(continued)

	References			
	Old Annex 11	211	820	11	Others/Guidelines
13. Incident Management All incidents, not only system failures and data errors, should be reported and assessed. The root cause of a critical incident should be identified and should form the basis of corrective and preventive actions.	11-17	211.100(b)	820.100		Q7A Good Manufacturing Practice Guidance for Active Pharmaceutical Ingredients GAMP 5, Operational Appendices O4, O5, and O7 Brazilian GMPs Title VII Art 588 ISO 13485 8.5; 8.5.1; 8.5.2; 8.5.3 Japan CSV Guideline (Guideline on Management of Computerized Systems for Marketing Authorization Holder and Manufacturing of Drugs and Quasi-drugs, October 2010), Sections 6.7 and 7.2 China GMPs, Sections 5 and 6 Thailandia CSV GMPs, Clause 526 Health Canada API, C.02.015 Interpretation #19 Articles 20 and 21 draft Annex 2 CFDA GMP

14. Electronic Signature Electronic records may be signed electronically. Electronic signatures are expected to: • have the same impact as handwritten signatures within the boundaries of the company;[g] • be permanently linked to their respective record, and • include the time and date that they were applied.				11.3(b)(7); 11.10(e); 11.50; .70, .100, .200, .300	Q7A Good Manufacturing Practice Guidance for Active Pharmaceutical Ingredients Electronic Signatures in Global and National Commerce (E-Sign), a US federal law (available at: http://thomas.loc.gov/cgi-bin/query/z?c106:S.761:) 21 CFR 58.33;.81;.35;.120;.185 Japan's Pharmaceutical and Food Safety Bureau "Using electromagnetic records and electronic signatures for application for approval or licensing of drugs," Section 4, April 2005 Article 22 draft Annex 2 CFDA GMP
15. Batch release When a computerized system is used for recording certification and batch release, the system should allow only Qualified Persons to certify the release of the batches, and it should clearly identify and record the person releasing or certifying the batches. This should be performed using an electronic signature.	11-19	211.68 211.186 211.192 211.188(b)(11) 211.188(a)		11.70; Sub Part C	21 CFR 211.68 The APV Guideline "Computerized Systems" based on Annex 11 of the EU-GMP Guideline 11-9; 11-14 EC Directive 2001/83 Brazilian GMPs Title VII Art 590 Thailandia CSV GMPs, Clause 528 Article 21 draft Annex 2 CFDA GMP

(continued)

	References			
	Old Annex 11	211	820	11	Others/Guidelines
16. Business Continuity For the availability of computerized systems supporting critical processes, provisions should be made to ensure continuity of support for those processes in the event of a system breakdown (e.g., a manual or alternative system). The time required to bring the alternative arrangements into use should be based on risk and appropriate for a particular system and the business process it supports. These arrangements should be adequately documented and tested.	11-15 11-16				PIC/S PI 011-3 GAMP 5, Operational Appendix O10 Brazilian GMPs Title VII Art 586, 587 Thailandia CSV GMPs, Clause 524, 525

17. Archiving	211.68(b)	11.10(c)	DOD 5015.2-STD, Design Criteria Standard for E-records Management Software Applications
Data may be archived. This data should be checked for accessibility, readability, and integrity. If relevant changes are to be made to the system (e.g., computer equipment or programs), then the ability to retrieve the data should be ensured and tested.			GAMP 5, Operational Appendix O13 GAMP GPG: Electronic Data Archiving, 2007 Brazilian GMPs Title VII Art 584

a O. López, "A Historical View of 21 CFR Part 211.68," *Journal of GXP Compliance,* 15(2), Spring 2011.

b *Federal Register,* 60(13), 4087–4091, January 20, 1995.

c All 21 CFR Part 812 regulations apply equally to both paper records and electronic records. The use of computer systems in clinical investigations does not exempt IDEs from any Part 812 regulatory requirement.

d O. López, "Requirements Management," *Journal of Validation Technology,* 1(2), Spring 2011.

e Test methods: With the Black-Box Test, the test cases are derived solely from the description of the test object; the inner structure of the object is thus not considered when creating the test plan. With the White-Box Test, the test cases are derived solely from the structure of the test object. With the Source-Code Review, the source code is checked against the documentation describing the system by one or several professionals. The APV Guideline Computerized Systems based on Annex 11 of the EU-GMP Guideline, April 1996.

f The term "critical data" in this context is interpreted as meaning data with high risk to product quality or patient safety. ISPE GAMP COP Annex 11–Interpretation, July/August 2011.

g The phrase "within the boundaries of the company" clarifies that such signatures applied to records maintained by the regulated company are not subject to Directive 1999/93/EC on a company framework for e-sigs, nor the 2000/31/EC Directive on electronic commerce, nor any associated national regulations of EU member states on such topics.

Appendix F: Case Study SCADA and Annex 11

Introduction

The introduction of the Annex 11, Revision 1, established the guiding principle applicable to the computer systems performing GMP-regulated activities.

There is no requirement in the EU GMPs to maintain electronic copies of records in preference to other media such as microfiche or paper. If the regulated user decides to maintain regulated records in electronic format, Annex 11 provides the GMP controls to perform such activity.

This chapter is a sample Annex 11 case study applicable to supervisory control and data acquisition (SCADA) systems managing manufacturing data in a GMP-regulated activity.

The case study focuses on relevant technical issues associated with the implementation of a SCADA system. Relevant procedural controls are discussed in Chapter 22. Project cost is not addressed.

SCADA* Basics

Cell controllers are used for manufacturing control or data acquisition. In their most basic form, these systems process inputs and direct outputs. Everything

---

* O. López, *Qualification of SCADA Systems*, Sue Horwood Publishing Limited, West Sussex, UK.

else is simply an activity supporting inputs and outputs (I/Os).* The primary concern for cell controllers is working accurately in the intended process. This is dynamically verified during the qualification of the cell controller and the integration with the process equipment.

Cell controllers fall into a specific category, such as a distributed control system (DCS), programmable logic controller (PLC), or SCADA. Historically, a DCS was meant for analog loop control, a PLC was meant for replacement of relay logic, and a SCADA system was used when data collection was needed. Presently, a DCS can replace relay logic, a PLC can implement analog loop control, and SCADA can do both. In addition to the above-mentioned categories, cell control can be implemented using personal computers. This category is called "soft PLC."

PLCs, as depicted in Figure F.1, are always linked to a process plant via a real-time link. To be able to record data, PLCs cannot exist in isolation. The PLC must be linked to a SCADA system. The combination of a PLC plus a SCADA system gives functionality close to a DCS.

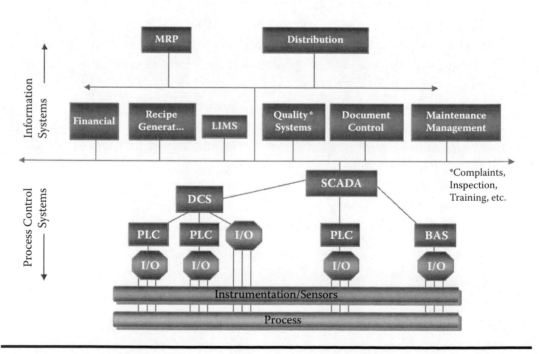

Figure F.1   SCADA configuration.

---

* Snyder, D., "Take Advantage of Control Options," *A-B Journal*, March 1997.

SCADA Systems

SCADA is a system operating with coded signals over communication channels to provide control of remote equipment. The supervisory system may be combined with a data acquisition system by adding the use of coded signals over communication channels to acquire information about the status of the remote equipment for display or for recording functions. It is a type of industrial control system (ICS). Industrial control systems are computer-based systems that monitor and control industrial processes that exist in the physical world.

SCADA systems historically distinguish themselves from other ICS systems by being large-scale processes that can include multiple sites and large distances. These processes include industrial, infrastructure, and facility-based processes.

A SCADA system typically consists of the following subsystems:

■ Remote terminal units (RTUs) connect to sensors in the process and convert sensor signals to digital data. They have telemetry hardware capable of sending digital data to the supervisory system, as well as receiving digital commands from the supervisory system. RTUs often have embedded control capabilities such as ladder logic in order to accomplish Boolean logic operations.

■ PLCs connect to sensors in the process and convert sensor signals to digital data. PLCs have more sophisticated embedded control capabilities, typically one or more IEC 61131-3 (international standard for programmable logic controllers) programming languages, than RTUs. PLCs do not have telemetry hardware, although this functionality is typically installed alongside them. PLCs are sometimes used in place of RTUs as field devices because they are more economical, versatile, flexible, and configurable.

■ A telemetry system is typically used to connect PLCs and RTUs with control centers, data warehouses, and the enterprise. Examples of wired telemetry media used in SCADA systems include leased telephone lines and Wide Area Network (WAN) circuits. Examples of wireless telemetry media used in SCADA systems include satellite (e.g., VSAT), licensed and unlicensed radio, cellular, and microwave.

■ A data acquisition server is a software service that uses industrial protocols to connect software services, via telemetry, with field devices such as RTUs and PLCs. It allows clients to access data from these field devices using standard protocols.

- A human–machine interface (HMI) is the apparatus or device that presents processed data to a human operator and, through this, the human operator monitors and interacts with the process. The HMI is a client that requests data from a data acquisition server.

- A historian is a software service that accumulates time-stamped data, Boolean events, and Boolean alarms in a database that can be queried or used to populate graphic trends in the HMI. The historian is a client that requests data from a data acquisition server.

- A supervisory (computer) system that gathers (acquires) data on the process and sends commands (control) to the SCADA system.

- Communication infrastructure connecting the supervisory system to the remote terminal units.

- Various process and analytical instrumentation.

Data acquisition begins at the RTU or PLC level and includes meter readings and equipment status reports that are communicated to SCADA as required. Data is then compiled and formatted in such a way that an operator using the HMI can make supervisory decisions to adjust or override normal RTU (PLC) controls. Data may also be fed to a historian, often built on a commodity database management system, to allow trending and other analytical auditing.

SCADA systems typically implement a distributed database, commonly referred to as a tag database, which contains data elements called tags or points. A point represents a single input or output value monitored or controlled by the system. Points can be either "hard" or "soft." A hard point represents an actual input or output within the system, whereas a soft point results from logic and math operations applied to other points.

Points are normally stored as value–time-stamp pairs: a value and the time-stamp when it was recorded or calculated. A series of value–time-stamp pairs gives the history of that point. It is also common to store additional meta-data with tags, such as the path to a field device or PLC register, design time comments, and alarm information.

SCADA systems may have security vulnerabilities, so the systems should be evaluated to identify risks and solutions implemented to mitigate those risks.

Case Study Background

The procedures, controls, instructions, specifications, and safeguards to be followed within computer systems controlling manufacturing processes are embodied in the computer program. The computer program drives the equipment and controls the process.

This case study consists of applications and the associated infrastructure for monitoring and controlling manufacturing processes. Each SCADA was responsible for a particular manufacturing line. The SCADA was linked, via network, to multiple PLCs. Each PLC manages one manufacturing equipment for an associated manufacturing line. Refer to Figure F.1.

Based on configurable products, each application was designed by an integrator specifically to manage the associated process equipment or cell using a scripting language.

Each manufacturing equipment is connected to the SCADA via the associated PLC.

Each SCADA has a data acquisition server accessed via the respective workstation. Typically, a workstation provides the user interface to the associated application. Each server is connected to the plant manufacturing area network. Specifically, two workstations, connected to the manufacturing network, are available to monitor all activities. These two workstations do not have control capability.

Security controls (Annex 11-12) were implemented at the workstation, server, and network levels. Operator interface is performed at the workstation level. Data collection is performed primarily at the PLC level and the data is transferred periodically to the primary repository at the server level (Annex 11-5). Collected data is saved in the relevant database. Formula management is performed at the server level. Formulae are transferred to the PLC when a job is initiated.

Of relevance to this test case is the sequencing, controlling data on product formulation, batch size, yields, and automated in-process sampling/testing procedures. These are performed at the PLC level and are elements that pertain to the master production records and are considered critical records required by the GMPs.

Other records to be saved are changes to alarm statuses and limits, events, warnings, alarms, and interlocks.

Annex 11 Applicable to SCADA Systems

Annex 11 applies to GMP-regulated activities managed by computer systems and critical e-recs that are created under the record requirement set forth in the EudraLex–Volume 4 GMP Guidelines. Records, which are electronically maintained following the provisions of Annex 11, are to be recognized as equivalent to traditional paper records.

The SCADA system, depicted in Figure F.1, high level functionality was built on a configurable product and associated infrastructure. Critical data is received and control information is sent via interfaces such as DCS, PLC, and Building Automated System (BAS). Data is sent to information systems via the site network. Recipe-related files, to be processed by the PLC, are received by the Recipes Generator System.

The areas in Annex 11 that impacted SCADA systems are as follows.

Risk Assessment and Requirement Document

The requirements established by Research and Development (R&D) were the foundations to establish, refine, and expand the manufacturing-related requirements (Annex 11-4.4).

Specifically applicable requirements in Annex 11 to this case include:

■ Built-in Checks (Annex 11-5)
■ Accuracy Checks (Annex 11-6)
■ Data Storage (Annex 11-7)
■ Printouts (Annex 11-8)
■ Audit Trails (Annex 11-9)
■ Security (Annex 11-12)
■ Electronic Signature (Annex 11-14)
■ Archiving (Annex 11-17)

In addition to the above requirements, the operational checks* were vital for SCADA systems "to enforce permitted sequencing of steps and events, as appropriate."† The sequencing of the application software was consid-

---

* O. López, "Operational Checks," in *21 CFR Part 11: Complete Guide to International Computer Validation Compliance for the Pharmaceutical Industry*, Sue Horwood Publishing and Interpharm/CRC, Boca Raton, FL, 2002, 121–124.
† US FDA, 21 CFR Part 11.10(f), "Electronic Records; Electronic Signatures; Final Rule," March 1997.

ered a set of instructions to the computer systems similar to a procedure in GMP-regulated activities.

A comprehensive list of SCADA requirements can be found at http://www.ispe.org/jett/scada-urs.doc.

Taking into consideration that the SCADA implementation was based on a configurable product, a risk assessment was performed to establish the intended use and validation extent of the SCADA system application, including the infrastructure.

The possible mitigations to vulnerabilities associated with each requirement and the validation extent (Annex 11-1) of the SCADA system application, including the infrastructure, were determined.

Specifically around security requirements of the SCADA, the concern was:

■ The lack of concern about security and authentication in the design, deployment, and operation of some existing SCADA networks
■ The belief that SCADA systems have the benefit of security through obscurity using specialized protocols and proprietary interfaces
■ The belief that SCADA networks are secure because they are physically secured
■ The belief that SCADA networks are secure because they are disconnected from the Internet

There are many threats to a SCADA system. One is the threat of unauthorized access to the control software, whether it is human access or changes induced intentionally or accidentally by virus infections and other software threats residing on the control host machine. Another is the threat of packet access to the network segments hosting SCADA devices. In many cases, the control protocol lacks any form of cryptographic security, allowing an attacker to control a SCADA device by sending commands over a network. In many cases, SCADA users have assumed that having a VPN offered sufficient protection, unaware that security can be trivially bypassed with physical access to SCADA-related network jacks and switches. Industrial control vendors suggest approaching SCADA security like Information Security with a defensive in-depth strategy that leverages common IT practices.

The above concerns were mitigated by following the Annex 11 elements associated with data integrity. Refer to Chapter 27.

Critical records were identified as the result of the risk assessment (Annex 11-1) and defined in the requirements document. Some of the critical records that were defined are

- P&IDs
- I/O List
- Identification of Critical Parameters
- Alarm Lists (priorities, types, areas, specific alarms)
- Recipe Lists (procedures, unit operations, and operations)
- Historical Data Collection List
- Engineering Parameters List
- Reports List or Descriptions

New requirements resulting from the mitigations were added to the requirements document.

The risk analysis was used as the input for the validation plan (Annex 11-4.1). The validation plan contained overall objectives, acceptance criteria, approaches, and procedures to be used to implement the SCADA system "in accordance with an appropriate quality management system" (Annex 11-4.1 and 11-4.5). An element of this plan was the data integrity controls (Annex 11-1).

Another input to the validation plan was the quality of the core SCADA product supplier* (Annex 11-3.2). The result of the assessment was considered suitable (Annex 11-4.5).

Based on the outcome of the audit, it was decided to use the core configured product documentation in support of the implementation of the SCADA application. This core product documentation consisted of the supplier's system documentation.

> 6.8.1 Vendor documentation, including test documents, may be used as part of the verification documentation, providing the regulated company has assessed the vendor and has evidence of:
>
> 6.8.1.1 An acceptable vendor quality system,
>
> 6.8.1.2 Vendor technical capability, and
>
> 6.8.1.3 Vendor application of GEP such that information obtained from the vendor will be accurate and suitable to meet the purpose of verification.†

---

* Supplier: An organization that enters into a contract with the acquirer for the supply of a system, software product, or software service under the terms of the contract (ISO 12207:1995).

† ASTM E2500-07, "Standard Guide for Specification, Design, and Verification of Pharmaceutical and Biopharmaceutical Manufacturing Systems and Equipment," October 2012.

Specification

As a result of using the supplier's core product documentation, instead of the typical Functional Specification, a Configuration Specification was developed. The configuration document contains information on:

■ Security configuration
■ Application software, infrastructure software, and infrastructure hardware descriptions (developer, revision)
■ Client and server configuration
■ Network configuration
■ System layout
■ Client settings
■ Global settings
■ Installation procedures for the server
■ Installation procedures for client
■ Other configurations not listed above

A traceability analysis was written (Annex 11-4.4) between the requirement and configuration documents.

Design and Configuration

Using the Configuration Specification, the developer's manuals, and SCADA hardware and system level software manuals, the system was designed.

The design was recorded in a design specification. Centered on the design specification, the SCADA was built and configured based on ANSI/ISA-88, the standard addressing batch process control. The critical data collected by the SCADA is to be uploaded to the Manufacturing Execution System (MES) and complete the production records.

The settings, configuration, and testing of the SCADA were initially performed at the integrator site.

The integrator performed software unit and integration testing. These tests were documented as described by the integrator applicable procedures.

After concluding the integration testing, an audit to these documents was performed and the Factory Acceptance Test (FAT) took place.

The objective of the FAT was to formally witness, by the regulated user, the conformity of the requirements document with the application.

It was verified, as well, that SCADA database files, or tables, were appropriately scaled versions of the production data sets. Test data must contain a well-designed representation of production data that allows all conditions to be tested and all defects uncovered so that they can be corrected. Test data was identified and retained.

A traceability analysis (Annex 11-4.4) was updated between the requirement, configuration, design documents, and FAT.

Installation

After the successfully executed FAT and revised integrator's documentation, the system was installed at the regulated user's site.

Installation related documentation was collected during the installation, including settings and configuration of hardware, software (application and infrastructure), and interfaces (e.g., PLCs and MES).

SAT*

The site acceptance test (SAT) activities, one SAT per manufacturing and associated cell controllers, combined the verification of the installation and verification/tests of all the computer systems and process equipment associated with the SCADA.

The SAT was performed by the integrator and additional validation personnel supporting the integrator. All test plans and procedures were reviewed and approved by the regulated user's quality assurance (QA) unit.

As the result of the successful audits to the core SCADA product, integrators internal development documentation, and SAT, it was decided not to execute again certain testing such as, for example, menus and reports.

The SAT consists of the installation and operation of all the equipment and associated software, including the SCADA:

- Man–machine–interface installation verification (Annex 11-6)
  - Boundary values
  - Invalid values
  - Special values
  - Decision point and branch conditions

---

* SAT: Inspection or dynamic testing of the systems or major system components to support the qualification of an equipment system conducted and documented at the manufacturing site.

- Security settings and verification (Annex 11-12)
- SCADA configuration verification
- Catastrophic recovery verification (Annex 11-16)
- Verification that all equipment and instruments have been installed according to PID and installation procedures
- Loop tests
- Identification of the core product revision and configuration files loaded to the corresponding SCADA system
- Identification of the infrastructure software to be loaded in the corresponding SCADA system, including SCADA database
- Identification of the infrastructure hardware to be hosting the applicable SCADA application and infrastructure software
- Verification of the network connections (as applicable)
- Data acquisition and database access controls

The operational test cases thoroughly, rigorously, and consistently challenge the SCADA system in that there is sufficient valid testing of all I/O values, data structures, process variables, and control flow logic.

- Loop tests and operational checks
- Network connection (as applicable)
- Trending and alarms processing
- Interface with other applications (e.g., SPC)
- Timing (as applicable)
- Database recovery
- Sequencing and operation, including Recipe Downloading

One of the main tests in the operational testing is the Recipe Downloading. Based on a production schedule, the operator selects the recipe to manage the manufacturing session. The controller loads the associated recipe from MES, via the SCADA, and loads the recipe to each PLC connected with the manufacturing line (Annex 11-5).

In addition to the above testing per cell, a performance qualification was completed to each manufacturing line to demonstrate compliance with the process requirements. Based on the European Medicines Agency* (EMA), the performance qualification was executed to verify that each manufacturing

---

* EudraLex Volume 4, EU Guidelines to Good Manufacturing Practice, Medicinal Products for Human and Veterinary Use, Annex 15–Qualification and Validation (Draft), February 2014.

line, as connected together, performed effectively and reproducibly, based on the approved process method and product specification.

A strict configuration management (Annex 11-10) was established during the FAT. The objective was to control the baseline and be able to ensure that the revision accepted at the integration site was the same version installed at the regulated user.

A traceability analysis was updated (Annex 11-4.4) between the requirement, configuration, design documents, FAT, and SAT.

Process Validation

Following the SAT and the performance qualification, a process validation was completed to demonstrate that the process, operated within established parameters, can perform effectively and reproducibly to produce a medicinal product meeting its predetermined specifications and quality attributes.

For the context of the SCADA system, the following areas were monitored:

■ Receiving, recording, storing, and processing with accuracy the electronically manufacturing information.
■ Arriving at the appropriate disposition decision based on the data received through the SCADA system.
■ Integration between all SCADA components and all interfaces.
■ Platform security.
■ Audit trail processing and reporting.

If SCADA database conversion, migration, or preloading with data is to occur prior to PQ testing, the verification of these activities and their associated data may be addressed in the PQ.

Operation and Maintenance

Supporting the operation and maintenance activities are SOPs as described in Chapter 23.

References

ASTM E2500-07, "Standard Guide for Specification, Design, and Verification of Pharmaceutical and Biopharmaceutical Manufacturing Systems and Equipment," October 2012.

EudraLex Volume 4, EU Guidelines to Good Manufacturing Practice, Medicinal Products for Human and Veterinary Use, Annex 15–Qualification and Validation (Draft), February 2014.

O. López, "Operational Checks," in *21 CFR Part 11: Complete Guide to International Computer Validation Compliance for the Pharmaceutical Industry*, Sue Horwood Publishing and Interpharm/CRC, Boca Raton, FL, 2002, 121–124.

O. López, *Qualification of SCADA Systems*, Sue Horwood Publishing Limited, West Sussex, UK, 2000.

References

Aide-mémoire of German ZLG regarding EU GMP Annex 11, September 2013.

Appel, K., "How Far Does Annex 11 Go Beyond Part 11?" *Pharmaceutical Processing*, September 2011.

APV, The APV Guideline "Computerised Systems" based on Annex 11 of the EU-GMP Guideline, Version 1.0, April 1996.

ASTM, E 2500–13 "Standard Guide for Specification, Design, and Verification of Pharmaceutical and Biopharmaceutical Manufacturing Systems and Equipment," 2013.

Cappucci, W., Clark, C., Goossens, T., Wyn, S., "Annex 11 Interpretation," *Pharmaceutical Engineering,* Volume 31, Number 4 (Jul/August), 2011.

CEFIC, "Computer Validation Guide," API Committee of CEFIC, December 2002.

Commission Directive 91/412/EEC, Laying down the principles and guidelines of good manufacturing practice for veterinary medicinal products, July 1991.

Commission Directive 95/46/EC of the European Parliament and of the Council of 24 October 1995 on the protection of individuals with regard to the processing of personal data and on the free movement of such data, http://eur-lex.europa.eu/LexUriServ/LexUriServ.do?uri=CELEX:31995L0046:en:HTML.

Commission Directive 2003/94/EC, Laying down the principles and guidelines of good manufacturing practice in respect of medicinal products for human use and investigational medicinal products for human use, October 2003.

European Commission (EC), "General Data Protection Regulation (GDPR)," January 2012 (proposed regulation to replace EU Data Protection Directive 95/46/EC).

EMA/INS/GCP/454280/2010, GCP Inspectors Working Group (GCP IWG), "Reflection Paper on Expectations for Electronic Source Data and Data Transcribed to Electronic Data Collection Tools in Clinical Trials," August 2010.

EU Annex III to Guidance for the Conduct of Good Clinical Practice Inspections Computer Systems, May 2008. http://ec.europa.eu/health/files/eudralex/vol-10/chap4/annex_iii_to_guidance_for_the_conduct_of_gcp_inspections_-_computer_systems_en.pdf.

EudraLex, Volume 4, "EU Guidelines to Good Manufacturing Practice, Medicinal Products for Human and Veterinary Use, Annex 11–Computerised Systems," June 2011. http://ec.europa.eu/health/files/eudralex/vol-4/annex11_01-2011_en.pdf.

EudraLex, Volume 4, "EU Guidelines to Good Manufacturing Practice, Medicinal Products for Human and Veterinary Use, Annex 15–Validation and Qualification," May 2014 (Draft).

EudraLex, Volume 4, "EU Guidelines to Good Manufacturing Practice, Medicinal Products for Human and Veterinary Use, Annex 16–Certification by a Qualified Person and Batch Release," 2001.

EudraLex, Volume 4, "EU Guidelines for Good Manufacturing Practices for Medicinal Products for Human and Veterinary Use, Annex 20–Quality Risk Management," February 2008.

EudraLex, Volume 4, "EU Guidelines to Good Manufacturing Practice, Medicinal Products for Human and Veterinary Use–Glossary," February 2013.

EudraLex, The Rules Governing Medicinal Products in the European Union, Volume 4, "EU Guidelines for Good Manufacturing Practices for Medicinal Products for Human and Veterinary Use, Part 1, Chapter 2–Personnel," February 2014.

EudraLex, The Rules Governing Medicinal Products in the European Union, Volume 4, "Good Manufacturing Practice, Medicinal Products for Human and Veterinary Use, Chapter 3: Premises and Equipment," 2007.

EudraLex, The Rules Governing Medicinal Products in the European Union, Volume 4, "Good Manufacturing Practice, Medicinal Products for Human and Veterinary Use, Chapter 4: Documentation," June 2011.

EudraLex, The Rules Governing Medicinal Products in the European Union, Volume 4, "Good Manufacturing Practice, Medicinal Products for Human and Veterinary Use, Chapter 7: Outsourced Activities," January 2013.

EudraLex, The Rules Governing Medicinal Products in the European Union, Volume 4, "EU Good Manufacturing Practice (GMP) Medicinal Products for Human and Veterinary Use, Chapter 9: Self Inspections," 2001.

EudraLex, The Rules Governing Medicinal Products in the European Union Volume 4, "Good Manufacturing Practice, Medicinal Products for Human and Veterinary Use: Glossary," 2007.

European Agencies Agency, Questions and Answers: Good Manufacturing Practice, "EU GMP Guide Annexes: Supplementary Requirements: Annex 11: Computerised Systems," http://www.ema.europa.eu/ema/index.jsp?curl= pages/regulation/general/gmp_q_a.jsp&mid=WC0b01ac058006e06c#section8.

European Directorate for the Quality of Medicine and Healthcare, OMCL Validation of Computerised Systems Core Documents, May 2009. http://www.edqm.eu/ medias/fichiers/Validation_of_Computerised_Systems_Core_Document.pdf.

European Medicines Agency (EMA), "Q&A: Good Manufacturing Practices (GMP)," February 2011.

GAMP® Good Practice Guide: Electronic Data Archiving, 2007.

GAMP® Good Practice Guide: Global Information Systems Control and Compliance, Appendix 2, Data Management Considerations, 2005.

GAMP® Good Practice Guide: IT Control and Compliance, International Society of Pharmaceutical Engineering, Tampa, FL, 2005.

GAMP® Good Practice Guide: Risk Based Approach to Operation of GXP Computerised Systems, 2010.

GAMP®/ISPE, Risk Assessment for Use of Automated Systems Supporting Manufacturing Process—Risk to Record, Pharmaceutical Engineering, Nov/Dec 2002.

GAMP®/ISPE, Risk Assessment for Use of Automated Systems Supporting Manufacturing Process—Functional Risk, Pharmaceutical Engineering, May/Jun 2003.

GHTF, "Implementation of Risk Management Principles and Activities within a Quality Management System," May 2005.

GMP Journal, "Q&As on Annex 11 (1-4) at the Computer Validation in Mannheim, Germany, in June 2011," 7, October/November 2011.

GMP Journal, "Q&As on Annex 11 (5-11) at the Computer Validation in Mannheim, Germany, in June 2011," 8, April/May 2012.

GMP Journal, "Q&As on Annex 11 (12-16) at the Computer Validation in Mannheim, Germany, in June 2011," 9, October/November 2012.

Grigonis, Jr., G.J., Subak, Jr., E.J., and Wyrick, M.L. "Validation Key Practices for Computer Systems Used in Regulated Operations," *Pharmaceutical Technology*, 74–98, June 1997.

ICH Harmonised Tripartite Guideline, "Good Manufacturing Practice Guidance for Active Pharmaceutical Ingredients, Q7," November 2000.

ICH Harmonised Tripartite Guideline, "Quality Risk Management, Q9," November 2005.

ICH Harmonised Tripartite Guideline, "Pharmaceutical Quality Systems, Q10," June 2008.

ICH Harmonised Tripartite Guideline, "Good Clinical Practice, E6," June 1996.

IDA Programme of the European Commission, "Model Requirements for the Management of Electronic Records," http://www.cornwell.co.uk/moreq.html, October 2002.

ISO 11799: 2003(E) Information and documentation—Document storage requirements for archive and library materials.

ISO 12207:1995,* "Information Technology—Software Life Cycle Processes," 1995.

ISO 13485:2012, "Medical Devices—Quality Management Systems—Requirements for Regulatory Purposes," February 2012.

ISO/IEC 27001: 2013, "Information Technology—Security Techniques—Information Security Management Systems—Requirements," 2013.

ISPE, "Regulatory Framework—EMEA," Dr. Kate McCormick, 2009.

ISPE, "Regulatory Framework—PIC/S and ICH," Dr. Kate McCormick, 2009.

ISPE GAMP®: *A Risk-Based Approach to Compliant GXP Computerised Systems*, International Society for Pharmaceutical Engineering (ISPE), 5th ed., February 2008.

ISPE/PDA, Good Practice and Compliance for Electronic Records and Signatures. Part 1 Good Electronic Records Management (GERM), July 2002.

---

* *Note*: The 1995 revision is not the most recent version.

Journal for GMP and Regulatory Affairs, "Q&As on Annex 11," 8, April/May 2012.

López, O., "A Computer Data Integrity Compliance Model," *Pharmaceutical Engineering,* Volume 35, Number 2, March/April 2015.

López, O., "Computer Systems Validation", In *Encyclopedia of Pharmaceutical Science and Technology,* Fourth Edition, Taylor & Francis: New York, Published online: 23 Aug 2013; 615–619.

López, O., *Computer Technologies Security Part I—Key Points in the Contained Domain,* Sue Horwood Publishing Limited, West Sussex, UK, ISBN 1-904282-17-2, 2002.

López, O., "Annex 11: Progress in EU Computer Systems Guidelines," *Pharmaceutical Technology Europe,* 23(6), June 2011, http://www.pharmtech.com/pharmtech/article/articleDetail.jsp?id=725378.

López, O., "Annex 11 and 21 CFR Part 11: Comparisons for International Compliance," MasterCotrol, January 2012. http://www.mastercontrol.com/newsletter/annex-11-21-cfr-part-11-comparison.html.

López, O., "An Easy to Understand Guide to Annex 11," Premier Validation, Cork, Ireland, 2011, http://www.askaboutvalidation.com/1938-an-easy-to-understand-guide-to-annex-11.

López, O., "EU Annex 11 and the Integrity of E-recs," *Journal of GXP Compliance,* 18(2), May 2014.

López, O., "Hardware/Software Suppliers Qualification," in *21 CFR Part 11: Complete Guide to International Computer Validation Compliance for the Pharmaceutical Industry,* Interpharm/CRC, Boca Raton, FL, 2004.

López, O., "Requirements Management," *Journal of Validation Technology,* May 2011.

McDowall, R.D., "Comparison of FDA and EU Regulations for Audit Trails," *Scientific Computing,* January 2014.

McDowall, R.D., "Ensuring Data Integrity in a Regulated Environment," *Scientific Computing,* March/April 2011.

McDowall, R.D., "Maintaining Laboratory Computer Validation—How to Conduct Periodic Reviews?" European Compliance Academy (ECA), April 2012, http://www.gmp-compliance.org/enews_03085_Maintaining-Laboratory-Computer-Validation---How-to-Conduct-Periodic-Reviews.html.

McDowall, R.D., "Computer Validation: Do All Roads Lead to Annex 11?," *Spectroscopy* 29(12)December 2014.

McDowall, R.D., "The New GMP Annex 11 and Chapter 4 is Europe's Answer to Part 11", European Compliance Academy (ECA), GMP News, January 2011, http://www.gmp-compliance.org/eca_news_2381_6886,6885,6738,6739,6934.html.

Mell, P. and Grance, T., "The NIST Definition of Cloud Computing," NIST Special Publication 800-145, National Institute of Standards and Technology, Gaithersburg, MD, 2011.

MHRA, "Good Laboratory Practice: Guidance on Archiving," March 2006.

NIST, "Guide for Conducting Risk Assessments," 800-30 Rev 1, September 2012.

PDA, Technical Report No. 32, "Auditing of Supplier Providing Computer Products and Services for Regulated Pharmaceutical Operations," *PDA Journal of Pharmaceutical Science and Technology*, Sep/Oct 2004, Release 2.0, 58(5).

PI 011-3. "Good Practices for Computerised Systems in Regulated 'GXP' Environments," Pharmaceutical Inspection Cooperation Scheme (PIC/S), September 2007.

Pressman, Roger S., *Software Engineering—A Practitioner's Approach,* McGraw Hill, New York, 2010.

Roemer, M., "New Annex 11: Enabling Innovation," *Pharmaceutical Technology*, June 2011.

Safe Harbor US–EU Agreement on Meeting Directive 95/46/EC http://www.export. gov/safeharbor/index.asp.

Schmitt, S., "Data Integrity", Pharmaceutical Technology, Volume 38 Number 7, July 2014.

Snyder, D., "Take Advantage of Control Options," *A-B Journal,* March 1997.

Stenbraten, A., "Cost-effective Compliance: Practical Solutions for Computerised Systems," paper presented at the ISPE Brussels Conference, GAMP - Cost Effective Compliance, 2011-09-19/20.

Stokes, D., "Compliant Cloud Computing—Managing the Risks," *Pharmaceutical Engineering*, 33(4), 1–11, 2013.

Stokes, T., "Management's View to Controlling Computer Systems," *GMP Review*, 10(2), July 2011.

TGA, "Australian Code of Good Manufacturing Practice for Human Blood and Blood Components, Human Tissues and Human Cellular Therapy Products," Version 1.0 April 2013.

US FDA, 21 CFR Part 11, "Electronic Records; Electronic Signatures; Final Rule," *Federal Register*, 62(54), 13429, March 1997.

US FDA 21 CFR Part 58, Good Laboratory Practice for Non-Clinical Laboratory Studies.

US FDA 21 CFR Part 110, Current Good Manufacturing Practice in Manufacturing, Packing, or Holding Human Food.

US FDA 21 CFR Part 312, Investigational New Drug Application.

US FDA 21 CFR Part 606, Current Good Manufacturing Practice for Blood and Blood Components.

US FDA 21 CFR Part 803, Medical Device Reporting.

US FDA 21 CFR 1271, Human Cells, Tissues, and Cellular and Tissue-Based Products.

US FDA, "General Principles of Software Validation; Final Guidance for Industry and FDA Staff," CDRH and CBER, January 2002.

US FDA, "Guidance for Industry: Blood Establishment Computer System Validation in the User's Facility," April 2013.

US FDA, Guidance for Industry: "Computerised Systems in Clinical Investigations," May 2007.

US FDA, "Guidance for Industry, Electronic Records; Electronic Signatures—Scope and Application," August 2003.

WHO—Technical Report Series No. 981, Annex 2, "WHO Guidelines on Quality Risk Management," 2013.

WHO—Technical Report Series No. 937, Annex 4, Appendix 5, "Validation of Computerised Systems," 2006.

Wechsler, J., "Data Integrity Key to GMP Compliance," *Pharmaceutical Technology*, September 2014.

Wingate, G., *Validating Automated Manufacturing and Laboratory Applications: Putting Principles into Practice*, Taylor & Francis, Boca Raton, FL, 1997.

Yves, S., "New Annex 11, Evolution and Consequences," www.pharma-mag.com, January/February, 2012.

Index

Note: Page numbers ending in "f" refer to figures. Page numbers ending in "t" refer to tables.